AMERICAN VAMPIRES

AMERICAN VAMPIRES

THEIR TRUE BLOODY HISTORY
FROM NEW YORK TO CALIFORNIA

DR. BOB CURRAN
ILLUSTRATIONS BY IAN DANIELS

New Page Books
A Division of The Career Press, Inc.
Pompton Plains, NJ

AMERICAN VAMPIRES
EDITED AND TYPESET BY GINA TALUCCI
Cover design by Wes Youssi/M80 Branding
Printed in the U.S.A.

To order this title, please call toll-free 1-800-CAREER-1 (NJ and Canada: 201-848-0310) to order using VISA or MasterCard, or for further information on books from Career Press.

The Career Press, Inc.
220 West Parkway, Unit 12
Pompton Plains, NJ 07444
www.careerpress.com

Library of Congress Cataloging-in-Publication Data

CIP Data Available Upon Request.

CONTENTS

INTRODUCTION

Perhaps no folklore entity is better known than the vampire. We've all encountered them in one way or another, whether it is through cinema, television, books, comic books, products, promotions, or dressed-up trick-or-treaters. Today, vampires are more popular than ever, serving up teenage angst in *Buffy the Vampire Slayer* and *Twilight,* or high-octane action in *Blade, Abraham Lincoln: Vampire Hunter,* and countless other franchises. Vampires are now a *business,* something so entrenched in our cultural perceptions that we can't really do without them. And because they're so familiar now, we all know what they look like and where to find them. They're gaunt aristocrats living in ruined castles somewhere in Transylvania; dissolute recluses lurking somewhere in misty New Orleans; hormonally challenged teenagers dwelling in some claustrophobic metropolis who attend an ancient but emotionally charged high school. *That's* what vampires are? That's what writers, film makers, and the media would have you believe, because that's the type of vampire that *sells.*

A belief in vampires has been with us for centuries, and during that stretch of time, it has adapted and developed as humanity has progressed.

Its roots stretch back into the mists of time and to the darkest perceptions and fears of our ancestors. It has little to do with the problems of puberty, the differences in social status, or dilettantism and privilege. Instead, it is the crystallized terrors of our forebears coalesced into one menacing shadow that has followed humanity through the ages.

There is much debate as to where the word *vampire* actually comes from. One theory suggests that it came from the word *upir*, which is the Russian word for "wicked person." In 1047, the word appears in an East Slavic letter referring to a Novgorodian (East Russian) prince as "Upir Lichy" (a wicked vampire). This might have been in regard to his taxation methods, that is, drawing the "blood" (wealth) from his people. Other sources say that the word first appeared in Bulgaria and Yugoslavia around the late 1600s, but nobody is really sure. The word *vampire* first appeared in the English language around 1734 in a travel feature entitled *The Travels of Three English Gentlemen*, which was published in *The Harliean Miscellany* in 1745.

Nonetheless, the concept of the vampire with which we are most familiar today originated somewhere in Eastern Europe or in Germany. This is not to say, however, that there were not vampiric beings long before that, or that other cultures do not have their own vampires, many of which are very different from the perception of the books and films. Vampires belong to a category of night visitors that often tormented our ancestors as they lay asleep. (These were called "mara" or "mares" by the Nordic peoples, and their visitations usually caused restlessness and awful dreams. These visitors included a number of demons, ghouls, and gaunts, who would cause physical harm if they could. In ancient Rome and Greece, these creatures included things such as incubi (male) and succubi (female): demons who would have sexual intercourse with the sleeper all through the night, leaving them tired and exhausted in the morning; the Lamia, who might smother the sleeper, strangling him or her in the bedclothes, especially killing small children; or a host of other night terrors who might attack the sleeping person in various ways. These evil dead might do physical harm to the sleeper—for example, the Irish folklorist Thomas Crofton Croker collected a story in County Limerick in which one being cut the throats of sleeping brothers with a razor. The idea of such creatures—which appear in many cultures—may have served as the motif for the concept of the vampire. In places such as Mexico, the Philippines, South Africa, and South America, sleepers are still visited by evil things—few of them bearing any resemblance to the commonly held perception of the vampire.

All of these vampire motifs describe a physiological condition. The notion of the Aswang (and similar vampires) may serve to explain nocturnal emissions in young men as they sleep and perhaps experience erotic dreams. It was not they who had created such visions—it was the Aswang in order to get their semen. Similarly, when someone wakes up tired and irritable after what appears to be a good night's sleep, it is the vampire that is to blame. All nocturnal ailments were often attributed to the work of vampires—a convenient handle on which to hang night-time and morning sicknesses and debilitation.

Besides leeching off of the resting, in a number of cultures, vampires subsist on bodily fluids, secretions, and whatever human energies that they can draw out.

The Penanggalan of Malaysia, for instance, is little more than the floating, blood-stained head of a woman who died in childbirth, traveling while dragging its entrails behind it. Again, the Aswang of the Philippines is a dragon-like creature that drinks both sweat and semen (no blood) from the bodies of sleeping men, sucking them up through a long, hollow tongue, which it lowers between the palm-leaf roofs of the forest huts. The tiny ape-like Tikoloshe of South Africa climbs on the bed and drinks from the soles and ankles of the sleeper's feet. In parts of Central America, tiny balls of light feed on the energy from the sleeping body through a process akin to osmosis.

Not all of the night-walking dead are malicious, though. Indeed, Romanian folklore draws a distinct line between two groups of corporeal phantoms who can visit houses during the hours of darkness—the moroi and the strigoi. The former are those who have been permitted to rise by a direct command from God because of their holy lives. They are permitted to enjoy the things that they knew in life, such as a hot meal, a glass of alcohol, or the company of their former partners and loved ones. At the end of one night they return to the grave, perhaps for all eternity. But if God could raise the dead, so could the Devil, and these were the strigoi, the malevolent dead who rose from the tomb to do evil. They might attack their families, relatives, and communities, and protections had to be put in place against their attentions.

Ireland, too, had an extremely similar belief system when it came to the walking dead who returned from their graves. The Blessed Dead, those who had lived exemplary lives or had died doing good in the service of their fellow men, were permitted to rise on certain holy days and for specific purposes. They could warn, offer advice, reward, rebuke, or even take a limited vengeance, but most of all, they enjoyed some of the comforts that they had when alive. They were also permitted to finish uncompleted tasks that their deaths had interrupted. For example, Grace Connor, an Irish seamstress from Cork, had agreed to complete a wedding dress, but died before she could finish it. However, because she had led a good life, she was allowed to come back and finish the work, so the bride could receive her dress.

My own grandmother, who lived in County Down, would sometimes set an extra place at the table on certain nights of the year in case one of the dead neighbors passed through. As far as I can recall, no one ever did, but it was bad luck to ignore the night-walking dead. An elderly lady who lived up the road from us often used to scatter the gleeshins (fine ash from the grate) from the bottom of her fire on the hearthstone on Halloween night; if it was disturbed in the morning, she knew that her dead relatives had been there and had danced on the stone.

But if the Blessed Dead walked the roads on some nights of the year, so did the evil dead. People who lived outside the church, who had not been buried with proper rites, who had done harm to their neighbors, or who had been selfish, could come back to torment their families and their neighbors. There was also the common idea that if a woman died during childbirth and the child survived, the woman might come back from the dead to take the child back with her to the grave. Children in these circumstances had to be constantly protected by holy ornaments, such as crucifixes, or by iron nails driven into the head posts of their cots. It was assumed that no evil thing could approach them as long as there was iron nearby.

But what *are* vampires? Surely after all the books, films, and television series about the subject we should know. A vampire is certainly a reanimated corpse that can come back to threaten the living; however, let's clear up a few misconceptions. First, not all vampires drink blood. As we read previously, some find sweat or semen more to their taste. Others simply drink energy. A Vietnamese vampire that resembles a bodiless human head with long antennae extending from the nose, gently strokes the legs of a sleeper with these, drawing up the sweat on which it subsists. It can also stimulate glands that produce more sweat. Other vampires in South America simply resemble a huge ball of fungus and wrap themselves around the feet of a sleeper, drawing energy from him or her just as a parasitic growth might. Before the sleeper wakes, the fungal ball shrivels up and retreats back into the surrounding jungle.

Although it looks both dramatic and erotic on screen, vampires do not usually drink blood from the base of the neck. This is probably a device added by certain writers such as Bram Stoker to add a touch of eroticism to the tale. But it's not practical; if a vampire actually bit into the jugular, it would kill its victim immediately and create a mess of blood everywhere. The vampire, however, can drink from other, less dramatic veins on other parts of the body. For example, it can drink from the crook of the arm, taking blood pretty much as a nurse would take a blood sample. The vampire bat of South America, for instance, drinks by gently lapping at the soles of the sleeper's feet, while certain types of South African vampires drink from a network of veins in the legs and ankles. None of this looks particularly erotic, so Hollywood opts for the more dramatic, which has slipped into our consciousness and is now a "given" in vampire lore.

Although we often think of vampires as ancient nobility, this is another uncommon motif. The idea probably originates with the idea of *Dracula*, created by Bram Stoker. Such a concept probably came out of the Anglo-Irish social structure of the late 19th century, the time during which Stoker was writing. During this period, a working class was emerging in England when the aristocracy and the nobility were viewed with a certain amount of suspicion. In Ireland, too, where the old aristocracy had owned the land for centuries, the working class was viewed with even more suspicion and dislike. Social and class divisions between the aristocracy and the working class, the landlord and the tenant, and the "haves" and "have nots," was becoming a problem in the late 19th century. The other celebrated "horror figure" of the 19th century, the infamous Jack the Ripper, was a shadowy figure in London murdering prostitutes. He was never caught, and he has now achieved a fearful cult status. But think how he is portrayed in common folklore—an aristocratic figure in a long cloak and a top hat—almost a caricature of Victorian nobility. Like Dracula, he is also the embodiment of the social division during that time. If one looks through *Dracula*, it's clear that the book contains hints of social commentary, all dating from around Stoker's time, hence the aristocratic background for the vampire count and for many other vampires since. Contrary to this idea, however, sees the majority of vampires coming from the lower echelons of society, that is, farmers, soldiers, shoemakers, wandering vagabonds, and so on.

The same goes when it comes to driving a stake into the body in order to "slay" the vampire. Once again, this looks particularly dramatic, and may have erotic overtones, but in vampire folklore, this is a risky business. In many parts of Romania, the stake is used not to destroy the vampire, but to *suspend* it. If the stake is drawn out at any point, then the vampire is free again. And one must be extremely careful about the type of wood of which the stake is composed. If it is made from the wrong type of wood, the stake will have little effect except to irritate the vampire. Therefore, great care must be taken in selecting the proper implement. In certain parts of Serbia, for example, the wood must be yew; in Russia it is oak; in Scotland it is rowan. So for the vampire-slayer, the choice can certainly be a tricky one, and is not as simple or straightforward as it initially seems!

One of the ideas that *is* closely associated with vampires is that they spread disease. Epidemics and plagues have always been connected with the Undead—whether this belief springs from the notion of decay or from the creature's unholy (and perhaps unhygienic) nature. In early and medieval times, disease had always been associated with the Devil and his minions, and vampires were counted among those. They carried the plague on their clothes and in their very touch—anywhere they had been held the beginning of some awful illness. Folklore has always reflected this. One such folktale from Scotland concerns the Vampire of Annandale. In the story, the Scottish king Robert I (Robert the Bruce) was dining with the Lord of Annandale when a local felon was brought in front of the Lord for sentencing. The man was greatly detested in the area and was suspected of being a witch. He had been held in the Lord's dungeons for some days. The Lord sentenced him to death, but the man appealed to King Robert for mercy. In an act of clemency, the monarch agreed to his request, telling his host that the man should be set free after he had departed. However, yielding to public pressure, the Lord waited until King Robert had gone and then had the man executed in defiance of his sovereign's wishes. Later, the man's phantom was seen in several parts of the locality and Annandale experienced a virulent plague that swept through the districts, taking young and old alike. The dead man, although he did not drink blood, was considered to be a vampire because he was spreading a plague. So virulent was the disease in Annandale that word soon reached the ears of King Robert. Upon investigation, he found out that his direct order had been disobeyed and instructed the local Bishop to perform an exorcism above the felon's grave. He also punished the Lord of Annandale by confiscating some of his lands. This seemed to put an end to the vampiric activities in the area, and the plague that affected the countryside passed. But the link between the return of the felon's corpse as a "vampire" and the spread of the infection were clearly linked.

The symptoms of certain diseases were also suggestive of vampire involvement. The gradual wasting away of the body seemed to give the impression that the individual's strength and vitality were being drawn off by some sort of external force. With a disease such as tuberculosis, the pallor of the skin and the gradual frailness of the body were often cited as "evidence" of a vampire's attention. Furthermore, the tightness of the chest, especially when lying down at night, resembled a weight crushing the victim. There were other symptoms, too: the marbled, pale skin; the glassy stare; and the coughing up of blood that formed in flecks along the edges of the mouth. It was all interpreted in a supernatural context; the victims were slowly turning into some sort of vampiric being themselves. This idea was paramount in many of the cases in rural New England during the late 18th century and for nearly all of the 19th. Even sometimes more so than the drinking of blood, the main aim of the vampire was to spread infection where it could.

The vampire also seems to be the embodiment of xenophobia within certain areas of the world. Anyone who was foreign, anti-social, or had strange ways about them was almost certain to become a vampire upon death. In Albania, anyone of Turkish nationality, Turkish descent, or who had relations with the Turks is almost certain to become a sampiro (Albanian vampire) and will stalk the night wrapped in a winding sheet. This may simply spring from a racial antipathy that the Albanians hold for the Turks. Both family and racial antipathies, however, provided a basis for many vampire beliefs and identified the possibility of individuals becoming vampires. Those who were different, and those who acted in a different way (especially with regard to practices concerning the burial of their dead), were vampires in the making. Those whose religion, funerary rites, or even food and clothing that were different were suspect. Even those who were antisocial might become members of the Undead—those who continually quarreled with their neighbors, those who were scolds, and those who engaged in unnatural sexual practices such as incest, all ran the risk of returning from the grave. In this way, many communities kept themselves, their practices, and their view of the world intact; the outsider, who could bring disruption, was excluded.

Despite the fictional idea of the Undead running amok through a town or a community and attacking at random, this was not the case. Although many communities lived in fear of them, vampires did not often strike in such a random fashion. Instead, they usually attacked what they knew: cattle, pigs, sheep, and even dogs became their prey, often creating poverty within a family. In many cases, the creature did not venture far outside its own circle of relatives for bloody sustenance, although certainly in specific instances it might attack other members of the community. Although many societies feared the vampire's blood-drinking habits and guarded against them, it was the fear of contagion that arguably troubled them the most.

Lastly and perhaps most chillingly, not all vampires assumed human form. The root of this belief centered around questions about what exactly a vampire actually *was*. Was it a corporeal entity that rose from the grave, or was it an insubstantial *spirit?* If the latter were the case, then could the spirit inhabit or *possess* an inanimate object? There are certainly stories—both folktales and literary fiction—concerning personalized objects, such as a comb, a hand mirror, or even a bottle, which has been in some way possessed by the spirits of their former owners. So if a vampire (or a person who became one), had owned the artifact, might it not be imbued with some of that essence? Thus, personal effects taken from the houses of those who were suspected of being vampires had to be treated with great care, as they might still contain some residue of their former owner. So the vampiric entity might not be the actual body of the dead person, but something with which they had been closely associated. These were just as deadly, for they drew energy from their surroundings and from any living being who had contact with them.

As a country, America seems to have drawn many of these mixed vampire beliefs to it. Immigrants flood in from various parts of the world, bringing their own beliefs and perceptions with them. These have mixed with some of the ancient beliefs of the Native Americans to form a rich tapestry of vampire folklore. It's a tapestry that reflects the myriad ideas of what a vampire might be. From state to state, tales of vampires sprang up and have continued through the years, each one displaying a subtle difference in how the creature was portrayed. And although we like to think of the American vampire perhaps living in the bustle of New York or San Francisco, or even maybe in the languid quasi-Gothic surroundings of New Orleans, much of the vampire lore can be found in quieter places such as Rhode Island, South Carolina, and Wyoming.

So let's take a journey through America and search for its home-grown vampires. There are plenty of them, but tread carefully, for they may not be what you expect!

TENNESSEE

Late in the year 1917, a road construction crew was widening a stretch of upper roadway that wound around a river bluff in Bradley County, Tennessee. Not far from Charleston, at a place where two dirt toads intersected each other to make a rough crossroads, they made a strange and macabre find. Turning over some earth in the center of the road, a workman uncovered the petrified body of an adult woman who had been buried many years before. The body appeared partially mummified by the minerals in the ground, which had preserved it to a reasonable degree. But there was something that unsettled the workmen: Petrified along with her body was a stake that had been forcibly driven through her chest and heart. This was clearly no ordinary burial. Stooping down, one of the crew members examined the stake and gave a gasp of amazement. It was certainly unusual—in fact, it was not a stake at all, but a bottom-leg support from an exceptionally handsome chair! Such a chair could have been the centerpiece of one of the finest homes in Chattanooga. So what was it doing piercing the chest of an unknown woman buried on a dirt road in remote Bradley County? It was a mystery indeed, but the chair leg was so distinctive that it yielded some of its own answers—down to the name of the men who had made it.

In early Colonial America, handmade chairs were always in great demand and the person who could make a fine seat was never short of work. In many rural communities, the chair had gradually become the staple of the craft business. Indeed, a good chair was the very center of the social world in many rural areas—it was the seat on which a mother nursed her young child; where women mended clothes in the lamplight; where the farmers and mountaineers rested at the end of the day; where neighbors exchanged gossip or ideas, and from which country patriarchs dispensed hard-won wisdom to their descendants. And because it held such a central place in the household, each chair had to *look* good. Arguably, the manufacture of such seats was both an important trade and a specialized art form. By the time that Allen Eaton published his *Handicrafts of the Southern Highlands* in 1937, southern and eastern Tennessee had boasted a proud history of rural chair-making for more than a century. Of special note in Eaton's book was Mary Ownby of Gatlinburg, who crafted her own chairs from start to finish. She selected a tree that she cut herself, splitting the wood and turning the posts by hand. Mary even fashioned her own tools—mainly chisels—to groove and decorate the chair, adding her own distinctive ornamentation to each one. She was certainly at the pinnacle of her craft, but she was not the only one.

The *real* antiques in the world of American chairs—those that would have been used by the early Tennessee settlers—were crafted by two brothers, Eli and Jacob Odom, in the high mountains near Shell Creek in Carter County. Their speciality was a distinctive slat-backed seat, beloved of the southern mountaineers, with shaved rear posts, curved slightly inward. It was known in the mountains as a "mule-eared chair," and was distinctive from the manufactured Hitchcock chairs that were in circulation at the time.

They arrived in Shell Creek around 1806 and set up their chairworks in a small cabin near the Creek. Because of their often distinctive importance in the community, chairs were not only sitting items in those backwoods days, they were used for trading as well. A handsome chair could be traded against something else, and it's thought that the brothers received such things as salt, sugar, molasses, meat, and coffee in return for their work. They created chairs of exceptional quality with support-posts made out of undried green maple and rounded struts cut from mountain hickory. As the maple dried, it shrank, holding the rounds firmly in place to create tighter joints. Using chisels and awls, the brothers then cut the intricate decorative pattern work that would come to characterize their chairs.

By the 1840s, their work was so famous that it was looked for everywhere in Tennessee. These were good times for the state, as more and more settlers poured in and a new wealth began to rise within some of the larger towns. New houses were starting to appear in places such as Chattanooga, many with sitting parlors, which required furnishing in a unique and decorative style. Hotels, too, were flourishing, many with long front porches where guests could sit. A good number of establishments boasted mule-eared chairs from the high mountains near Shell Creek. In time, the gentry of Charleston, taken by the "rustic charm" of the mountain chairs, began to acquire them as fashion items of furniture for their own homes. Wagonloads of slat-backed chairs were soon driven east from Carter County to Tusculum and Kingsport in order to grace the fine abodes of the new southern wealth.

But it was not only the gentry who acquired the Odom chairs. In many mountain cabins, they became the center of the household, placed in front of the stove where the mountaineers could sit, rest, and chat about the day's events. Such people didn't pay for the chairs in the way the rich folks did— this is where the bartering and trading previously mentioned comes into play.

So, as the workman knelt over the body on the side of a lonely dirt road, his eyes widened in astonishment as he recognized the pattern work of Eli and Jacob Odom on the chair leg. And what about the female corpse that it pinned down? Maybe one or two of the road crew, all local men, could at least hazard a guess. And it's here that we must delve into the murky and uncertain world of rural folklore and supposition.

It's difficult to say who the woman was; although the folklore of Charleston is littered with references to her, no mention is made of her actual name. She is usually referred to as "the woman from Hiwassee" or "the witch lady," often in a disparaging tone. Perhaps this serious omission stems from the face that, among mountain folks, as in many other cultures, a given name was a powerful thing. Speaking a person's name in a certain way could sometimes give the speaker a degree of control over the person, but in other cases, it could just as easily draw the unwelcome attentions of that particular person. Maybe the witch-woman was thought to be so powerful that even speaking her name would bring her down upon the speaker, and this resulted in the name being lost.

There are vague stories of her appearance and they are certainly not the most flattering. Descriptions speak of a fairly elderly lady with darkish skin as dry as that of a snake and a mouth as foul as a muddy hollow. She kept to herself up in her lonely cabin and seldom ventured to Charleston except to buy meager supplies. Birds refused to nest in the trees around her door and no dog would come near her. There are those who say that she never washed and others who say that she was a little lame. These may have been no more than stereotypes of a witch figure, but nevertheless everybody agreed that she had fearsome powers.

Her knowledge of natural things was reputedly formidable. She was, in the common parlance, a "yarb lady" who prepared poisons and potions from the plants that she found on the mountainside around her home. She made cures for various ailments, but with the darker side of her knowledge, she concocted deadly philtres and love potions, such as a medicine that could strike a man blind for life or could cause an unwilling girl to lose her inhibitions. The witchy woman was feared, but there was a certain allure about her powers. It was said that she could make men wealthy or successful and a woman alluring, simply by the use of certain herbs and incantations. So although they shunned her by day, folks secretly made their way up to the cabin on the ridge above the Hiwassee to buy favors or to have a curse issued against their enemies.

However, it was widely believed that the woman had far greater powers than simple herbs and potions. It was believed that she went about the countryside in the guise of a crow or a black cat, spying on her neighbors, learning their secrets, and creating mischief for them. And, it was whispered, drinking their blood. There were rumors all around Charleston and beyond that she was some sort of vampire and that she attacked men while they slept. Some said that they had witnessed her take the form of a great black bird that flapped away through the darkness, seeking victims. These were people who had crossed or mocked her or who had turned her away when she occasionally came begging. It was also said that she came in the form of a great black rat, which would often attack sleeping children in their cradles.

Moreover, some of the charms and potions that she used involved human blood, particularly menstrual blood. This was influenced by old beliefs that such blood was highly potent in a supernatural sense (it was believed to be the foundation of life itself) and therefore of immense use for Black Magic purposes. The idea of blood, used in hideous charms, invariably linked the woman to the idea of vampirism in the popular mind.

However, there have been those who have said that there is no evidence for the woman's alleged vampirism at all. The late Frank G. Trewhitt (who had family connections to the land on which the body was found), wrote the following in the *Tennessee Folklore Society Bulletin*: "The land on which the body was found belonged to my great-grandfather and was passed to his sons. If they ever had heard any vampire tales hereabouts, I would have been told." Though today, stories about her blood-drinking still persist around Charleston folklore circles.

Whether or not the woman *was* a vampire, the body was found in a remote place, impaled with a piece from a chair made by the Odom brothers, so how did she die? The most common story is that a disease epidemic spread through Charleston, carrying away both young and old. Such epidemics were common in many American cities and towns during the early-to-mid 1800s, but this one seems to have been especially virulent. This was a time before significant medical advances, and the origins of such illnesses—unsanitary living conditions, poor diet, and bad housekeeping practices—were unknown. Besides drinking blood and leeching human energy, vampires were strongly associated with plague and disease, and as the sickness took hold, the unsettled population looked around for somebody to blame. Who better than the strange woman on the bluff above the Hiawassee, rumored to be a vampire? She had hexed the neighborhood with her witchy ways, and for this she needed to be punished. Only then would the disease that afflicted the countryside come to an end.

Tradition says that a mob made their way to the cabin and dragged the woman from it, intending to set it on fire. Until the body was found, there was no record as to what had befallen her. It is interesting that when uncovered, she was buried facedown with the chair leg protruding from her chest. In some parts of Eastern Europe, this was the recognized way of burying a vampire and preventing the creature from ever finding its way out of the grave and menacing the world of the living, should the stake ever be withdrawn. If it clawed blindly in front of it, then it would only succeed in digging itself deeper into the earth. Vampires were also buried at a place where roads crossed, so that if by any chance it *did* manage to break free, it would become confused by the roads running off in different directions and it would not know which way to turn. And what better place to bury such a creature than in an earthen road where passing feet, hooves, and wagon wheels would keep the earth hard-packed, preventing the evil thing from finding its way to the surface?

Another intriguing question is: How did a beautiful Odom chair, much sought-after by the upper-classes of Tennessee society, find their way in to a cabin high above the Hiawassee River? And how did they fall into the hands of such a disreputable woman?

The chair, made by Eli and Jacob Odom was possibly passed down throughout the years, or the chair could have been given to her by someone in return for favors and without any knowledge on the part of the Odom brothers. If this is the case, then we will probably never know how it came into the witch-woman's possession.

As for the rest of the chair that the leg belonged to, it had allegedly "done the rounds" of the state, or so the gossip said. And the tale about how it worked its wicked magic never varied. At first, it is remarkably comfortable as the occupant settles back into it. Gradually, the person becomes more uncomfortable the longer he or she sits in it, and he or she becomes extremely tired and seems unable to rise. The victim may be unaware of this, and the vampiric lethargy may be passed off as simply weariness; later, when the chair has sated itself, its prisoner will be released, only to return later to have more energy and vitality drawn off again by the hideous seat.

Some stories say that it was last seen on the porch of a hotel near Charleston, the last one of a number of similar seats that had been put out for residents. Other tales say that it was seen among the furnishings of an elderly house in Greeneville; other sightings speak of it on the creaky porch of a rooming-house in Gatlinburg; in a college-house at Tusculum; in a shop in Kingsport that sold antiques. It has been seen in many locations all over the eastern state and certainly many stories are told about it. Its baleful influence stretches right across Tennessee.

Besides, any attempt to destroy it might provoke supernatural consequences. And in some versions of the tale, the wood of the chair is supernaturally impervious to blows with hammers and hatchets, so it cannot be
destroyed. By the same token, however, nobody seems to want to keep it
for long. Despite the grandeur of the seat, they are all too aware of the spirit
of the witch-woman exerting its influence. The only way to get rid of it, it
seems, is to give it to someone else.

And folklore even suggests that it might have moved outside the confines of the state—perhaps further north. There is even a rumor that it
might have been shipped abroad to Europe. In truth, nobody knows exactly
where it's gone. If I were you, I'd take a good, long look at the chair you're
currently sitting on.

The idea that at least some part of human consciousness can live on in
inanimate objects is not all that uncommon in folklore. The basic belief is
that if inanimate objects are strongly associated with an individual for a
length of time, they absorb some of the characteristics of that person. In
some instances, the soul of a deceased person may have attached itself to
some object that the person used in life, and this has formed the basis not
only of many folktales, but of several ghost stories as well.

The Irish folklorist and storyteller Michael J. Murphy (who served as a
collector for the Irish Folklore Commission) recounts a number of similar
tales from various parts of Ireland. The items range from a bone comb that
continually exuded the smell of apple blossom throughout a room, which
signaled the favorite scent of the owner, to a pair of sturdy leather boots
that began walking around at about 5 o'clock in the morning, the same time
as their previous owner would have arisen. Many of these items were
everyday things that might be found around a house, but had been imbued
with something relating to those who handled them. And it was possible
to deliberately imbue some inanimate object with part of one's personality—
maybe even for malign purposes. However, such an activity smacked of
dark witchcraft.

In American folklore and tradition, the most common item that took on some of the personality of a living person was the Cussing Coverlet. According to hill tradition, this was one of the staples of Appalachian witchcraft and it was not something of which mountain people often spoke.

All through the mountains, many women made patchwork quilts—either in quilting bees run by the various hill churches, or alone in their cabins by lamplight at the end of a long day. Many of these quilts, which were used to cover wood-frame beds, were works of art. There were certain standard designs, of course, but some women, particularly those who lived away in the remoter hollows, often designed their own. Some even sewed a memento into the work—a lock of hair, pieces of old garments, or baby clothes—all the things that went to make up their lives and had made them who they were. Like the mountain chairs, it was possible to name the woman who had sewed and embroidered a quilt from the pattern on the Coverlet. And as individual styles determined the quilt, so did the hopes and dreams of the sewer as her fingers worked the stitches. And in some cases, all her hates and frustrations were built into the embroidery as well. It was possible to weave a curse into the very fabric of the quilt so that it might do harm to others.

What better place, it was argued, for a spell to be made than in the stitching of a quilt? And what more intimate things could a person have than their coverlet wrapped around them against the chill of an Appalachian night? All the better for the stitched spell to take effect. Thus, the mountain witch could stitch her evil or her curse into the intricate weave of the quilt, perhaps mixing in some evil thing, such as noxious mountain herbs like snake root, pokeweed, or wild parsnip leaves. Only when it was placed on the bed would the curse *really* take effect.

The Cussing Coverlet worked in one of two ways. First, it could wind itself around the sleeper, choking the person to death. It would then rearrange itself as an ordinary quilt once more, giving no clue as to why the sleeper had died.

It might also act in a vampiric way, drawing the energy from the person sleeping beneath it into itself, like a sponge. In the morning, the person would rise, tired and ill-slept, possibly exhausted by nightmares as well. Eventually, the Cussing Coverlet sucked away all of his or her vitality and left the individual as an empty shell or even dead. And there was no way of detecting the Coverlet unless one had a practiced eye and could see the spells woven into the cloth.

It was further said that certain mountain midwives, healers, and wise women had the "knowing" of making such quilts—what undetectable spells and incantations to sew into the item—and their services could be purchased if need be. One of the most famous in Tennessee was the notorious Granny Bacon in Blount County, an area famous for its patchwork quilting. According to the Tennessee folklorist Dr. Joseph Sobel, she was sought after throughout the state by families seeking to resolve feuds and quarrels through dark and supernatural means. It would appear that she was something of a skilled needlewoman, and acquired "the knowing," which she adapted into her patchwork in order to make money. She was not a witch *per se*—there are other references to her as a healer—but she had certain skills that she chose to use for nefarious purposes when her neighbors clandestinely called on her to use them. Her quilts were deadly, vampiric things that could gradually draw the life from anyone who slept below them. And yet they were stunningly beautiful, all incredibly fine examples of mountain artistry and craftwork. But something of the evil intent had gone into them and had made them dangerous. Although most of the "old timey quilts" have long passed into extinction, there are still some of Granny Bacon's (and those of some other mountain witches) about even today.

North Carolina

In the wild, mountainous country near the tiny village of Boho in south-western County Fermanagh, Northern Ireland, tiny roads interconnect, leading across the stony uplands to queer, isolated hollows and fields. Some roads will take you across the uplands to Swanlinbar, others down toward places such as Wheathill or The Five Points near Florencecourt.

If you were to follow one of the narrow earthen lanes that lead upward into the fields, you would eventually come out high up on the side of a steep hill and close to the ruins of what seems to be a prehistoric fort in which lies a well. It is tucked away among large stones, thick brambles, and thorn bushes, and it always appears to be in deep shadow, even on the brightest day. Although the water in it seems clear, few farmers in the area let their livestock drink from it or will drink from it themselves. In Ireland, and in some other parts of the Celtic world, it is known as a Famine Well.

As their name suggests, Famine Wells in Ireland are connected to the great Potato Famine, which ravaged the countryside between 1845 and 1852. Around 1589, the English adventurer Sir Walter Raleigh planted the first potatoes in Ireland as a garden crop at his home in Myrtle Gove. From that small planting, potatoes spread across many of the fields in Ireland and became the county's staple. Potatoes could be grown in very little space— several drills or rows were all the Irish peasantry needed—and with very little effort. They were both filling and nourishing and, even when heated, could still be held in the laborer's hand and eaten as he worked.

In 1845, the potato crop failed spectacularly. It was coupled with a generally bad wheat and barley harvest in both England and Ireland. In 1847, the famine was at its worst. Almost everyone expected the Famine to pass, but the disease was in the soil, and each time the Irish turned their land, they dug the blight in once more. The effects of the blight would reoccur year after year as late as 1852 (in fact a less virulent form of it still remains in the soil even today). However, even as it began to die away slightly, its consequences for the Irish people were still devastating. Throughout the "Black Years" of 1847 and 1848 many died and many more emigrated. The roads were filled with people traveling between locations, seeking employment, and seeking food. The Irish countryside had become a nightmare of death and disease. It was not only the hunger that killed people, but a whole series of illnesses associated with it. By 1852, more than a third of the Irish population were either dead or fled to other places.

The Famine had an impact on the folklore of Ireland; memories and associations of that terrible time were woven into the tapestry of Irish belief and storytelling. For example, there is the supernatural phenomenon of the Hungry Grass. This is supposedly a lank and sickly grass that often grows on the grave where a Famine victim has been laid to rest. All across the Irish roads and fields, a number of the unfortunate were buried where they died, often without any Rites of the Church.

If one inadvertently steps on a patch of Hungry Grass then one is immediately seized by the Famine Hunger and may very well die from it, just as the victim in his or her grave did. The only remedy is to carry a small piece of bread, which one must insert between the lips as soon as the hunger strikes.

Even the smallest morsel will be effective. However, such places could be dangerous, and there is even a place known as Hungry Hill in County Cork that rises above Bear Haven and Bantry Bay. It is said that a number of unfortunates trying to reach Cork Harbour died and were buried there, and that, consequently, large patches of the Hungry Grass are in evidence.

The idea that the Famine dead had somehow "polluted" the land became extremely widespread in many parts of Ireland. Indeed, the idea went from simple patches of grass-covered land to wells and springs along roadsides and remote mountain places. It was thought that the unfortunates had drunk at these places and had somehow transmitted the Famine into the waters of the well. Those who drank from it thereafter would become "infected" with the Famine element. In fact, in some tales, the Famine Well takes the goodness from whoever samples its waters, drawing it into itself. In effect, the Well actually drank from its victims in the same way that a vampire might, leaving them weak, hungry, and exhausted. Moreover, it created a craving in the person to drink from it again, and would draw him or her back once more to its waters.

The idea of water, wells, spirits, and blood merged together in an idea that the well was devouring or drinking the sacrifice. Such a notion had an almost vampiric quality about it, as if the well was a living thing and was demanding both blood and life. It was as if the spirit who was worshipped there and the actual well had become one entity.

This idea was all very well in Celtic countries such as Ireland and Scotland, but could such a notion transfer itself to the United States? The answer is that it could and it did, and became prominent in places such as North Carolina.

The English arrived in the late 1580s when Sir Walter Raleigh established the ill-fated but celebrated Roanoake Settlement, which was probably wiped out by local Native Americans. There was little interest in the area until around 1653, when settlers from Virginia began to establish more permanent towns around the Albemarle Sound (which they named after

George Monck, Duke of Albemarle) in present-day Stanly County. Albemarle would assume the name North Carolina in 1691 and become a fully-fledged colony in 1712. The settlers who arrived there found themselves largely isolated from each other and from the other colonies throughout the area, for although there were some major towns, the region was mountainous and thickly forested, and did not lend itself readily to integration.

Although it was initially an English colony and would remain so for many years, it was Scots-Irish settlers who latterly determined the character and culture of the new state. Most of them were Protestant and large numbers were Presbyterian (many were Fundamentalists), and a good number were also from poor farming stock in their own country. It is estimated that between the years 1710 and 1775, more than 250,000 of them arrived in the colonies and settled throughout the developing states with large concentrations in the south and the Appalachian region. They all brought the culture and traditions of their homeland to the New World.

When these immigrants arrived in North Carolina, they found the English well established there. Much of the prime farming land had been doled out to incoming settlers from England and was occupied by second- or third-generation families of that descent. So, the new arrivals traveled further into the mountain country—into the Great Smokies, a part of the Appalachian chain—where the land was still untamed and had not been claimed by former settlers. They settled in the remote valleys and hollows where they set up isolated and reclusive communities, which still maintained many of the old ways that they'd brought with them from their mother country. Many of these beliefs and customs appeared strange or "quaint" to outsiders, but they embodied the characteristics of what formed the hardy people who had made the mountains their home.

Life in the mountain country was certainly hard; a harsh environment with many natural obstacles such as disease, wild animals, and dangerous Natives often made up the settler's world. It required a person with a determined character and hardy physique to withstand all the obstacles that the environment threw against those who ventured into the mountain wilds. It also required a resilience that came from deeply held traditions. It was these traditions that invariably shaped the characters of the mountaineers and enabled them to stand against the vicissitudes of their new environment. Old beliefs and perceptions were not all that readily disregarded.

In many ways, the landscape of North Carolina was not terribly far removed from that which they had left in Scotland or Ireland. It was mountainous and covered in forest with hollows and glen-like valleys tucked away in folds in the countryside, through which creeks and rivers ran. It had shadowy hollows with tiny lakes, ponds, and swampy areas. And of course there were wells. Many, like the ponds and minor lakes, were tucked away in remote hollows or on the high, near-inaccessible sides of hills and mountains.

These wells were sometimes perceived by local Native Americans in roughly the same way that they were seen in Ireland and Scotland. Local legends said that they were the abode of capricious spirits, or that they were gateways to another realm from which their waters issued. They were often treated with both reverence and awe.

Scattered throughout the Appalachian Mountains are a number of summits known as "balds." There are summits or crests that are covered with a thick vegetation of mountain grasses or mossy heath where one would normally expect heavy forest. How and why such summits have occurred is an ecological mystery. However, these mysterious hills were viewed with apprehension by local Native American tribes.

The names of some of these mountains reflect a long and complicated history, and some of them are known by the epithet of "woolly heads," because their summits are covered with a light gorse. Others take their names from dark tales that are connected to them. For example, Grier's Bald, about 45 miles from Asheville, North Carolina, is named after a strange, mad, and very sinister hermit, David Grier, who lived there around 1802. He shut himself away from the world after the rejection of his marriage proposal by the daughter of local military man and Grier's former employer, Colonel David Vance. Grier withdrew into the wilds and, according to rumors, trafficked with dark spirits on the mountain summit in order to win the girl (who had by this time married someone else). He lived up on the Bald in splendid isolation for almost 32 years, subsisting on what he hunted and a portion of the $250 that he had obtained for services when he had worked for Colonel Vance. There seems little doubt that such isolation drove him mad. When others began to encroach on his territory, he responded both angrily and aggressively and eventually killed one of his neighbors, Holland Higgins, who "trespassed" on his mountain. Brought to trial in 1834, he was acquitted on grounds of insanity, but was killed shortly afterward by one of Higgins's friends. Other versions of the tale say that he was killed by an iron-worker whom he'd threatened and who subsequently lay in ambush for him. The killing was dismissed as one of self-defense, so feared and abhorred was the strange hermit within the local community. His unquiet spirit is supposed to haunt the mountaintop as a penance for his dealings with dark powers, and the influence of these forces is still said to linger there.

Although Grier was certainly a strange character, he was not alone. Many such people—whether they were hermits or not—were to be found among the mountains of North Carolina, some of them associated with the balds. The mysterious Moses Fenn (or Fennel) is another strange character who allegedly lived among the hills during the 1840s and who frequented their upper reaches. Fenn was supposedly a wolf hunter who dwelt in a makeshift shack somewhere in the forests around Wayah Bald or Tusquitee Bald, which are both now part of the Nantahala National Forest. Moses Fenn emerges as a vague character about whom little is known, but according to popular lore was more Indian than the Indians themselves. He allegedly took several wives (mostly Cherokee) and was something of a shaman among some of the local tribes. His dealings with white men, however, were very few and far between. At times, he would disappear into the mountains (particularly the balds), and not seen for long periods. He would also sometimes tell wild tales of secret kingdoms lost among the hills or far underground, which he had supposedly visited. However, stories about him are so varied and contradictory (and he also appears to have been slightly crazy) that perhaps little attention should be paid to his claims. They do, however, refer to an interesting perspective on Cherokee folklore.

Many of the legends of local Cherokee tribes have maintained that these balds are hollow inside. Moreover, their interiors contained "countries" in which people, creatures, and forces dwelt. From time to time, these beings would come to the surface world and, though they did not remain here long, they often left evidence of their visit. Late at night, Cherokee hunters would see the flickers of fires along the mountains, suggesting that "people from below" were hunting on the surface of the world, or they might find curious tracks through the forest, which were suggestive of something strange and perhaps inhuman traveling that way—something that had maybe come from the lower worlds beneath the mountains.

The Cherokees, for example, spoke of Judaculla, a great giant that had come to the surface and left mysterious glyphs on a rock near the Devil's Courthouse on Whiteside Mountain. Similarly, Spearfinger, a creature that was somewhere between a witch and an ogress, emerged under cover of darkness from her underground lair to do harm and to kill as many as she could with her spear-like forefinger. In addition to this, there were the Nunnehi, strange little people who lived under the hills or in the deep forests and only came out to hunt at night. They were so temperamental that to encounter them might be extremely dangerous. They might lead you back to your own camp, or they could just as easily take you back with them into the underworld and you would never be seen again. Closely allied to these Nunnehi were the Moon-Eyed people, who only hunted by the light of the moon. As their name suggested, their eyes were large and round and their sight was weak; they were pale skinned because they lived so far underground and only came to the surface on rare occasions. Unlike the temperamental Nunnehi (who could, on occasion, be very benign), these creatures were extremely dangerous, ferocious, and inimical toward humankind and were to be avoided at all costs.

How had these beings come to the surface world, especially when they lived so far beneath the ground? The answer lies in the water-courses and sink-holes that dotted the region. Such creatures supposedly found their way to the surface by following ancient rivers and deep water sources, and probably returned to the depths by the same route. Water flowed through the hollow hills, emerging in the surface world. Wells, particularly in the remote hills, were also used and were considered to be a favorite method of entry to our world.

Native American lore also mentioned spirits and invisible forces that lurked at such wells, which could be just as dangerous as the underground folk. Such forces lingered close to springs and deep holes from which they often drank. These were the old spirits of nature or the ghosts of dead warriors, and were usually extremely hostile toward humans. They dwelt in the trees and bushes that grew around the edges of the wells and sometimes even in the water itself. Those who were foolish enough to ignore the warnings around such places and came to drink there might find themselves attacked and even drowned in the well-waters. Others might be induced to drown themselves under the malign influence of the spirit there or be dragged down into the other world, deep inside the balds.

It was, of course, extremely unwise for a brave to sleep anywhere near the well, as the spirits were always on the prowl there. They could drink the energies from the sleeper as he lay close by, just as easily as they could the water in the well. Those who slept by such wells often woke up exhausted and disorientated from the attentions of the spirit. It was not only the invisible spirits who attacked hunters while they slept, for the Moon-Eyed people sometimes chose to drink human blood in order to restore their own energies for a hard night's hunting on the surface. Thus, for tribes such as the Cherokee, who hunted among the mountains and the balds, such places were extremely dangerous and should be avoided.

The legends of the Indians and the stories of the white Celtic settlers who came to the hills of North Carolina often blended together very easily. The idea of the Famine Well, which could drive those who drank from it

mad with the Famine hunger, and perhaps draw their very energies from them, soon meshed with the Cherokee notion of dangerous spirits and blood-drinking folk who lived far underground and used such places as a means of access to our surface world.

Wells, of course, held a special significance to both sets of peoples. They were the reason why Indians constructed their villages in certain areas and also why the settlers put down roots in a certain place. The availability of fresh water was essential to life and settlement, and in the remote hill country of North Carolina, this was even more important. But they now could be a source of terror as well, harboring strange beings and forces that might be supernaturally dangerous to human life. Certain wells had to be avoided, particularly those among the North Carolina balds. With their strict religious viewpoint, the Presbyterian settlers in the hills soon attached the name of the Devil and other evil entities to some of these Indian places.

One of the most striking is a small well that exists on the side of Whiteside Mountain near the The Devil's Courthouse. The site, which is 10 miles northwest of Brevard and 28 miles southwest of Asheville, is well named, for it is a great slatey-gray area of rock on which nothing will grow and on which the devil is said to sit from time to time. Its name reflects the preoccupations of the original Presbyterian settlers in the countryside. The well is said to be the one from which the Evil One drinks during the course of his malicious ponderings.

The site is also not all that far away from Judaculla's Rock, and it is said that the well is also the haunt of the Cherokee monster, who subsists on both human flesh and fresh blood. In fact, in some Cherokee myths, the being squats on top of Whiteside Mountain watching all that is going on in the world below with a squinting, toad-like eye. Like the Devil, Judaculla drinks from the well and often lurks, invisibly, close by, ready to attack anyone who might be tempted to sample the water there. Similar to the Famine Wells back in Ireland and Scotland, the well has vampiric qualities and can draw the energies of those who bend down to drink there into itself. Those who press its water to their lips will soon feel a strange lethargy creeping over them, which will last for some time. Again, they will feel a need to return to the place and drink from the well as the vampiric site works its magic upon them. Whether this is the result of the Devil's influence or whether it is that of Judaculla is unclear. It is even said to be the unquiet spirit of a dead Cherokee who was condemned to remain by the well, where he had committed the offense of eating dog meat, and, subsequently will attack anyone who comes there in order to eat their flesh and drink their blood. Whatever the story, the Cherokee (and the later Celtic-European settlers as well) stayed away from the place. There have also been a number of disquieting stories concerning it, which have come to us from more recent times.

One such tale concerns a hunter named Ira Wallace. It is said that he was a man to be avoided; from time to time he was seized by unholy appetites and often drank the blood of the animals that he killed. It was also alleged that, given half a chance, he would have drunk human blood as well. This terrible craving was attributed to him using the well on Whiteside Mountain and being somehow "infected" by the spirit there. Descriptions of him, such as they are, suggest that he was gaunt and pale, with long and stringy hair—a bit like a wild animal. Periodically, he would come into places to buy meager provisions (it was noted that he never seemed to buy much food and it was speculated that he lived on other things up in the mountains). People would try to avoid him as best they could. Then, he would vanish up into the hills again and would not be seen for months. There was evidence of his presence though: the dead carcasses of animals that were sometimes found by other hunters, creatures with their throats torn out, and the savage marks of a hunter's knife on their dead bodies. It was said the travelers had sometimes glimpsed him in his awful work of viciously killing the animal down in some hollow or along a river track. This, some people said, was the work of the well upon him, and as long as he drank from its tainted waters, he would be like this. It was also said that it was the well that had somehow claimed him in the end, though no one knows what happened to him for sure.

Another such well is to be found on the slopes of Cold Mountain, located in the Shining Rock Wilderness about 15 miles southeast of Waynesville. The mountain and the surrounding wilderness was once part of the Biltmore Estate, owned by George Washington Vanderbilt II and, after his death, his widow turned the region over to the United States Forestry Service as the basis of the National Forest Park. The Wilderness is uninhabited and comprises a beautiful landscape of mountain and forest. On the property was said to be a particular well, which had all the attributes of that on White-side Mountain and which was avoided by local Indian tribes. Local Indians passing through the region might have used this well, and were seized with a dreadful lethargy that would prove fatal if they succumbed to it. In fact, there are several stories concerning the site in both Cherokee and settler lore.

At the end of the 19th century, a settler and trapper named Eli Ross supposedly lived with an Indian woman somewhere in the Cold Mountain area. He was found inexplicably dead out in the wilds around the beginning of this century. His death always was regarded as a strange one, as there was not a mark on his body, and it could not have been the result of an Indian attack or that of a wild beast. The body, however, seemed rather emaciated and the skin was a papery yellow, as though Ross had been drained of all his goodness and vitality. It was assumed that he had died of some form of fatal heart seizure or something similar, but there are those who say that he died with a queer look of horror on his face, and his death might have been caused by drinking from the well or from some connection to it.

Just as mysterious, and perhaps just as deadly, is a water source on Cling-mans Dome on the North Carolina-Tennessee border. It is one of the highest points on the Appalachian Trail, east of the Mississippi River, and is part of the Great Smoky Mountains National Park—only Mount Mitchell and Mount Craig are higher points. The Dome is named after Colonel Thomas Lanier Clingman, a celebrated fighter in the American Civil War (when he commanded the 25th North Carolina Infantry), who also explored the area extensively in 1850. It was named in Clingman's honor by the geographer Arnold Goyot in his maps of the area.

Clingman was not the only surveyor of the region, and several other maps of the Dome (also known as the Black Dome) exist, compiled by other explorers, showing old Indian trails across the region. The Cherokee called the place "Kuwahi," which means "the place of mulberries," and they believed that the Dome was hollow and stretched over a hidden land. On some of the maps, a well is marked, which the Cherokee believed led down to this land where unseen forces lived. Such forces, it was said, could also come to the surface world, although they could not stray too far from the well, but lingered invisibly in its vicinity. Some early maps purport to show the location of the well, although, confusingly, they all show different locations for it. No one is exactly sure where it is, but it is said that one will certainly know when he or she has drunk the water from it.

According to Cherokee folklore, the well is haunted by a spirit or force that has its home in the underground world somewhere under Clingman's Dome, but which comes to the surface on numerous occasions. The force is vampiric in nature and can "draw the good" out of anyone who uses the well. Doubtless, some of the later settlers in the area adapted the story in their own way, adding to its malignancy and to the potency of the tale. The being is also said to have the power to carry small children, the old, and the weak down into the well and deeper into its own dark world where it can hold them captive and feed on them. There is said to be no escape from the underground lair, and those who vanish around the Dome are never seen again, although sometimes on quiet, still nights their voices are heard crying for help from somewhere deep inside the height. Consequently, hunters and settlers have stayed away from the area in the past, though hikers along the walking trails might still be at risk. Through the years, there have been stories of hikers vanishing in strange circumstances. This may be just an old and possibly false belief, but perhaps it is better to avoid venturing from such trails altogether.

These are some of the major wells in the North Carolina region, but they are not the only ones. There are smaller, unrecorded places that have existed since the early days of the Spanish, French, and English colonists. It is suspected, however, that the stories concerning them might be of slightly later origin. In all probability, they are the fusion of old Cherokee legends with the myths of the incoming settlers to the region, and they have blended together to form a part of the folkloric tapestry of the North Carolina landscape. Combined with the stories concerning the surrounding balds, they give an eerie character to the area and create a developed, but quite mysterious mythology there. And although the idea of a vampire might seem strange, they are the legends of the North Carolina people.

So when hiking through the balds or through the wider Smokey Mountain region, it is extremely wise to take note of the wells that lie along the route. If you are caught thirsty out along the trail and are forced to look for water, who knows what might be lurking in the shadows of some remote waterhole? Maybe the well in County Fermanagh should serve as a warning!

SOUTH CAROLINA

Arguably no other region in America is as beautiful and as eerie as the Tidewater Country along the coasts of the Carolinas. Intercut with rivers such as the Waccamaw and the Great Pee Dee, the area abounds in deep and mysterious swamplands. Is it any wonder that such a region has drawn tales of pirates, smugglers, and lost treasure? There are fearful tales of runaway slaves who fled far into the marshes, never to be seen again. Although some undoubtedly drowned in the quicksands and swampy ground, legends say that some survived and turned feral in the wilderness. These individuals might have turned vampiric and cannibalistic and preyed along some of the small coastal settlements of the Tidewater Country. Others mated with queer creatures living in the deep swamps to produce hideous offspring that continue to dwell there today. But there are other elements to the eerie swampland atmosphere than vanished slaves and lost treasure.

From around the late 1600s, settlers in the Low Country found that rice imported from Asia grew extremely well in the valley swamps along the rivers. During the 1700s, rice became the economic basis of South Carolina, mainly for export to England where demand for it was high. The area thrived, making the Low Country one of the most prosperous colonies in all of the

United States. They initially began experimenting with various strains of the crop, but the damp climate of the region frustrated them and all experiments failed. However, they began to recognize the advantages of importing slaves from the traditional rice-growing areas of West Africa, who were used to working with the crop. For obvious reasons, the Rice Kings showed more of an interest in the origins of the slaves they purchased than did many other American colonists. The Rice Kings were willing to pay high prices for slaves from the "Rice Coast" or the "Windward Coast" of Africa or from Sierra Leone.

Most of these slaves were Gullah people. The origin of the word *gullah* is uncertain, but it referred to a distinct type of people found along the "Rice Coast" of West Africa. Some ethnographers have argued that it refers to Angola, an area from where at least some of these people might have originated. Other state that it refers to a tribe of people known as the *Gola*, who came from a region between Sierra Leone and neighboring Liberia. Another name for such slaves, "Geechee," might come from the *Kissi*, a people found in both Guinea and Sierra Leone. Other have suggested that their name might be American-Spanish, as the Spanish often referred to the Carolina people as *Guale*. Whatever the origin of the name, the Gullah made the ports of Charleston, South Carolina, and Savannah, Georgia, into two of the busiest and wealthiest ports in the South. They imported slaves mostly from Sierra Leone who came by way of Brazil, however, the trade was growing and more direct routes were being established.

In 1750, two Englishmen named Henry Laurens and Richard Oswald opened a "slave castle" (slave-holding enclosure and trading post) on an island in the Sierra Leone River, known as Bance or Bunce Island, trading directly with America. With them, the Gullah brought their own culture, which thrived and expanded all through the Low Country region.

White rice planters built grand houses for themselves on the islands and along the rivers, leaving the running of their plantations to "rice drivers" or black overseers. Gradually, a new Afro-American culture began to develop in the area—one that had a strong African basis, which was reinforced by the numbers of new slaves coming in from the Rice Coast. This feeling of "Africanness" was perhaps more pronounced than among the slaves in, say, Virginia or North Carolina, where the settlements were smaller and where contact with white overseers and white owners was much more frequent. This, of course, helped to preserve many of the traditions and beliefs that had been brought from Africa on the slave ships. These mingled with some of the more white perceptions, which many of the slaves had picked up from the planters; thus, Low Country traditions, although primarily African in tone, also held elements of white Christian traditions.

The great rice plantations were sprawling affairs. Many of these dwellings were splendid antebellum mansions, standing in their own well-manicured grounds, a number of them reflecting the histories and aspirations of their owners. For instance, the beautiful Litchfield Plantation was established by the Simon family, who came from Litchfield, England, in the early 1700s. They purchased more than 2,000 acres of land around Pawley's Island from Thomas Hepworth as their estate. The plantation house was built around 1740. The sprawling estate was divided around 1794, with one half (now called Willowbrook) being retained by the Simons and the other (which kept the name Litchfield) passing into the hands of the Tucker family of Georgetown, who had recently arrived from Bermuda. The Tuckers were to prosper on their new property, and by the 1850s, the plantation produced almost one million tons of rice per year with freighters sailing up the Waccamaw to the Litchfield landing to take on cargoes bound for Europe. Nowadays, as the river mist wraps itself around the edges of the old plantation, the faint sound of a gate bell continually ringing and demanding admission calls can be heard, even though the bell and clapper have long since been removed. And on the roads along the Neck, a spectral horseman still thunders through the mist in the direction of the plantation house, not pausing in its headlong flight.

All this is thought to be connected to the unquiet spirit of Dr. Henry Massingbird Tucker, who owned Litchfield between 1859 and 1897. Medically trained, he served for four years as a volunteer surgeon in the Confederate forces. He was an exceedingly complex man, showing great individual acts of kindness to the slaves on his land, who called him "the Ol' Doctor," yet capable of great cruelty toward them as well. A great Episcopalian, he severely punished those who did not attend his church, depriving them of food and allowing several of them to starve to death. After the Civil War, he served as a local doctor in the lands along the Waccamaw Neck. He died

in 1904, and is buried in Georgetown Cemetery. However, his restless spirit refuses to leave Litchfield, and on foggy evenings, the vampiric form of the doctor returns to its former home, demanding admittance by ringing the ghostly bell, just as when he was alive.

At Wambaw Creek, on the swift-flowing South Santee River, stands the elegant Hampton Plantation founded by the French Huguenot Horry family during the 1730s. However, it is not a Horry phantom that is seen in the grounds of the house, but rather the ghost of John Henry Routledge (or Rutledge), a later owner who committed suicide there after being slighted in love. His spectre is said to haunt both the house and the grounds, looking mournful and dejected as if brooding on his past misfortunes.

And on the North Santee lies the overgrown ruins of the once-elegant Peachtree Plantation. Built by Thomas Lynch in 1762, it was burned to the ground in 1840 when it was leased by Stephen Duval Doar. It is said to be haunted by several ghosts. One of these is said to be the daughter of Thomas Lynch, Jr. (who was a signee of the Declaration of Independence), who died of yellow fever; her overgrown earthen funeral marker still stands in the ruinous grounds. The spirit of Lynch, who went mad with grief at her demise also haunts the grounds.

The American Civil War hit the Rice Kings extremely hard. As an important Confederate port, Charleston was blockaded by the Union navy, preventing a great deal of its trade. Blockade ships, known as the Stone Fleet, were brought close to the port with the intention of sinking them. Although some of them were driven off course, some actually did sink and prevent entry to Charleston Harbor. Moreover, Union forces conducted attacks all along the coastline, burning and pillaging where they could, sometimes along the edges of the great plantations.

After the War was over, exports of rice from South Carolina never really recovered. The cultivation and shipping of rice was becoming far too expensive and many of the big plantations faced bankruptcy. The era of the Carolina Rice Kings had passed, and many of the big estates were forced to sell.

Today, many of these grand houses have been restored and are now museums, hotels, or conference centers owned by the state or by private companies. But there are still said to be a few, abandoned and hidden away in the swamplands, perhaps along some half-forgotten creek, lost in both mist and memories. These give off a mouldering grandeur, together with an air of vampire lore and mystery, which is hard to dismiss. There are, of course, stories of travelers through South Carolina who have come upon them by accident, and have often been unable to find their way back to them once they've returned to civilization once more.

And of course such near-forgotten abandoned buildings draw all sorts of local legend and folklore. The Gullah people who live in the area have their own stories, based on their own folklore, about such abandoned places. They say they are the lair of "swamp devils," strange inhuman creatures that are the spawn of dark swamp entities and runaway slaves. Tales of the walking dead and beings akin to zombies are frequent.

European folklore and Gullah beliefs have fused together in the swamplands to provide a rich tapestry of legend and lore. However, the basic beliefs remained essentially African and West Indian in nature. For instance, some slaves spoke of an experience called "kana tavario" in which the spirit of a dead ancestor visits the living world in order to complete some unfinished business or to hold conversations with descendants. The spirit of the dead person comes and squats upon the chest of the sleeper so that it can communicate directly with him or her, drawing energy from them during the course of the conversation. The sleeper later awakes exhausted. Among the Zimbabwean Shona people, the word *madzikirira* is used to describe something that visits a sleeper during the night and draws off energy. In South Carolina, the being is referred to as a Hag and the experience as being "Hag ridden."

Interestingly, there is a somewhat similar belief in Far Eastern folklore, especially Mongolian, where the phrase *khar darakh* is used to describe the experience. This means "pressed by the black or dark" and refers to a spirit that comes back from the dead, either voluntarily or at the direction of a black magician, to commune with the living. They squat upon the chest of the sleeper drawing energy from them.

Throughout the Low Country of South Carolina there was a distinct trace of African lore and superstition all across society. The old forest gods and spirits of the mother country still slumber beneath the surface of the everyday world. There is still a belief in root doctors and in rootwork (herbal practices that are often connected with magic). Around the time of World War II, root doctors flourished all over the Carolina Low Country, mixing herbs and potions and dispensing charms. Possibly the most famous was Stepheney Robinson, famously known as Dr. Buzzard, who died in 1947. The title "Dr. Buzzard" was not exclusive to one individual, and was passed down among Gullah root doctors as a sign of status and power. In fact, Robinson was said to have been the son of another Dr. Buzzard who had practiced in the Low Country for many years. After Dr. Buzzard died, his ghost was said to take revenge on some of those who had crossed him during his lifetime. It was said that Dr. Buzzard would sometimes appear at the foot of their beds wearing the blue-tinted sunglasses he sometimes wore when alive, and through these he would drain the energy from the sleeper.

Although one of the more famous conjure men in the South Carolina swamplands, Dr. Buzzard was certainly not the only one. Even during World War II, there were a good number of root "doctors" living among the remnants of old plantations, all with fanciful-sounding names such as Dr. Fly, Dr. Crow. Dr. Turtle, and Dr. Bug. All of them claimed to have knowledge far and beyond that of ordinary people and to be in contact with the old gods and spirits that dwelt in the swamps, which they could manipulate for their own purposes. Dr. Buzzard, it was said, could summon the dead and make them do his will if he so chose.

Such a tradition of magic, dark gods and the dead stretched way back into South Carolina's colorful history, and had its roots in the slave trade. Indeed, it was not only in the largely rural Low Country that such traditions flourished. In places such as Charleston, the dangerous John Domingo resided. The Black Constable, as he was known, lived in a curiously shaped house that had been owned by a Dutchman who had a reputation as a necromancer. There was even some talk that he might have somehow been involved with vampires.

The street on which he lived had been extremely respectable and had once been the abode of many of the old Charleston families of quality. By the time John Domingo arrived, however, it had a distinctly "run down" feel to it and had such an evil name that few decent people cared to go there. The house where Domingo lived quickly gained a formidable reputation for evil. Local legend stated that a number of people had vanished in its vicinity and that bodies had been found close by with the blood drained from them. Strange noises and voices came from it, as well as queer smells.

Domingo made his own laws and his neighbors were forced to respect that. An old man who lived next door to him saw what Domingo kept in his back yard and it terrified him, but he was forced to shrug his shoulders and say nothing because he "feared for his blood." What did that mean? Had the neighbor glimpsed some sort of vampiric creature lucking there? Something that the Black Constable kept well away from human view? There were rumors of a thing living in the shadows of the yard and that Domingo had killed several people in order to feed the thing. Rumors around the city said that it was something without a skin, and that it was extremely voracious.

But it wasn't just vampires lurking about in his yard; there were other things under the Black Constable's control that had vampiric tendencies. For instance, a man across the road from Domingo disputed over a well on his property that the Constable sometimes used. He forbade Domingo from using it, so the Constable sent a creature of light that resembled a rainbow to suck the well dry. After that, water never came again. Others believed that it might be a blood-drinking or energy-drinking spirit.

The Black Constable's end came in a rather dramatic and terrifying manner. At the very height of his pride and power, he was acting as an unofficial law officer. One evening, he pursued two burglars who were violating homes in the district. The robbers tried to escape, but Domingo caught them and brought them back to Market Street where a small crowd was waiting. Stepping ashore, he held each one up by the scruff of the neck. Nobody around saw anything except the Black Constable. His eyes certainly seemed to be fixed on something directly in front of him, and his darkened skin began to pale slightly For a moment, he stood upright, a look of bafflement crossing his face as if he could not really comprehend what was happening. Foam mixed with some blood began to run down from the corners of his mouth and he rose up onto his toes as if something were pulling him upward. Several bystanders swore that they saw the marks of long and inhuman fingers on his windpipe, even though there seemed to be nothing there. Letting go of the two thieves, Domingo started to claw at the air in front of him. The blood began to flow more freely from his mouth as though something might be drawing it from him. For a moment, he seemed to dangle in mid-air and then his body appeared to be thrown backward to the ground. Before anyone could reach him, he seemed to age a good number of years right in front of them, becoming an old and wrinkled man, and his face had turned the color of a withered cucumber. A local doctor came and pronounced John Domingo dead. Even as the bystanders looked at the cadaver, it seemed to shrivel up even more until it was merely a withered representation of its former self. Several times after his death, he was reputedly seen walking down the street and disappearing into the doorway of his strange house. His name lingered in the area and many rumors still claimed he was a vampire, years after his death.

For the Gullah people, the main supernatural danger is the plat-eye. Initially, it's thought that the plat-eye was simply an evil spirit that dwelt in a certain place, but it has taken on a variety of shapes. It is said to be the spirit of somebody who hasn't been buried properly or who has been exceptionally evil, so the ground has refused the corpse. If a victim makes eye contact with the creature, then the plat-eye has the power to draw the energy from them into itself. The plat-eye is supposed to wait in the shadows of a moss-covered tree for someone to pass, and then it will leap out and confront them, eventually drawing their souls from them. Plat-eyes can, of course, take other shapes. Sometime they appear as great snakes, gliding through the swampy gloom, or they can take the form of an irritating insect that annoys travelers, sometimes leading them into dangerous, marshy areas where they might drown. In other instances, the plat-eye can take the form of a horrible looking creature that can petrify its victims with its stare. The name is said to come from a great extended eye that emerges from the center of the Being's forehead and can look all around it.

All through the South Carolina swamplands there are tales of haints (ghosts), plat-eyes, and boo-daddies, all of whom seek to prey on the living in various ways. The notion of the boo-daddy is interesting, because it signifies either a sorcerer or a supernaturally created being who often requires either the blood or energy of victims in order to maintain itself. In other words, a vampire. There is also a female equivalent known as a boo-hag, which is just as dangerous. It was thought that a witch or sorcerer could become either a boo-daddy or a boo-hag simply by taking off his/her skin. The being could then fly through the air and attack the living across the countryside. The existence of such beings was widely believed among the Gullah people, and the idea might have originated in the old forest gods and monsters that haunted the African nights, memories of which were still maintained within the slave religions. Gradually, however, the notion became slightly modified with certain Christian elements added. A crucifix fixed to a window or door might drive the boo-daddy away, but it wasn't always a reliable protection, as the boo-daddy's African origins might not recognize it. There was, however, one sure way in which the living could protect themselves and their property against haints and boo-daddies.

For the Gullah, color has significance. Various colors symbolize various aspects of their lives, and the color associated with the supernatural in the Gullah mind is blue. To some, it can mean witchcraft and dark magic, but to others it was the color of protection against ghosts and evil things. Thus, to paint the front porch of a house with a light blue coloring was considered an infallible protection against witches and boo-daddies in South Carolina. Indeed, a shading of light blue paint that was used was sometimes described as "haint blue" because of this association. Once the doors and windows were painted, the boo-daddy, boo-hag, or any other evil thing couldn't enter. Even to touch the painted area caused the creature pain. A smudge of such paint on the body would also serve to protect the individual, or so the tradition said.

It was also said that the boo-daddies and boo-hags traveled around the South Carolina swamps in small flat-bottomed boats. Indeed, it was said that they preferred this method of travel to flying, as they could more easily see what was going on all around them. Small lanterns were sometimes attached to the ends of these boats to guide them through the swamps at night and they sometimes appeared like moving groups of fireflies drifting among the overhanging trees. There are a number of folktales concerning this type of boo-daddy or boo-hag. The following tale is one of the most celebrated.

Bobby P lived with his father (Pa) in a little cabin deep in the swamps. His mother was dead and it was only the two of them, but they lived a reasonable life. However, as Bobby's Pa got older, both of them began to long for a woman to tidy up and look after them. His Pa thought that it was high time that Bobby was married. But where could he find a girl out in the swamps? Throughout the next year, he took himself to the dances and the settlements nearby and met with a few of the girls there. They say that he proposed to several and even got accepted by a few, but when it came to the actual marrying, they got cold feet and Bobby was left to go back to the cabin.

One day at a grocery store, he had a strange meeting. An old woman came out of the deep marshes in a little flat-bottomed boat from which she sold milk and eggs. She and Bobby talked, and it turned out that she had a granddaughter who was about Bobby's age. It seemed like the answer to all of Bobby's prayers.

When they first met, she was everything that Bobby had hoped. Bobby suggested that they should get married by a visiting priest. So they went to Beaumont and were married, and Bobby brought the girl home to live with him and his Pa for a time. However, the girl was skittish and wouldn't settle, as if there was something really troubling her. It turned out she didn't like living with Bobby's Pa, so he put down money on a little house of their own.

One night after a large meal, Bobby felt tired and stretched out on the couch while his new wife settled down in a rocking chair on the front porch to do some sewing. As she did so, she hummed a little tune that made Bobby drowsy. He fell sound asleep and slept until morning. When he woke up, he noticed that his wife looked particularly hot and sweaty.

And that was the way it seemed to continue. During the day, the girl cooked and looked after the house, but as the evening came around Bobby would suddenly get very tired and would either go to bed or fall asleep on the couch and awake in the morning to hear his wife come in and go to bed. She would sleep for a little while and then get up as fresh as ever to go about her work. He tried to question his wife about it, but each time he raised the subject, she became cranky and would either divert the question or refuse to answer it.

In the end, he spoke to his Pa and told him what was happening. Bobby's Pa was extremely worried, for he had heard of things that lived deep in the swamps that had the appearance of humans, but were not. They were vampires, and had no great love for humankind. He sent Bobby to a hex-woman to consult him about his wife. When she heard his story, she told Bobby that he had been drugged by a boo-daddy or boo-hag, and that he might be in great danger. She gave him an herb that would counteract the effects of the drug. She also told him to pretend to be asleep and to see what happened.

Bobby did what she said and took the herb, which allowed him to eat the food that his wife gave him without feeling drowsy. Even so, he pretended to fall asleep on the couch as the hoodoo woman had instructed him to do. As usual, his wife took a seat on the rocking chair and hummed her little song. When she though he was asleep, she crept past him and up to the attic, where she kept a large spinning wheel. Bobby followed her and peered through a crack in the door. To his absolute horror, he saw his beautiful wife sit down at the wheel and spin off her skin, leaving only a creature of red muscle and blue veins, completely bald and with very sharp teeth. As he watched, this terrifying creature rose up and escaped out through a skylight window and away into the swampland night.

The next day, he went back to the conjure woman and told her what he'd seen. The old lady nodded and told him that this was either a boo-daddy or a boo-hag, a shapeshifting fiend that had taken human form. At some point, she would turn on him, drink his blood, and gnaw his flesh. However, there was a way to defeat the thing.

She told Bobby to buy himself blue paint and to wait until the being had flown away into the swamps. Then he was to paint the blue color around every doorway and every window, leaving not the tiniest bit unpainted. When that was done, he was to gather up the boo-creature's discarded skin and to fill it with salt and pepper. Once she put this on again, it would burn her from the inside out.

Once again, Bobby pretended to be asleep and his wife stole up to the attic to her spinning wheel. When she had gone, he began to paint every window and every doorpost with a blue color. Then, he nailed the windows closed with thick iron nails.

The boo-creature returned just as the first fingers of dawn were touching the sky. Her mouth was covered with dried blood where she had been drinking from sleeping folks out in the swamp. As soon as she touched the skylight window, she gave a terrible shriek as the blue paint turned her away. She began to beat on the glass with her skinless hands, trying to find a way in. As Bobby watched, she began to test each window and door to find a chink through which she could enter. At last, she found a tiny piece of window ledge that Bobby had neglected to paint and began to squeeze herself through very painfully, her skinless form being torn on the rough edges of the wood. He heard her fall to the ground with a whimper. Outside, daylight was crawling across the swamplands and the conjure woman had told him that the creature had to get back into its skin before the sun was fully up.

She bounded up three flights of stairs to the attic room. Once there, she tried to pull on her human skin, but the salt and the pepper that Bobby had put there burned her flesh. By now the sun was already up, and as she flew out over the swamp, she exploded in a welter of skin and gore.

Bobby never married again—after his experience he reckoned that bachelorhood was a much better option. But each night he would stand on his front porch and watch lights come and go deep in the gloom of the swamps, and he knew that the boo-daddies and boo-hags were moving about in their flat-bottomed swampboats, each with a lantern on its end.

There are a number of stories similar to the one above in the swamp country. In some respects, such stories reflect the mystery and eeriness of the swamps coupled with the half-remembered traditions that were brought from Africa by the slaves. African witches allegedly drank blood or drew off the energies of their enemies, like a vampire.

There are a number of references in the slave accounts collected around Murrell's Inlet by the Writer's Project to "blind Aunt Daddy," who seems to have been a significant character in the wider Low Country. She appears to have been a slave woman of considerable age and was stone blind. Among the Gullah, as with many other cultures, physical deformity or physical disability was sometimes suggestive of a supernatural aspect to the person concerned. Aunt Daddy's blindness may have given the impression that she was in contact with forces other than those of this world and that she was a witch. It was believed that, like John Domingo, she could travel around the countryside in various shapes, drawing both blood and energy from her neighbors in order to sustain her.

Some of the references to her come from a servant named Lillie Knox, who was interviewed by Genevieve Willcox Chandler around the late 1930s. Lillie had been a house servant to the Chandlers and, at the time of her interview, she was roughly 10 years younger than Genevieve. She knew all about boo-daddies and plat-eyes.

She claimed that in Gullah folklore, the boo-daddy or boo-hag often drank from the most available orifice, the nose. The only way to divert the boo-daddy's attentions, according to Lillie, was to hang a sieve on the bedroom door.

This is a common belief concerning vampires in many cultures, and is not unique to the Gullah. Vampires, being inquisitive and fastidious creatures, will be drawn to some small repetitive task that will keep them occupied until the sun rises, and they have to return to the grave.

According to Lillie, the sounds made by a boo-daddy deep in the swamps were distinctive and would let swamp-dwellers know that the creature was on the prowl. Allegedly, it barked like a fox, howled like a dog, and hooted like an owl. Cynics will of course say that the sounds were made by ordinary animals, but to the Gullah, they were indisputable proof that the boo-daddies were prowling areas of the swamplands.

Besides the usual tales of men who had married boo-creatures, Lillie also knew about ruined shacks and abandoned mansions far away in the swamps where such beings congregated, which she called "haint houses." The only people who could enter these places, unmolested by the vampiric creatures there, were those who had been born with a thin membrane of skin across their faces, which comes away after birth. In many cultures, this membrane has magical properties and often acts as a form of protection against evil spirits. Babies born with a caul are considered special, and in Gullah lore, it might have immunity to the attentions of boo-daddies.

As mists writhe through the South Carolina swamplands and queer noises are heard in the depths of the marshes, it is easy to see how the Gullah people formed their beliefs. Even if one was not Gullah, it was difficult to suppress a shudder as the Carolina night crept in from the sea. Who knows what lies out there in the dark, along the lonely swamp roads?

LOUISIANA

A s far as vampires go, Louisiana might be just the place to find them. Past New Orleans, a brooding, magical city filled with shadowy streets, courtyards, and alleyways, lies a wilderness of cypress swamps, a place of hidden, misty bayous, abandoned and overgrown cemeteries tucked away in remote groves, and mouldering antebellum houses, some hung with Spanish Moss, dreaming in the last vestiges of the fading grandeur of the Old South. What better place to find the unquiet, vampiric dead? Little wonder that writers such as Anne Rice, Robert Bloch, and H.P. Lovecraft have set some of their more eerie tales there.

Louisiana is a real melting pot of cultures and traditions, yet it does not seem to readily lend itself to conventional ideas of the Undead. By "conventional," we mean the traditional notion of the vampire as portrayed in books and films. So forget the ideas of Anne Rice, as Louisiana vampire beings are slightly different.

For a number of years, the predominant culture in the state was that of France (up until 1803, it was a French Colony), a country that does not really have a major tradition of vampirism. Nevertheless, other influences have crept in and now form a rich vampiric tapestry, which lies just beneath the surface of Louisiana society. Vampires in this state tend to be fused with other entities to form hybrid monsters or were-creatures. Like Louisiana, these Undead and terrible things have often originated in an amalgam of cultures and perspectives, so in order to understand where they might come from, it is perhaps necessary to take a brief look at the complex colonial history of Louisiana.

People have immigrated into the Louisiana area since 3400 BC. During this period, when the hunter-gatherers began to organize themselves and build mound-dwellings, Louisiana boasted the earliest (and largest) mound complex in America at the Watson Brake site near Monroe. These Mesolithic peoples settled in this area, spawning cultures that would follow them in the region throughout the centuries—periods that gave rise to some of the Native American groups in the area—the Appalousa and the Chitimacha among many others.

The first Europeans arrived in the area in 1528 when Pánfilo de Narváez led a Spanish expedition to the Mississippi River. In 1542, an expedition led by Hernando de Soto passed north of the state, encountering Caddo and Tunica natives, before moving south again, down to Mississippi to the Gulf of Mexico in 1543. De Soto found that the natives all along the river were incredibly hostile and the Spaniards were very poorly equipped (their crossbows had stopped working and they were low on provisions). Significant numbers of his expedition were wounded and more than 11 were killed. After his experiences in the region, de Soto reported back to Spain that future expeditions should avoid the area where possible.

And so, for a time, European interest in Louisiana was negligible. However, in the later 17th century, when French expeditions traveled south for sovereign, religious, and commercial objectives it was renewed. The French began to establish themselves along the banks of the Mississippi River, extending their influence down to the Gulf of Mexico. In 1682, the explorer Rene-Robert Cavelier, Sieur de La Salle, entered the area and named it "Louisiana" in honor of the French king, Louis XIV. The French rapidly began to establish fortified settlements, the largest being Fort Maurepas (now Ocean Springs, Mississippi, near Biloxi). This was founded in 1699 by Pierre Le Moyne d'Iberville, who was brought from French Canada for the task. He formed much better relations with the local Native Americans than the Spanish had been able to do, and soon the Fort and settlement were well established. Louisiana was a massive territory, extending along both sides of the Mississippi River toward French Canada and encompassing the present-day states of Mississippi, Missouri, Arkansas, Oklahoma, Nebraska, Kansas, Wisconsin, Illinois, Iowa, Indiana, Minnesota, Michigan, and North and South Dakota. Such a large area was set up with one specific purpose in mind—to trade with the Spanish colonies that lay to the west and in Texas to deter any Spanish advances. El Camino Real (the King's Road)—or the old San Antonio Road—was set up as a trade route in order to convey goods and supplies into the Spanish colonies in Spanish Tejas. Its terminus was based at Natchitoches. This settlement soon became a bustling river port, transporting cotton and similar goods into the west, and many great plantation houses grew around it. And another town, serving surrounding plantations, was also growing fast; New Orleans was quickly becoming a major port. The massive area of Louisiana was rapidly adopting a French ethos, which was beginning to rival the Spanish west.

The French, of course, were not the only immigrants. Along the banks of the Mississippi from around 1720, Germans had begun to settle—there is still an area of the Mississippi shore, through St. Charles, St. John the Baptist, and St. James Parishes—which is still known today as The German Coast. Their influence stretched even further back into the swamplands where there are areas known as Bayou des Allemandes (German Bayou) and Lac des Allemandes (German Lake). They also settled all the way through the area to a site known as the Arkansas Post (Encores Rouges), now part of the Arkansas National Park. This was a large German settlement, although a census conducted in 1790 showed only roughly 10 pure German families living there. It's thought that the Germans found living at the Post somewhat intolerable.

Many of the German families in Louisiana came from the Alsace region on the French/German border, and were largely of farming stock. The majority, however, came from the Rhineland area and from the German-speaking cantons of Switzerland. They had settled there under the aegis of the Company of the Indies (Le Banque Generale Privee, also known as the Mississippi Company), a private land-holding bank. When the Company folded in 1731 (as part of the Mississippi Bubble) they took over and became responsible for their own holdings.

In 1763, a large part of Louisiana was signed over to the other major power in the area—Spain—at the Treaty of Paris, which concluded the Seven Years War in Europe. Much of the territory to the west of the Mississippi was handed to Great Britain following the French- Indian Wars. The Spanish now controlled New Orleans (the Old Quarter of the city still boasts Spanish architecture), and this would prove important when a new wave of French immigrants would arrive. They were Acadians from French Nova Scotia in Canada, who had been driven out of their homes by invasions by the British and had traveled south hoping to settle in the areas around New Orleans. Led by Joseph Broussard (known as Beausoleil) the refugees had tried to settle on the island of Dominica in the Caribbean before moving to New Orleans and finding it in the hands of the Spanish. More than 200 of them arrived in the city on February 27th, 1765, on board the *Santo Domingo* and were initially welcomed by the Spanish. However, life in a Spanish-dominated city slowly became intolerable for the independent-minded Acadians, and they gradually withdrew out into the swamps and bayous of the countryside to the southwest, becoming what are known today as "Cajuns" (a corruption of Acadian). There were Spanish settlers too—mainly from the Canary Islands—called *Islenos* (islanders). They began arriving between 1778 and 1783, and some of them drifted out into the bayou country; many, however, stayed close to New Orleans. The area was now becoming a rich cultural mix of Cajuns, Spanish, and Germans, but there was yet another element that would add to this heady interracial stew.

In 1719, two French ships—the *Duc du Maine* and the *Aurore*—arrived in the port of New Orleans carrying an important cargo. Both were slave ships and they brought the first African slaves into Louisiana. Many of these slaves (and those who would follow them) came from the West African coast, from a region that is now known as Benin. Others came from Angola. Later, slaves would also arrive from what is now Cote d'Ivoire (Ivory Coast) and Senegal—according to French shipping records more than 2,000 slaves were brought from these areas between 1718 and 1750. Trade and administrative links between French Louisiana and Senegambia (the area that is now covered by Senegal and Gambia), facilitated the ready import of slaves. New Orleans became a major slave port on the southern coast supplying slaves to the plantations and great houses further inland. Life on these plantations was not always pleasant, and according to legend, groups of slaves would run away into the swamps where pursuit would be difficult and where they could continue to live without disturbance. It's also thought that many of these slave groupings mixed with and intermarried with groups of Cajuns, Islenos, and Germans already living there, thus forming an even richer cultural mingling in the bayou regions. There is evidence that all of these cultures merged with each other in various ways; music is one example. One of the staples of Cajun music, for which southwest Louisiana is famous, is the accordion. It came from the Germans who were already living in the bayous before the French arrived. The music consists of two types—the formal French Cajun waltzes and two-steps, which certainly come from the French settlers, and the blues-soaked zydeco (swamp rock), which has all the features of slave music. The two are often intertwined and white musicians often play the frottoir (a vest-like instrument made of corrugated aluminium worn by zydeco musicians in Cajun bands).

The cultures also shared their differing cuisines. The most famous dish usually associated with the Louisiana cajuns—jambalaya—is thought to be French. Actually, it contains elements of both Spanish and Creole slave dishes. Some have argued that it was an early attempt by the Spanish settlers to make paella without using saffron (which was expensive to import), so tomatoes were used. Others state that the dish is simply a variation of the Jollof dishes (also called *Benachin* meaning "one pot" in the Wolof language of Gambia) of West Africa brought over to America by the incoming slaves.

But it was not only music and food that the various peoples shared; it was also their folktales and their belief in supernatural and mysterious things. The French did not have a widespread belief in vampires; in fact, the conventional idea of the vampire played no great part in their folklore. But they did have a great belief in monsters. In the woods of Provence, a giant, human-like ghostly creature known as Le Grand Bissetre hovered over lonely pools, making a mournful cry as it did so. To see this creature, or even to hear its cry echoing through the forest, was a bad omen, as it would guarantee a slow and lingering death, during which all the good was "sucked" from the individual's body by some mysterious malady. Although this being was not exactly a ghost, it was regarded mainly as a kind of monster that could do physical and mental harm to those who saw it. Le Grand Bissetre has often been dismissed, using such explanations as marsh gasses and swarms of insects carrying sickness in marshy places in the woods, but none of these could satisfactorily take away the actual terror of the legend concerning the thing. This terror was probably also brought to the swamps of the New World. The low-lying boggy land, which lay around New Orleans and which stretched into the swamps, may have rekindled memories of such creatures lurking in the countryside back in France.

There were also malignant forms of fairies known as *fee*, which often attacked young children in their cradles, as well as the very old and sick. Belief in them was usually found among the French, but there were tales among some of the Spanish, particularly among those who had lived close to the French borders. These beings sometimes dwelt close to water and were especially vicious, especially during the summer months. There was little protection against them, said the French legends, save the power of the Holy Cross or the prayers of a priest, and they too could draw the breath from a sleeper—especially if that sleeper was an infant—for their own malign purposes. Although many of the fatal activities of the fee have been explained away by a gradual understanding of water-borne diseases, it is easy to see how some of these stories and beliefs could have transferred themselves into the swampy low-lying marsh country of southwest Louisiana and how some elements of them could appear in "vampire tales."

The Germans, on the other hand, had a rich tradition of vampire stories and tales of the walking dead. They knew the Undead under a number of names—*nachtzehrer* (night waster), which had been used mainly in the north of the country, and *blutsauger* (blood suckers), which was a term used in the south. The *nachtzehrer* was something of a dangerous nuisance that attacked family members as they slept, and had a penchant for ringing church bells in order to keep the community awake. The *blutsauger* was one of the dead who sucked the blood of sleepers. The general term of *shroud-eater* was also used, denoting the way in which a revenant might devour its way out of its winding sheet. It has to be pointed out, however, that not all German vampires simply drank blood. Many caused terrible dreams that were just as deadly, as they left the dreamer wasted and exhausted in the morning and might ultimately result in his or her death. They also spread disease in a community and tormented livestock. Like everywhere else, the types and activities of German vampires varied, wavering between the returning, malignant dead, and outright night-time monsters. Like the Dutch *nachtmerrie,* these creatures belonged to a class of being known as *night visitors,* which were not altogether human (or which had never been so). Such "visitors" could take the form of old pagan gods in the guise of *Nacht Ruprecht* (a strange creature of vegetable origins with a face of twisted roots and vine, always accompanied by a humanoid companion named George Oaf) or *Zwarte Piet* (Black Peter), a sinister shadowy creature who might steal away the souls of the innocent. Such beings did not necessarily drink blood, but created terror in those who were getting ready to settle down for the night. There were also blood drinkers; in the north of Germany, a goblin-like creature called an *alp* climbed on the beds of sleepers to draw blood from trailing arms or from exposed areas of flesh. Like other night visitors, the alp also had the power to affect dreams. Alongside this vampiric being was the *neuntoter,* a type of vampire who was driven away not by garlic (as in the films), but by lemons. Lemon juice, and even the smell of lemons, could repel this night monster. In order to dissuade such night creatures, a rope or a sheet with a number of knots was sometimes left by the bed or along a road leading to the sleeper's house. The idea was that the night visitor would have to stop and would be forced to unpick the knots in the rope or sheet for most of the night, until the sun came up, and it would have to return to its grave, thus leaving its potential victim alone.

In the gloomy swamplands of 18th-century Louisiana, however, tales of the night visitors, whether it might be the blood-drinking alp or Nacht Ruprecht, must have taken on a kind of immediacy, which may have unsettled the early immigrants into the bayou country. Tales of such beings might have merged with the stories of the French Cajuns and of Le Grand Bissetre.

According to the Hausa people (the largest ethnic group in coastal West Africa), deep within some of the forests lived the Bori, although, exactly *who* or *what* the Bori were is open to question. We must be careful, too, because among the Hausa peoples, Bori is also the name of a spiritual force that can possess an individual, and an entire belief system has been built around it. However, for some of the Hausa, Bori was something physical that lived deep in the forests and usually stayed away from men. Alternately, there was a gathering of evil spirits; a coven of witches or indeed a congregation of the dead. It was also said that they were a different type of people, not exactly human, with their own ways, their own religion, and their own customs. Some traditions held that there were more than one grouping of them, each with its own language, traditions, and "rhythms" (the sound of their drums). And although it was held that Bori, were disembodied spirits, it was also believed that they could possess individuals in order to gain physical shape. The same was true with dead bodies, which they could reanimate if they so chose. It was not normal to see a walking dead man emerge from the forest gloom. This might be one of the Bori and their influence was very strong. Similar to European vampires, they could spread death and sickness wherever they wandered and could sometimes draw healthy, living people back with them to the forest depths.

In some traditions, for example, the Ashanti from the Ghana region, there were other things that dwelt in the forests, too. These were things made of leaves and roots that were molded into human shape. They could be briefly glimpsed moving among the shadows of tall trees, but were never directly seen in sunlight. Similar to the Bori, they often preferred the night. They were, according to some, the old vegetation and forest gods that had once ruled Africa way back in some former time. Once they had accepted the worship of men, but now for some reason they had turned against them and often sought out ways to do humanity harm. They were entities to be avoided, for they could lead men astray and to their deaths. Some of them were small, some the same height as men, and others still were giants who could crush a man simply by flexing the root-like fibers of one hand. Not all these entities were masses of tangled roots though. Some were like ghosts and could float through the forests on the wind, lighting on their victims from above. Others had leathery wings like bats. And there were those among humankind who leagued with them in return for power—witches and wizards who worked evil against their communities. These "witchy people" or "voodoo hags" were either slaves or masters of the forest entities and worked with them to promote evil. These were the kinds of dark creatures that lurked in the minds of the African slaves as they first came to the swamps of Louisiana. And again, it is easy to see how these beliefs merged with the dark, boggy, forested countryside that they found there.

In these gloomy marshlands where the Louisiana vampires were born, all of these ideas came together in a kind of supernatural gumbo and gave such creatures their shape and form. Rural vampires in Louisiana, therefore, tend to be a combination of many of the nightmares of each culture rolled into one. These creatures prowled the lonely bayous, almost like wild animals manifesting themselves to lonely settlers or travelers at will, sometimes during the day, as well as at night. But, just to complicate matters, there were other, more conventional, types of vampire as well.

In districts within cities such as New Orleans, where arguably some of the more traditional cultural ideas manifested themselves, vampires seem to be slightly more recognizable in their appearance and customs. Thus, perhaps Anne Rice is right to portray her vampires as the dissolute scions of old Louisiana families or as members of the Undead who had traveled to the city from parts of Europe. Indeed, in areas of such cities, European traditions were still paramount and the inhabitants still viewed the vampire as the walking corpse of medieval folklore. Old European practices still continued. For example, there was a custom of "sitting with the dead" for several days before burial and roughly seven days afterward. Such custom seems to have been common in a number of European countries and was done for a variety of reasons. In a time when there were no real doctors to pronounce a person dead, the actual instance of death might be problematical. A person might fall into a "deep swoon" or experience a cataleptic episode and be taken for dead. During times of widespread disease and plague in both towns and cities, such "deaths" appear to have occurred with fair regularity. Those who had apparently succumbed to illness were interred as quickly as possible to prevent the plague from spreading, although they may not have been clinically dead at all. And of course, even in times of no disease, people might be pronounced dead under the most spurious of circumstances. In both England and Ireland (and in parts of France and Germany as well), the tombs of some great local families had bells connected between the living rooms of their houses and the nearby tombs of family members. Should the person who was mistakenly interred come to in the tomb, he or she could summon help by pulling on a bell rope and alerting those within the house.

Many of these devices still exist in large houses; I was in a house in the Irish Republic that had a large and ornate bell hanging in its front drawing room, which was connected to a family mausoleum within the building itself. I was told that the bell had, in fact, rung twice—once it was answered and a woman was saved, but on the second instance, members of the family had been too fearful to answer it. This has, of course, given us our common expressions, "saved by the bell" and "dead ringer." However, not all families had such devices and the custom of "sitting with the dead" took place to ensure the person did not return to life.

Of course, the idea of a corpse suddenly rising up before being placed in the grave or ringing a bell from an otherwise silent tomb has eerie connotations and could have fed into the idea of a vampire lurking among the graveyard shadows. Old, common European beliefs were often called into play to explain such returns from the grave: a corpse not properly buried according to the rites of the Church; a dog barking at the coffin (a German belief); being the seventh son of a seventh son (which was believed to leave one open to becoming a vampire in some parts of Europe); or a horse shying away from the gravesite of someone. These were all the conventional marks of a possible vampire, and the methods to alleviate them dated back to medieval Europe: decapitation of the corpse, burial face down, the placing of a sickle on the neck, and so on. Also, certain funerary articles can be placed on the graves of suspected vampires to prevent them from rising (wreaths of garlic, wolfsbane, and crucifixes). Some of these can be seen adorning the fronts of the famous "oven tombs" in places such as St. Louis Cemetery No. 1—which gained some notoriety through Anne Rice's books, and the fact that it houses the grave of Marie Laveau, the famous "Voodoo Queen" of New Orleans. As the cemetery name suggest, these were largely European burial sites (although a number of Creoles are also buried there), and these apostrophics reflect such tradition and belief. The vampires that might lurk there are of the conventional kind, and ones that we would readily recognize.

There is an extremely curious story concerning the Ursuline Convent on Chartres Street in the French Quarter of the city. The Convent was founded in 1727 and nuns arrived from France to assume their duties in New Orleans. However, it is said that they arrived with some very special items.

For some reason, they brought with them several coffins that they kept in the convent and transferred to a second building built in 1745. The coffins were rumored to contain vampires, through how they had come into the possession of the nuns is unknown. In some accounts, they were the bodies of former Sisters who had been bitten by vampires and for whom the others were seeking a cure. Other legends cite different reasons. The new convent was designed by Ignace Francois Broutin, who had designed the original convent. As with the first, he designed a secret room in which the coffins could be stored. And there they lie to this very day. It is said that from time to time, the nuns permitted the vampire ladies to rise and walk about. This could be done during the day as well as at night-time—in Europe it was believed that some vampires could exist in daylight—and the vampires might often mingle with ordinary people who are going about their business in the city. However, after a certain time, they had to return to their caskets, which the nuns kept for them in the secret room. Other versions of the story say that these beings were women who had become vampires within the city and whom the Ursuline nuns had taken in and cared for. According to some versions of the legend, some of these women even married and lived for part of the time with their husbands in various areas of New Orleans. Nonetheless, they still had to return to their caskets at certain times, perhaps without the knowledge of their husbands. The convent is no longer in use (in 1912 the nuns moved to a new building uptown) and part of the building remains as an archive for the Diocese. However, it is still a persistent legend in the neighborhood that somewhere in an attic or in a secret room, there are still coffins in which the vampires lie. Of course, the story may be no more than a fable without any real substance—some commentators have argued that it was no more than a tale spread by Protestants in the city in order to cast a slur on the convent and on the Catholic Church—although its proponents argue that there is at least *some* grain of truth in it.

In other parts of the city where the Creole and African cultures dominate, such as the Vieux Carre, Canal Street, and Dumaine Streets, vampires take on a much more exotic form and may have more in common with those in the more outlying bayou areas. Here, the influence of voodoo and African religions have played a part in shaping the perception of the Undead. In the Cane River area, and around the Melrose/Yucca Plantation just beyond the city, vampires take on a distinctly more zombie-like "feel" to them. These are not the recognizable figures of European lore, but the shambling rotting dead of African nightmares. These, according to tradition, were creatures that could eat human flesh, as well as drinking blood. They might also change shape at will, often taking on the form of a great reptile such as a snake or lizard—a suggestion of the serpent worship in the Voodoo religion. They might enter a room or a house through a keyhole or a crack, and for this reason many of the keyholes in the houses within the Creole quarters of New Orleans were blocked in order to prevent vampires from entering. Vampires, in the guise of snakes, can sometimes also slither under doors, often resuming their ghastly, rotting zombie-appearance as soon as they enter a building; for this reason, the undersides of doors are also blocked.

Among certain Creole groupings, it is believed that if a person tastes human flesh either deliberately or inadvertently, he or she is bound to become a vampire after death. This may connect vampires and zombies (who are also said to be flesh-eaters) in the Creole mind. And like many of the European vampires, they are associated with disease and dirt.

One of the most notorious New Orleans cemeteries for these vampiric walking dead was the St. Peter Street Cemetery in the Vieux Carre, bounded by Toulouse, Rampart, Burgundy, and St. Peter Streets. This ancient cemetery had a fearful reputation all across the city. It had been designed as part of the city area by the military architect Adrien de Pauger, who had laid out many of the streets in the Vieux Carre around 1721, and it was the first of the burial grounds on the banks of the Mississippi. Its closeness to the river—and to the residential district—created all kinds of problems. The actual level of the graveyard had to be raised, using dirt from ditches that had been dug all around it. A wooden palisade surrounded the site, but this did not prevent a few of the graves from the balconies and even sometimes from street level. And as the city was hit by various epidemics, the plots soon filled to bursting point. All sorts of people were buried there. By the end of the 1740s, cemetery neighbors complained that they were unable to endure the sight (and the stench) of bodies poking out from under tombstones or half-buried in the graves into which they had been squeezed. Some people claimed that the dead rose up and shambled about and sometimes wandered out of the cemetery after nightfall in order to attack those passing by. A 5-foot high brick wall was built around the graveyard in order to deter these "night walkers." Built by the money of the rich and the sweat of the poor, it was dedicated and blessed by a bishop on All Saints Day of 1741; this meant that no wandering corpse could cross it and attack anyone in the city beyond. This was probably the first "celebration of the dead" in New Orleans. However, the unquiet dead made their presence felt with regard to the cemetery and its new holy wall. In 1788, a series of catastrophes occurred around the gravesites—the first occurring when the Mississippi River burst its banks and flooded the place as well as a great area of the city itself. This was followed by a serious fire on Good Friday, which burned a large number of houses to the ground. It is said that part of the "holy wall" around St. Peters Street Cemetery collapsed and that the dead wandered out of the graveyard after nightfall and attacked people as they attempted to deal with the calamity. With them came an outbreak of disease, which spread quickly throughout New Orleans. The deaths from the plague added to the number of bodies that were packed into St. Peter Street Cemetery. However, such disease also had the effect of diminishing the population, and over time the number of burials in the overcrowded graveyard gradually decreased. St. Peter Street was unceremoniously covered with lime—ostensibly in the hope that it would strop the spread of any disease, but in reality, some say it was to stop the vampiric, rotting dead from getting up and wandering about during the night.

Today, no tombstone remains to mark the site of any burial in the Cemetery. The place was closed as a burial site in 1788, although burials still continued there for a number of years afterward. Some of the funerary markers were transferred to St. Louis No. 1, which became the new burying ground for the area. Stories concerning shadowy forms still circled the old ground after dark, though. It is also whispered that some of these ghostly shapes have transferred themselves to the St. Louis Cemetery on Basin Street between Conti and St. Louis. Vampires, it would seem, still haunt the French Quarter.

But, although the shadowed streets of New Orleans contain their own dangerous ghosts and each district of the city holds its own dark secrets, it is out in the swamps and bayous, way beyond the city limits, that bizarre vampires truly hold sway. And the brooding landscape does nothing to quell the traveler's apprehension as he or she journeys through this territory. Driving out of New Orleans along Interstate 10, it is unsettling to know that sections of the road are actually supported by piles driven into the swamp where all manner of beings might lurk. Just outside the city lies the second largest area of swamp and bayou in Louisiana—the Honey Island Swamp, named after the swarms of honeybees that are found there. Only the Atchafalaya Swamp near Lafayette is bigger. The region is an "overflow swamp" fed by the Pearl River, which flows into it and covers an area of 35,000 acres.

The place certainly has slightly sinister overtones. Clumps of cypress, red maple, water elm, and tupelo gum trees rise up out of the watery depths like malignant sentinels, creating a gloomy twilight that stretches all through the swamplands. The near twilight is enhanced by large areas of duckweed floating on the top of the water, creating a blanket of deep green, and the seemingly unending curtains of lacy, pearl-grey Spanish Moss, which hangs from the branches of the trees. Here and there, little creeks run off into the depths and twisting trails lead across navigable land into the very depths of the wilderness. And here and there the roofs of small (and possibly abandoned) cabins can be seen from the roadway and through the trees. These may have been erected to facilitate the fishing camps that are set up along the creeks and swampholes going further into the marshlands. Abandoned fishing camps are scattered through these swamplands, suggesting that humans have been somehow all but overwhelmed by an encroaching nature. And there are stories of small and almost abandoned villages hidden away deep in the swamps. These have been built by runaway slaves and evil-doers from the nearby major slave port of New Orleans, who set up communities in the swamps just beyond the reach of the authorities. There are also a number of former plantations close by, and slaves also ran away from these from time to time, disappearing into what was then trackless waste and seldom being heard of again. If these individuals *did* form some of these near-abandoned settlements, exactly *what* lives there now?

There have always been tales about places such as the Honey Island Swamp. As the traveler journeys deeper into the marshes, past the fallen cabins tucked away among the trees, the sense of a brooding presence grows stronger, as does the feeling that one is being watched. Decaying vegetation fills the air with a sweet, rotten smell, often suggestive of old cemeteries and hidden, badly overgrown graveyards. Little wonder then that such regions have become associated with monsters and the Undead. And the creatures that lurk in the swampy depths—part devil, part vampire—are not the beings that are found in the cities, but are rather a wilder, more exotic, mixture of beliefs and perspectives—French, Creole, African—but are nonetheless deadly for that. A number of these beings are a fusion of vampire and werewolves—sometimes referred to as *loup garou* (from the Latin *lupus*, meaning "wolf" and possibly the Frankish *garulf*, meaning a man who is supernaturally more than he seems, perhaps able to transform himself into something else). The term *loup garou* (also referred to in parts of America as *loogaroo*) is generally taken to mean a werewolf, but in some cultures it can mean slightly more and in the swamps of Louisiana it is referred to as *rougarou*, which can sometimes mean a combination of werewolf, vampire, and witch. Such things exist in the swamplands, such as the Honey Island Swamp.

One of the most popular tales concerning these swamps is the legend of "Old Handsome." The name is ironic and full of black Louisiana humor, for "Old Handsome" is anything but good-looking. Instead, it is a "booger" or a "hant" that lives deep in the swamps. It is both a monster and one of the Undead. It can both drink human blood and eat human flesh, and has lived in the swamplands for several centuries. Some legends suggest that "Old Handsome" is a sort of ghost of a slave who fled from a plantation and became lost in the Honey Island Swamp. He died, but his body was taken over by forces that had dwelt among the trees since the earliest times and turned it into a kind of vampiric monster. Some say that it appears in the guise of a great reptile—like an alligator—other accounts say that it has the guise of a thing made out of tree roots and foliage, which can actually lurk under the surface of the swamp.

In other versions of the story, "Old Handsome" appears as the spectre of a French pirate who operated off the Louisiana coast. In order to avoid capture in New Orleans, he traveled into the swamps and bayous where, like the slave in the previous version, he was somehow possessed by the ancient powers that lurked there and became a ravening monster. In this version, the being resembles a kind of smoke or mist (the swamps are full of fogs and mists that are often associated with "hants," which follow travelers deep into the wilderness and attack them when they least expect it). In this, he takes the guise of a *feufollet,* a kind of Will-o-the-Wisp–type entity that can lure travelers into dangerous places and then kill them. In other versions of the tale, this vampire assumes the form of a great reptile that waits just beneath the surface of the waters to trap the unwary. It is said that "Old Handsome" can suddenly rise up out of the water or appear from a dark area among the trees ready to attack and drink blood, and in this way it parallels the provincial French idea of Le Grand Bissetre or some of the German horrors that lived in the gloom and half-light. Certainly the swamps have an almost primal feel to them and they are never really silent or empty—the air is filled with the continuous sound of cicadas and the furtive movements of animal life.

Around New Orleans lies the former plantations from which many of these slaves escaped; some of these boast stories of their own. The most accessible of these great houses is Destrehan, only a 10-minute drive from New Orleans International Airport and about 30 minutes from the French Quarter of the city, standing on River Road. It is the oldest documented plantation home, still standing in the Lower Mississippi Valley. This also has the reputation of being one of the most haunted plantation houses in the area, and is supposedly home to a vampire who was a member of the family who lived there in former times.

The house was built in the French Colonial style between 1787 and 1790 for Robert Antoine Robin de Logny by a mysterious master builder known only as "Charles." It is thought that this gentleman may have been Charles Paquet, a freed "man of color" who kept slaves of his own. The house boasts hand-carved cypress posts on its upper gallery. However, it is not clear that it actually *was* him who built Destrehan.

When de Logny died in 1790, the house passed into the hands of his son-in-law Jean Noel Destrehan, who purchased it for a nominal sum. Jean Noel was a Creole but of an extremely noble family—his sister Jeanne Marguerite was married to Etienne de Bore, the first mayor of New Orleans. Destrehan would become a Louisiana state senator. He and his wife Marie Celeste de Logny would have 14 children necessitating an expansion of the house. He added several wings including two *garconnieres* (from the French word *garcon* meaning a "boy"—these were essentially bachelor pads where men of quality entertained their lovers and mistresses or where young men sometimes stayed within sight of their parents).

In January 1811, New Orleans experienced one of the largest slave uprisings in United States history. It began about 30 miles upriver from the city on the plantation of Michael Andre. Urged on by old witch women and Voodoo men, the slaves rose up, severely wounding Andre and his son. The rebels began marching toward the city and River Road, where they were joined by a number of other slaves; a large group of them—about 200 in total—began to advance on the city and on some of the other plantations. Two days later, the Louisiana militia put down the insurrection by killing a number of the leaders and taking the rest prisoner. They were taken back to Destrehan where a summary court was convened. All were found guilty— most were sent back to their own plantations, but some were given a bloody and painful execution. Following in the traditions of the French Revolution, a number of the rebels were beheaded and their gory heads mounted on wooden poles near the house and along the River Road. Their unquiet spirits are still said to walk there. Among those killed were several old voodoo women and the spirits of these gather around the house in a guise of bats or dark birds, ready to drink the blood of the unwary individuals that pass by. Some of them take the form of flying heads with filed and sharpened teeth, which will spring on the traveler, bearing him or her to the ground, before beginning a gory feast.

Jean Noel Destrehan died on his plantation on October 4th, 1823. His descendants, who continued to live at the plantation house until 1910, included the enigmatic Nicholas Noel Destrehan, who was Jean Noel and Marie Celeste's son. Nicholas Noel was a handsome and dashing figure—he went about in a black cape and dark clothes—but he was also rumored to be very wicked. He learned old African magic from some of the slaves on the plantation, and adapted this to keep him young and handsome. However, his life was haunted by catastrophe. He married a 15-year-old girl, Justine Fortier, who died shortly after the marriage; he later lost his right arm when his cape became snagged in some plantation machinery. Although he married again, he did not survive long after and died of Yellow Fever in 1836. However, he was supposedly possessed with the vampiric spirit, which settled on the plantation house following the slave revolt. In fact, it is said that, while living in the *garconniere,* the vampire spirit had taken hold of him and he was a blood-drinker while still alive. He is still said to travel all through the plantation in the shape of a bat or an owl, seeking out prey for himself.

Although he acted like a wealthy plantation owner, Nicholas Noel never actually owned Destrehan, and at the time of his death was nearly bankrupt. He did, however, accumulate a mountain of family debt while living there; with creditors closing in, it seemed that Destrehan might have to be sold off to meet some of this. The property was actually in the hands of Jean Noel's daughter Elinore Zelia Destrehan, a pretty young Catholic girl who, in order to save the plantation, married the much older, curmudgeonly Protestant Stephen Henderson. Indeed, Destrehen had already been put on the market, much against Nicholas's will, but after Zelia's marriage in 1816, the "For Sale" notices disappeared.

However, the family was a haunted one, and during the next several years, Zelia began to look pale and drawn, which some neighbors put down to the callousness and brutality of her husband. Others, however, suggested that it might be because of the vampiric attentions of Nicholas Noel who came and went from the property as he pleased. In 1830, Zelia (around 30 years old) suddenly and inexplicably died while on a trip to New York. The cause of death was left blank on the death certificate and speculation was rife. Stephen Henderson was named as her sole heir. He died in 1838, declaring in his will that he should be buried with his wife and that all his slaves should be freed and allowed to return to Africa if they wished. This was a number of years before the Emancipation Proclamation, and this last proviso was swiftly overturned by the Louisiana legislature.

Throughout his days in the house, Stephen Henderson had never been well—some people said that it was his age, but others said that it was the attentions of a vampire (possibly Nicholas Noel Destrehan), which lurked somewhere in the environs of the place. His family was, however, extremely anxious to dispose of it and, in 1839, sold the plantation of Judge Pierre Adolph Rost, the husband of Zelia's younger sister Louise Odelle. The Rosts undertook a series of extensions to the main house, making it even grander, but they were never very happy there. The family later became connected by marriage to the nearby Ormond Plantation when Nicholas's daughter Adele married Samuel McCutchon of Ormond. During the American Civil War, Rost was appointed as Ambassador to France by the Confederate President Jefferson Davis, and the family left for Europe in 1861, leaving Destrehan abandoned. It was later seized by the federal government. For more than four years, Union soldiers lived in the house and there were stories that some of them vanished, perhaps dragged away by the vampire hidden somewhere in the building. Destrehan acquired something of a sinister reputation during this period.

The Rost family returned in 1866 and took over their former properties, including the plantation house. Their youngest son Emile was one of the last of the line to live in the house before selling it to a sugar manufacturing corporation in 1910. The house was largely closed up and was given over to its memories and its ghosts, which perhaps included a vampire. And just to emphasise the fact, some of the rooms in Destrehan were used in the film adaptation of the Anne Rice book *Interview with a Vampire.*

The neighboring plantation of Ormond, which would later become connected to Destrehan through marriage, also had its legends and mysteries. Slightly "younger" than Destrehan—though not by much—Ormond was built by Pierre d'Trepagnier on land that had been granted by Don Bernardo de Galvez, the Spanish governor of New Orleans, as a reward for services in the American Revolution. The house was built in the same style as some of the great Colonial plantation houses of the West Indies and became a family home. The exact date of its construction is unknown, but it is thought to have been slightly later than the neighboring Destrehan. Not long after it was raised, however, a mystery occurred.

The family gathered in the great dining room for a meal one evening in 1798 when the master of the house, Pierre d'Trepagnier, thought he saw something moving outside the window. A servant motioned him to look; the master stepped out of the room and out of the house in order to speak to whoever it was, and vanished into thin air. He never returned and no one knows what happened to him.

Like its neighbor, Ormond was not a "lucky house." It was bought in 1805 by Colonel Richard Butler who named the place "Ormonde Castle" after an ancestral home in Ireland. However, he did not live there, stating that the place had a "sinister air" about it. Like its neighbor, there were tales of ghosts and vampires about the house and the plantation, and these may have unsettled Butler. He sold Ormond to his business partner, Samuel McCutchon.

During the American Civil War, Ormond suffered as the McCutchon family faced financial setback and parts of it were sold off at public auction. A pall of some kind tended to hang over the place, and once again there were tales of ghostly blood-drinkers living somewhere in the old slave houses on the plantation. In 1898, the place was bought by Senator Basile LaPlace, Jr. He allegedly made enemies with the local Ku Klux Klan and was murdered on October 11th, 1899. Ormond, with its legends of vampires and "hants," was put up for auction once again and passed into the hands of the Shexnaydres, who moved a large family into it and lived there between 1900 and 1926. After they left, Ormond was pretty much neglected and became the dwelling of a number of tenants, including tramps and hobos, who lit fires and drank in some of the once-great rooms. This continued until 1943 when the house was taken over by Mr. and Mrs. Alfred Brown who began renovations and brought Ormond back into some semblance of its former grandeur. Following the Browns' death, the place was sold to Betty Le Blanc, a prominent businesswoman in New Orleans. She had great plans for the house, but died of cancer in 1986 before she could complete them. Her son Ken Elliot is currently resuming the renovations and has opened the house to the public for the first time.

Although these two great houses are perhaps the most famous in the New Orleans area and have provided some of the inspiration for the Anne Rice books, large plantations are scattered all across Louisiana, each with their own particular history and ghostly legends. Some of these also concern vampires. For example, in Carville, 16 miles south of Baton Rouge, stands Indian Camp, which has a history of disease and where half-dead figures were once rumored to come and go. The house was built during the late 1850s, but was leased shortly after by Dr. Isadore Dyer of Tulane University Medical School, and was used as an open treatment center for Hansen's Disease (leprosy). However, Dr. Dyer had neither the money nor the inclination to develop and refurbish the house, so it became run-down and slid into genteel decay. In the end, conditions had become so bad that 80 patients were compelled to take an 80-mile trip upriver to New Orleans to better facilities and abandon the house altogether. In fact, the state of the place had become so bad that for a number of years they had been cared for in the old slave quarters, which were less than sanitary. Moreover, there were whispers of vampirism among "patients of color" who were held in these appalling conditions. Indian Camp gained a reputation as a "hant house" and nobody would venture near it after dark for fear that *something* in the shadows would slit their throats and drink their blood.

The site was purchased in 1896 by the State of Louisiana as the location of the Louisiana State Leprosarium, and, in 1921, the United States government took it over as the national center for the treatment of Hansen's Disease. Even so, the dark reputation of those former days still lingers on in the shadows of the main building and stories surface from time to time of leprous vampires still haunting the area seeking victims. Some of these have been possessed by dark, blood-lusting spirits, which still lurk on the sites of old slave houses. Vampires, it seems, are not all that far away from the great plantation houses of Louisiana and even some of these have traces of African/slave culture about them.

And out in the bayous, there are tales of strange spirits lurking among the moss-draped trees. Tucked away in remote corners of the parishes are tiny lakes and waterways, which may be haunted by blood-drinking ghosts. For example, Palquemines Parish is about as far south and about as remote as you can get in Louisiana. It's where the Mississippi River empties into the Gulf of Mexico and in a quagmire of weed-choked bayous and marshlands. Somewhere in this wasteland is said to lie the legendary Deadman Bayou. Tucked away in a remote corner of the parish is supposedly a hidden bayou from which the top of some kind of mausoleum protrudes above the waterline. The bayou itself is said to be a flooded cemetery. The mausoleum at Deadman Bayou, however, is reputedly the home of something that is Undead and that travels out into the surrounding countryside to feed on the living—taking both their blood and energies and leaving them tired and drained when they wake. No one in the surrounding area knows to whom this monument was raised—although it is certainly an ornate structure with extremely ornate frescoes—or what other graves lie under the bayou waters, but it is thought that it is the resting place of some great family. When the water in the bayou is low, it may be possible to travel out to view the ruin close up, although it is considered inadvisable to do so. There is the tale of a shrimper named Roland (or Ramon) Perlander who traveled out to the place in a pirogue (a flat-bottomed Louisiana boat) to investigate the submerged monument for a bet. He set out late in the evening when a mist was rising on the surface of the bayou. He poled off into the gathering fog and was never seen alive again. What happened out there in the swirling murk is unknown—did he reach the sunken mausoleum, or did something overtake him in the fog? Several weeks later, his body was found in a backwater creek completely drained of blood! Had something vampiric emerged from the mysterious tomb as he approached it and attacked him? And why are there no records of who lies within the monument?

Similar tales to this emerge in Evangeline Parish further north. More than 15 square miles of the parish is covered by swamps and water and a network of bayous makes up large areas there. Mention has already been made of Cemetery Bayou, which was supposedly covered with water during the Great Mississippi Flood of 1927. However, it is not the only such expanse and, although possibly the most important bayous in the region are Bayou Chicot and Bayou Teche, there are small, hidden bayous tucked away in quiet corners of the parish that hold secrets. Bayou John, located somewhere near Big Mamou, for example, supposedly covers a forgotten graveyard and the ruins of a church are said to lie beneath its waters and give the bayou its name. Tradition says that the graveyard contains the bodies of those who died in a Yellow Fever epidemic, but nobody can give the date of the catastrophe. However, some of these bodies may rise and threaten those who live nearby. A bit like the story from Palquemines Parish, tales are told of individuals who have disappeared close to the bayou. These include people such as Arne Guillory who, like Ramon Perlander, mysteriously vanished among the Spanish Moss–draped trees in the vicinity of the eerie bayou, and was later found drained of blood.

St. Charles Bayou—a tiny bayou that supposedly lies near Reddell—is said to contain a *feufollet*, which is said to drag passers-by beneath its water.

Once they are drowned, it removes the "goodness" from their bodies, leaving them little more than an emaciated and desiccated husk. There have, of course, been a number of stories of disappearing travelers and the discovery of bodies floating in the bayou water. Cajun vampires perhaps? Something else lurking in these remote areas? Something that is maybe older than the bayous themselves?

As the Louisiana night closes in over bayou country, things stir among the moss-draped trees and in the rotting, abandoned shacks and mouldering plantation houses. Some of them might have originated in the nightmares of a number of cultures—French, German, African—some are a fusion of all of these. And as we travel through the winding waterways and hidden lakes, are we so sure that the shadow moving behind the hanging curtains of Spanish Moss is *really* something that belongs to this world?

VERMONT/RHODE ISLAND

Arguably, and perhaps unsurprisingly, vampirism in America originated in colonial New England. The influx of various immigrants from Europe—British, Dutch, German, Portuguese, Romania, and Poland—brought indigenous traditions, and created a rich melting pot in which many beliefs could flourish and develop. The German and Dutch settlers came to the New World with a supernatural portfolio of *nachtzehrer, shroudeaters,* and *bloedzuigers,* the unquiet dead called back to life, who might attack the living and drink their blood. Such ghostly traditions blended well with Indian myths of nameless creatures, which were halfway between some sort of monster and a phantom. Both the Wampanoag of Massachusetts and the Narragansett of Rhode Island spoke of a thing that had the form of a man, but hid in the shadows between the forest trees. It would attack hunters and travelers that it chanced to encounter. Its distinguishing feature was its large eyes that enabled it to see in the forest dark. Neither arrow nor tomahawk could kill or injure it, and to speak its name was to call it from the forest depths. Exactly what this creature did with its victims is unknown, but it was unwise to cross its path. It is easy to see how a belief in such a being could readily fuse with some of the mythologies of the incoming settlers. The Cherokees also had tales of old witches and wizards who thrived upon their murdered victims. Such Indian motifs undoubtedly passed into the folklore of the incoming colonists. They, too, had horrors that lay in abandoned cemeteries, ruined tombs, and neglected mausoleums, which lay in remote areas in their own native countries.

Another element in the colonial mix was religion. A stern Christianity characterized and guided the lives of many settlers and the Devil was everywhere. He was in the forests, remote valleys, and dark caves that were scattered around their settlements, ready to strike at any time. Their only shield against such a being was their faith. And because they came from different backgrounds with varying viewpoints regarding salvation, there were many differing faiths that the new colonists might espouse in order to avoid Satan's claws.

From the days of the pilgrim fathers in 1620, the early colonies of America framed their world through religious experience and supernatural intervention. Thus, in 1692, Massachusetts Bay Colony was facing its most serious political and religious crisis, and their anxiety was expressed, not in political activity, but through a series of witchcraft trials at Salem. Therefore, the early Colonial world was heavily influenced by faith and signs, and wonders were all around.

In the 1740s, the radical preacher George Whitefield traveled along the American coast preaching to packed congregations in the beginning of what was called The First Great Awakening, sometimes dismissively referred to as the New Light Stir. From this emerged groups with radical theories regarding salvation, sin, and the world: the Strict and Particular Baptists, the Separates, Universalists (who denied the existence of Hell), Evangelical Calvinists, and many others. Some groups espoused views, which, today might be considered strange; the early Brownists (followers of the English preacher Robert Browne), for example, held that the Devil was a woman, and, consequently, no woman could enter Heaven (saintly females were turned into men upon death). Mother Anne Lee's Shakers, who had fled from England in 1774, believed that lust was the Original Sin, so any contact between men and women (even eye contact) was forbidden. On the contrary, the Perfectionist named Shadrack Ireland believed that the Second Coming was imminent, and instructed his followers to lay themselves out on stone slabs in sealed underground chambers beneath the Massachusetts hills, so that when the Great Trumpet sounded they could walk out, whole and ready to face God. It is easy to see how unshrouded bodies lying in stone crypts might have formed the basis for the idea of the walking dead in New England.

For many of the faithful, sin and evil (and the avoidance of both) were the twin preoccupations of life. Once Salvation had been achieved, Satan would stop at nothing to bring God's children down, and apparently his agents were everywhere. The Indians who lived in the woods were undoubtedly agents of the Evil One. Thus, when the Indians attacked their settlements, it was unquestionably the work of Satan against the Chosen. And God permitted such atrocities to occur because of the sins of the colonists, whether real or imagined. Such raids were a chastisement upon the settlements, but they were also a powerful reminder of the evil that dwelt out there in this new land.

Disease formed yet another problem in the colonial experience, and it was one that continued until the mid-1800s. The conditions in which many of the early settlers lived were poor and unsanitary by modern standards, and many people lived on the edges of swamps, lakes, and bogs—perfect breeding grounds for all sorts of ailments, many of them fatal. Consequently, epidemics of various kinds swept through the colonies, taking away mainly the weak and vulnerable as they passed and, once again, given the religious fervor of the time, their spread was interpreted as God's judgement upon a sinful people. Because of the swampy conditions and the poor sanitation, tuberculosis and typhoid, along with many forms of respiratory and lung infections, flourished in many parts of the colonies, the contagion sometimes carrying away entire families.

On May 19th, 1780, a spectacular event occurred that shook New England to its core and galvanized many of the radical churches. Many of the

hill congregations had experienced a renewal of religious fervor, as itin-
erant preachers traveled among them, preaching on the damnation of sin
and the imminence of evil. Then, at mid-day, the sky suddenly went dark
and the sun disappeared. In fact, it was so dark that birds flew home to
nest, flowers closed their petals, and people had to use candles in order
to see anything. The sky was even blacker than it was on a regular night.
What caused the famous New England's Dark Day is unknown. It may have
been a solar eclipse, but it was probably a combination of smoke from forest fires, a heavy fog, and cloud cover. The total darkness extended as far
as Barnstaple, Massachusetts, and was even experienced in Pennsylvania
and New Jersey. For the Godly, though, there could be only one interpreta-
tion: the end of the world was coming and Christ was about to return. In
Hartford, Connecticut, the fledgling state legislature was already meeting
in session when the light failed; thinking that it was the Day of Judgement,
the speaker called for the sitting to be suspended. However, one representative, Abraham Davenport, called for candles and the meeting proceeded.
The darkness lasted until about midnight when it finally dispersed and the
stars could be seen again. Christ certainly hadn't come, and the world was
still the same.

The effect on the Godly congregations was, however, electric. If the
darkness was not a sign of the Second Coming, then it was something else.
Many said it was a warning from God to the colonies regarding their sins.
It was a hint at things to come if men did not mend their ways and follow
holy precepts. In some parts of New England, everything was treated as a
sign from God or the sign of the Devil's work. Satan had redoubled his efforts to drag the colonies down to a lost eternity and his agents were even
thicker on the ground. As if to prove this assertion, in the months following
the Dark Day, many colonial villages and towns experienced epidemics of
both typhoid fever and tuberculosis.

Is it any wonder that from this rich stew of folklore, religion, and disease, the idea of the vampire emerged almost fully formed? And there might
have been a moral dimension to its appearance, for the animated corpses
were usually of those who had died in sin or who wished to draw the Godly
members of their family away with them to the grave, and, perhaps, into

Satan's power. The effect of the Dark Day only served to strengthen the religious fervor that had established itself within the New England mind, and to establish the imminence of the Devil as a real and potent force on day-to-day life.

Perhaps one of the first people to write on vampire beliefs in America was the anthropologist George R. Stetson. His article, "The Animistic Vampire in New England," appeared in *The American Anthropologist* in January 1896. He centered his arguments around the remote areas of Rhode Island—settlements such as Exeter, Foster, Kingstown, and East Greenwich—where, in his day, some of the older superstitions and beliefs still flourished. He quickly drew attention to the isolation and poverty of the place.

T he region referred to where agriculture is in a depressed condition and abandoned farms are numerous, is the tramping ground of the book-agent and the chromo-peddler.... Farmhouses, deserted and ruinous, are frequent and the once productive lands, neglected and overgrown with scrubby oak, speak forcefully and mournfully of the migration of youthful farmers from country to town.... Here Cotton Mather, Justice Sewall and the host of medical, clerical and lay believers in the uncanny superstitions of bygone centuries could still hold high carnival.

Between 1780 and the mid-1800s, plagues of tuberculosis, typhoid, and smallpox swept many of the tiny communities already devastated, as Stetson points out, by poverty and a decline in their agricultural base. Poor diet and a harsh life often took their toll on the more vulnerable, leaving them open to the attentions of such contagions.

It was not only humans who suffered from disease in these areas. In an area heavily dependant on agriculture, crops were also susceptible to infestations. Whole fields could be ravaged by the onset of a pestilence, financially ruining families and leaving whole communities prey to starvation. Between the years 1790 and 1815, the South County of Rhode Island, famous for its apple growing and cider making, suffered a series of severe apple blights. Fruit withered and died on the trees. as even relatively prosperous families struggled to survive. Poverty was everywhere, and death followed.

In his article, Stetson mentions a curious custom in which such illnesses had been involved. Following certain epidemics, bodies of the victims seem to have been exhumed and inspected. According to Stetson, citing a local doctor, this practice (burning the heart and some internal organs of a tuberculosis victim) was common in many parts of rural Rhode Island, and was designed to prevent the corpse coming back to torment or injure other members of its immediate family.

O f the origin of this superstition in Rhode Island or in other parts of the United States, we are ignorant. It is in all probability an exotic like ourselves, originating in the mythographic period of the Aryan and Semitic peoples, though legends and superstitions of a somewhat similar character may be found among the American Indians.

Along with the belief in returning revenants, which had been carried off by disease, was a sense of moral justice. Although these things might be agents of the Devil, God sometimes *permitted* them to return for a specific purpose—to show His displeasure as a warning. They were also connected with illness and pestilence as part of his judgement. This could form the basis of at least *some* of the vampiric appearances, and would serve as an explanation to why Godly families might be so persecuted.

One of the earliest instances of alleged vampirism in New England comes from Manchester, Vermont, and dates back to the late 18th century. It is the case of Rachel Burton, and an account of it appears in the personal papers of Judge John S. Pettibone, although the report is taken from an unnamed source. The account, written sometime between 1857 and 1872, is of uncertain date, and is still held by the Manchester Historical Society. It perhaps reflects an underlying religious morality on the subject of marriage, which may have characterized sections of early Vermont society.

On March 8th, 1789, Captain Isaac Burton married Rachel Harris in Manchester. She was from a reasonably wealthy family in the area, and was widely described as a young, healthy, beautiful girl. The union was lauded in the Manchester community, and the Captain found an ideal partner. Unfortunately, the marriage did not last long. A bout of tuberculosis passed through the region and Rachel Burton succumbed to it, dying slowly and painfully. During her illness, she coughed up large quantities of blood, her skin became pale and marbled, and she went into severe decline. Less than a year after she had married Isaac Burton, on February 1st, 1790, Rachel passed away.

At first, Isaac Burton was distraught at the loss of his pretty young wife, but shortly after her death, rumors began to circulate that, as Rachel lay ill, he had sought solace in the arms of another woman. Allegations of the affair seemed to take on more substance when the Captain proposed marriage to Hulda Powell, daughter of Esquire Powell, a local landowner. Despite an unspoken disapproval, the Captain and Hulda were married on January 4th, 1791.

A few months into the marriage, Hulda Burton also began to display symptoms of the strange wasting fever that had taken Rachel. Desperately, Isaac threw a greater part of his wealth at the occurrence by summoning two doctors from Manchester to investigate his wife's condition. Although they gave learned opinion, and prepared tonics for the declining Hulda, they were of little use and soon Captain Burton's second wife was confined to her bed, just as his first had been. Tales say that she became delusional— she claims she saw Rachel Burton in her room, her lips caked in hardened blood and smelling of dirt. Maybe this was a delirious reaction to the whispers and the implied disapproval concerning her marriage, or perhaps it was something else, but it had an alarming effect on Isaac Burton and on his wife's relatives, who took turns looking after her when the Captain was unavailable. Despite all the doctor's ministrations, Hulda Burton continued to deteriorate.

One of the relatives who sat by her bed was an elderly and venerable aunt, greatly respected in the community, but steeped in the traditions of former years. As he spoke to the old woman one evening, Isaac Burton was offered a rather chilling explanation for what ailed his sickly wife. Bluntly, the aunt told him that she believed some wicked spirit was somehow drawing both the blood and the energy from Hulda's body. Isaac expressed his horror at such a theory; he asked what motive such a spirit would have for attacking his wife.

"It is the one that has gone before," replied the old woman darkly. "The one that can't rest in her grave for the jealousy that she bears my niece. She wants you to herself." What could he do, he asked? She told him there was a way that had been practiced in these parts countless years before—something she called "a burnin'"—but it would need the approval of the Selectmen who oversaw the running of the town. The body would have to be exhumed, and certain vital organs would be formally burned in public view. Only then might Hulda recover but, even then, such recovery was not certain. It was certain that if nothing was done, Hulda would die and the spirit would perhaps attack other members of the family.

At a loss, Isaac Burton approached an old friend, who was also a Selectman, named Timothy Mead. Mead had already heard about the belief in the remoter parts of Rhode Island, which were looked on as "barbarous practices," and was not inclined to support the exhumation. Vampires were only an old superstition, which had originated in Europe in times long past. Furthermore, Rachel Harris had been a respectable girl from a respectable family, and there was no need to connect her with such a hideous superstition. The matter remained where it was, with Hulda now growing steadily weaker by the day. The old aunt's supposition seemed vindicated, however, when she complained of an intense weight on her chest each night, as though somebody was sitting on it. Moreover, she now had flecks of blood around the sides of her mouth, as if somebody were drinking it from her. Both Isaac Burton and several relatives dozed in a chair each night beside her bed while she slept fitfully, only to be wakened by her cries and screams that Rachel Burton was in the room with her.

It can be argued, of course, that the progress of the tuberculosis in the body will produce a variety of symptoms. For example, the victim might cough up blood (the blood flecks on the lips), or create respiratory and chest problems, such as a tightness of the chest and difficulty in breathing (the sensation of weight on the chest). Further, the condition is often accompanied by pallid, marble-like skin, giving a ghostly impression. These can be attributed to the medical condition, but to Isaac Burton and many other people around the Manchester area, it meant only one thing: a vampire and the work of the Devil.

He approached Timothy Mead again. This time the Selectman was very much aware of the rising tide of rumor and fear within the town and, after a special meeting of the town's legislature, the exhumation was granted. On a February morning in 1793, Rachel's coffin was brought from the iron-hard earth, and was taken to the forge of Jacob Mead, the local blacksmith. In spite of their fear, a good number of people had gathered—some reports say between 500 to 1,000 people—to see what the exhumation had disclosed. The casket, once open, revealed a bloated corpse that was barely recognizable as the beautiful Rachel Burton. However, around the mouth were the dark brown stains of dried blood, which were quickly noticed and seized upon by the crowd, some of whom cried out that the bloated nature of the body was because of it being gorged with human blood. To many of those present, this was incontrovertible evidence that Rachael was indeed a vampire.

The heart, liver, and lungs of Rachel Burton were removed and cast into the searing coals of the blacksmith's forge. The stench that arose from the burning organs was almost overpowering, and several onlookers declared that they heard a faint sigh as the charnel smoke curled skyward. Others thought they saw something like a black serpent climb upward through the smoke and vanish as it dispersed.

With the grim exorcism completed, the crowds departed. If Isaac Burton had expected his wife to recover, he was sorely disappointed. Although she appeared to rally briefly, Hulda Burton had been weakened by her ordeal and did not survive. On September 6th, 1793, she succumbed to the disease that had wracked her for more than a year. Although she died, the strange malady did not pass on, and it was assumed that the attentions of the vampire had been finally fulfilled.

Isaac Burton continued to live in Manchester and married again—in fact, he married twice more. He and his fourth wife Dency Raymond lie together in a section of Manchester's old Dellwood Cemetery. Some of the graves have been relocated there from an older graveyard on the village green near today's courthouse in which many old unmarked graves still remain. There is no grave marker in Dellwood for Rachel Burton, so perhaps she lies somewhere by the courthouse.

The story of Rachel Burton, the "wronged wife," who returned from the grave to take a bloody and wasting revenge upon her successor, spread through New England like wildfire. It reinforced old beliefs—first about the imminence of evil, and second about the necessity of living a good and proper life and the avoidance of sin. In Rhode Island, such stories provided the staple of folklore and may have inspired some other incidents in the state. Vampirism would flourish in Rhode Island for more than 100 years through the celebrated "Vampire Ladies," who allegedly prowled the nights. We'll get to them a little further along in the chaper.

Along a narrow country road in North Cumberland, Rhode Island, lies a small and overgrown cemetery, supposedly dating back to Revolutionary times. Badly neglected, the encroaching overgrowth serves to cover a number of tombs and funeral markers, including the last vestiges of the once-prosperous Staples family. Here, among the broken stones and tumbled funerary urns, lie the unquiet bones of Abigail Staples, who died toward the end of 1795 at the age of 23. It is thought that she died of consumption (tuberculosis), but her death does not appear to have brought an end to her involvement with her surviving family.

On February 8th, 1796, Stephen Staples approached the Cumberland Town Council with an unusual request. He wished to conduct an "experiment," which involved digging up the body of his daughter Abigail, who died several months earlier, in order to see if it might save the life of his other daughter Lavinia Chace.

Abigail had been a moody, wistful girl, sometimes given to romantic dreams of marriage and family life. When her sister married Stephen Chace, its thought that Abigail harbored a little resentment toward the marriage—after all, she, a born romantic, still remained unwed and uncourted. Her dreams, however, were cut short by a bout of consumption that passed through Cumberland. Shortly after her death, however, her sister Lavinia began to exhibit similar symptoms, and began to deteriorate. She was confined to her bed for a time, and often drifted in and out of sleep. During her slumber, she had visions that a dark figure crouched at the very end of the bed and jumped onto her chest, crushing it with its weight and drawing the breath from her body. All were convinced, however, that the nightmare would pass with the sickness. One morning, her husband was disturbed when Lavinia sat bolt upright in the bed and uttered "Abigail." She then sank back to sleep, but her outburst had troubled the young man.

Stephen Staples listened intently to the young man's concerns. He knew the legends of the vampires that existed among some of the townspeople, but he tended to put little faith in them. However, the account came at an interesting time. There had been several instances of tubercular fever in some of the neighboring villages and, in keeping with the ethos of the time, several local ministers had proclaimed this as God's visitation upon a wayward people. Satan was very near at hand, they warned, and would make his presence known very soon. So although Stephen placed little credence in such ghostly things, there was still a corner of his mind that was unsure. In the end, he decided to place the decision in the hands of the authorities.

The Council's first reaction was one of skepticism. One of the more formidable members present was Captain Ben Westcott, an old soldier who had been decorated during the War of Independence. Although he sympathized with Stephen Staples over the loss of his daughter Abigail, and expressed his concern over the illness of his daughter Lavinia, Westcott suggested that perhaps a better remedy would be to pray for the latter's swift recovery. From the chair, councilman John Lapham stated that the matter was actually beyond their field of expertise, and that it properly belonged in the realms of ignorant superstition and folklore. Nevertheless, the Council was well aware of the sermons of preachers in the area, and how they had stirred up notions of ever-present evil and devilry. Sensing their uncertainty, Stephen Staples pressed the matter, saying that if the Devil were close at hand and ready to strike, so might demon vampires. Stephen Chace then made an impassioned plea, begging them to act in the community's good, if only to dispel the terror that had gripped so many people. Let them dig up

Abigail's corpse and inspect it, and if nothing was amiss, they would rebury with decency. Somewhat reluctantly, the Council authorized the exhumation. However, the "experiment" had to be conducted more or less in secret. Furthermore, no record was to be kept of the exhumation.

Mindful of the Council's request, Stephen Staples made his way to the tiny graveyard on the edge of the Staples' property, together with three hired men, after nightfall. By the light of lanterns, they unearthed Abigail's body. No record exists of what they found, but according to local lore, whatever young Stephen Chace saw when the coffin was opened almost drove him mad, and had him wandering about the countryside, muttering to himself, for the rest of the night. Although he recovered, he refused to go anywhere near the burying ground. Stephen Staples never again spoke of that night or what he had witnessed, but he was a changed man, gaunt and silent with dark, hollow eyes. He was constantly troubled by terrible nightmares. It is also said that one of the workmen who unearthed the coffin committed suicide shortly afterward.

What became of Lavinia Chace is unknown, as she simply disappears from the pages of recorded history. She might have recovered, or she, too, might have succumbed to the pestilence. No marker indentifies her grave to say when or how she died, and no mention of her is made in any subsequent account. In fact, as the Town Council would have wished, the whole incident has been consigned to history. There is no record of any similar occurrences in the area, and it is unclear if there were any similar deaths.

However, a History Channel special showed a curious headstone erected to Simon Whipple Aldrich in the Union Cemetery Annex, which bears a curious inscription: "Although consumption's vampire grasp had seized thy mortal frame."

Simon Whipple Aldrich was the youngest son of Colonel Dexter Aldrich and his wife Margery, who died on May 6th, 1841, presumably of tuberculosis. However, the strange mention of the word *vampire* in the inscription has intrigued historians; why should it be included on the headstone? It may, of course, be just a turn of phrase, but it may also be the trace of a memory from the dark time of Abigail Staples, and perhaps part of the legacy that she bequeathed to the community.

The Staples case may have established the notion of vampires firmly in the Rhode Island mind, because shortly after, the first of the celebrated "Vampire Ladies," Sarah Tillinghast, allegedly made an appearance in Exeter, Rhode Island. In many respects, the Tillinghast story matches that of Abigail Staples. The similar protagonist was the dreamy and moody Sarah, who whiled away some of her girlhood days by visiting old cemeteries in which many who had been killed in the Revolutionary War lay. The area around Sarah's home had been used by American snipers against the British, and her father, Snuffy Tillinghast, had actually fought against British and Hessian troops.

Snuffy was a reasonably prosperous apple-farmer, and with his wife Honour, he had raised many daughters. In the later days of 1799, his prosperity, his family, and his way of life were to be severely tested by what he believed to be supernatural forces. It all began with a nightmare. One night, just before the apple harvest, Snuffy Tillighast awoke sweating. He had experienced an awful dream in which he was walking through his orchard. It was harvest time and the branches were laden with apples. Suddenly, from somewhere close by, he heard the voice of his daughter Sarah calling to him. As he turned to see where she was, a cold wind suddenly sprang up, blowing through the orchard and chilling him to the bone. Branches creaked and leaves blew everywhere. The voice faded, and in the dream Snuffy turned back to work at the trees; as he did so, he saw that the leaves on about half of them had turned brown and were withering, the fruit rotting on their branches. The stench of decay spread through the orchard and, as he looked, he saw that half of his harvest was completely rotten.

The dream haunted Snuffy for many days afterward, and he was sure it was a prophesy of things to come. It came again and again and, in the end, he went to see his local minister, Benjamin Northup, to see if the preacher could determine exactly what the vision portended. The clergyman was of little help—he told Snuffy not to worry, but to keep praying. It was nothing but anxiety about the crop. Snuffy was hardly comforted by the minister's words, but he tried to do as he was told and put it all to the back of his mind.

The harvest passed and, greatly relieved, Snuffy and his family settled in for the winter.

Sarah had always been a moody child and, as the winter set in, she seemed to draw more and more into herself. She sat about all day reading old books, and when she did go out, she was often found wandering down in a tiny cemetery, which had been created on the corner of her father's land. She chose to stay in her room during mealtimes instead of joining the family at the dinner table, and she appeared to be growing weaker and weaker. Soon it became apparent that Sarah was ill, and as the days went by, it also seemed that she was not long for this world. At the end of 1799, she was dead. The cause was, of course, given as "consumption," and she was laid to rest in the family plot, a little way from the house. That, however, was not the end of her involvement with the family.

A few weeks after her death, the Tillinghast's youngest son James came down for breakfast one morning looking decidedly peaked. Assuming that he'd been gorging himself on some of his father's green apples, Honour chided him gently as she made breakfast. James protested his innocence and said that his chest hurt badly, "where Sarah touched him." The mention of her daughter's name brought a mixed range of emotions in Honour. Gently, she told the boy that Sarah was dead and that he had only been dreaming about her. Even as she did so, she could hear the unhealthy rattle in his chest. She put him back to bed and piled his bed high with blankets to keep him warm, feeding him nourishing broths. In the nights that followed, he talked again and again about Sarah coming to visit him in his room and sometimes touching him. James did not linger long, and followed his sister into the ground.

Shortly after, James's sister Andris, then age 14, also took ill, as well as another sister Ruth. Both died, and it seemed that an unknown blight had suddenly hit the Tillinghast family. The father went to see Reverend Northup again, but once more gained little comfort from the visit. The clergyman simply told him to leave the fates of both himself and his family in God's hands and to pray. Snuffy returned home a worried man. Worse was to follow.

The Tillighast's eldest daughter, Hannah, age 26, was married and lived several miles away with her husband in West Greenwich. However, this didn't stop her from visiting her mother and family whenever she could in order to give Honour some help with the chores. However, on several nights when she left the house after a visit, Hannah was sure that she was being followed. Shadows moved under the trees and there were furtive and unexplained movements and rustlings in the roadside undergrowth. For a moment, she had thought it was her sister Sarah, but Sarah was dead. That night, however, she had dreams that Sarah was in the bedroom with her. On her next visit, she told her mother about the nightmares. Honor was now convinced there was evil somewhere close by, and that it was stalking her family. She begged Hannah not to speak of it, and told her that if perhaps they prayed together it might go away. But it didn't, and Hannah soon came down with the illness, gradually wasting away. She died in the late spring of the following year.

Honour now began to experience the same vivid dreams as her children. They always followed a similar pattern—she was stifling from a waft of stale and fetid air, which swept all through the bedroom. Sitting up in bed, she saw her daughter Sarah standing at the far end of the room, looking at her mournfully, but with a great longing in her eyes. Honour found herself rising from bed and walking slowly toward the phantom, who opened her arms. Then Honour woke up, bathed in sweat. She told herself that there was really nothing to worry about, it was only a dream, but she nor Snuffy were all that sure. Their fears were further compounded when their 17-year-old son Ezra took to his bed and lay shaking with a fever. He too spoke of dreams of Sarah, but these were simply put down to the sickness.

Things took on a slightly more sinister tone with the arrival of a visitor named Jeremiah Dandridge, an old man greatly respected in the community and across other parts of Rhode Island as well. He had come to offer his condolences on Hannah's recent passing. During the course of the visit, Honour began to detect something else in his conversation—something Dandridge seemed hesitant to mention. The old man had very fixed views of the world, particularly when it came to the supernatural. He said that there was an old story that those who died from the consumption some-times returned to torment the living in the form of a vampire. He had heard of a case in Vermont several years before where a corpse had been dug up and was found bloated with human blood. And there had been another more recent instance in Cumberland where a family had been tormented by the unquiet phantom of a relative. In each case, the families had also been tormented by dreams that often foreshadowed yet another tragedy. His words troubled Honour greatly and stayed with her long after Dandridge had left. It was an old superstition—and Jeremiah Dandridge was prone to give credence to such things—but what if it was actually true?

Long into the night, Snuffy and his wife talked over the situation. They were getting no help from the community or from the Church, so Snuffy decided to take matters into his own hands. The case of Rachel Burton in Vermont, which Dandridge had mentioned, placed the seeds of a grisly idea in his mind. There might still be a way to save what remained of his family. The following night, together with two hired men, he made his way out to Exeter Cemetery where the body of Sarah lay. With them they took shovels, a mattock, ropes, and a flask of oil.

Throughout the night, the men worked at digging up coffins of all the children from the hard ground. All of them had been in the earth for more than six months and when the caskets were opened the bodies inside showed various stages of decay—all, it's said, except Sarah. When the lid was removed from her casket, she was, according to popular lore, lying as if in repose. Her eyes were open and gazing blankly at the night sky above, and there was a slight flush on her cheek. Upon seeing her, one of the workmen fell to his knees and began to pray. The other farmhand stepped back as though the girl might spring from the coffin and seize him. Looking at the horror, Snuffy Tillinghast ordered them to return to the cart and fetch the oil. Taking a large hunting knife from under his coat, he allegedly cut his daughter's breast and, as the men returned with the oil, he tossed something on the ground in front of them. It was Sarah's heart and liver. Pouring the oil over them, Snuffy brought out a tinder and flint and set fire to the small heap of internal organs. An acrid smoke rose through the graveyard and then, somewhere away among the trees, a breeze seemed to sigh. As the heart turned to ash, the men, still shaking, judged that the danger was past. Reinterring all the coffins, they left the cemetery as the sun began to rise.

As a result of Snuffy's actions, Honour recovered completely and was able to bear two more children, and all of the remaining youngsters outlived their parents. In many ways, however, Snuffy Tillinghast's strange dream had come true—in it he dreamed that he had lost half his apple harvest and out of his children, half had died.

The Tillinghast graves can still be seen today. They lie in a quiet wooded cemetery, close to what was once Snuffy's farmhouse, just off Victory Road in Exeter, Rhode Island. The original stone markers are, however, difficult to detect, lying half-hidden in the encroaching growth. Snuffy's is no more than a squat stone swamped by the tall grasses with only the initials ST to identify it. Nearby stands a stone for his wife Honour, who died in 1831, and beyond that are several graves of some of their children. The final resting place of Sarah Tillinghast, however, is unmarked.

The Tillinghast case (and that of Abigail Staples) firmly established Rhode Island as a vampire-ridden state. Sarah Tillinghast became one of a series of reported cases that continued into the 19th century, all of which followed roughly a similar pattern. These instances that became known as the Rhode Island "Vampire Ladies" included Nancy Young (1824), Juliet Rose (1874), and Mercy Lena Brown (1892). Although the specifics of Mercy Brown's case broadly follow all those who had gone before, it is a striking one, because it was so late (almost into the 20th century), and because it is thought to have partly influenced Bram Stoker in his writing of *Dracula*. Stoker toured America with the Irish actor Sir Henry Irving around the time of the Brown case and, after his death, his widow found newspaper cuttings of that period.

From time to time, the newspapers seized on some of the practices that were carried out in some of the Rhode Island and Vermont settlements. The Mercy Brown vampire story attracted some journalistic interest, particularly in the *Providence Journal*, which had a wide circulation in Rhode Island. Indeed, in its March 21st, 1892 issue (around the time Mercy's body had been exhumed), the *Journal* ran a special article on vampirism, in which it claimed vampirism was not a Rhode Island tradition, but one that had been imported from Europe. Stating that the burning of a vampire heart to alleviate supernatural harm may have originated among the Hindus and Danubian peoples, the article goes on to say that it was brought into places such as Rhode Island by way of Hungary and White Russia. Describing the case in some detail, the *Journal* goes on to state that the rite of exorcism (the burning of heart and organs) is hideous, comparing it to the practice of the inhabitants of the Upper Congo in Africa. Apparently, it was even suggested that Mercy's brother Edwin, who was suffering from consumption at the time, should eat the ashes of the burned organs in order to save himself. This course of action, it seems, was inspired by certain beliefs from Serbia. Whether or not this was done is unclear. The article provoked a series of letters from Rhode Island residents, commenting on the event and drawing attention to some others of which their authors had heard.

And of course where local newspapers picked up on the story so did the wider press. New York papers such as *The World* began to run articles on what was happening in Rhode Island, along with several other New York and Washington broadsheets under headlines such as:

Vampires in New England—Dead Bodies Dug Up and Their Hearts Burned to Prevent Disease.

Similar headlines appeared in many other editions of the New York press. The idea was, in the minds of New York and Washington editors, to create the impression of gullible backwoodsmen who desperately clung on to the (false) perceptions of former years while they (New Yorkers) were far too sophisticated and savvy to believe in such nonsense. Several of the papers attempted some sort of "learned critique" of the subject, quoting extensively from Stetson's article and other anthropological texts. The tone, however, remained condescending.

One of the last of the so-called Rhode Island "Vampire Ladies" would appear to be the rather unfortunate Nellie Louise Vaughn, who died in West Greenwich on March 31st, 1889. She became a victim of much press speculation, even into comparatively recent times. She died at the age of 19 and her grave is allegedly situated in a small secluded cemetery on the twisting Plain Meeting House Road in West Greenwich The cemetery is a large one and contains graves that date back to the 1700s.

Nellie's story seems to parallel many of the others—illness and death, a ghostly figure, and dreams within her family. But it is the inscription on her headstone that attracted the most attention: "I am Watching and Waiting for you." No reason has ever been given for this particular form of words— maybe they are purely innocent and were directed toward a living family; maybe even toward a secret lover, but many people later seized on them as a sinister warning. Little attention was actually paid to them for a long time, and then, in the mid 1960s, during the course of a lesson on local folklore, a teacher at the local Coventry High School told his class of an alleged vampire's grave out in West Greenwich. The site was identified, and suddenly the strange inscription took on an added significance. Stories began to circulate that Nellie had been buried alive, that her form was seen in the vicinity of the church on certain nights of the year, and that no vegetation or moss would actually grow on her grave or headstone. Students first identified the grave, then the press took an interest. All through the 1960s and early 1970s, sporadic articles appeared in a host of magazines concerning alleged "vampire activity" in West Greenwich.

The story was given fresh interest in 1993, when ghost hunter Marlene Chatfield paid several visits to Nellie's grave. On the second visit, accompanied by her husband, she claimed that she heard a female voice telling her "I am perfectly pleasant." She claims to have been the voice of Nellie Vaughn herself. She also claims that she met a woman in the graveyard who said that she was a member of the local historical society and who told her that Nellie was not a vampire. Once again, there was a flurry of interest among national magazines, many centering on the queer inscription on the headstone. Naturally, with such coverage, hundreds of ghost seekers and occultists found their way to the West Greenwich churchyard to view the grave and perhaps even hold rituals there when no one was looking. Christian groups made their way there in order to "exorcise" the evil that was deemed to still remain there. In the end, the site was littered with bottles and other rubbish, and the headstone was smeared in graffiti and eventually had to be removed. Irreparable damage has been done to both the burial ground and the adjacent church, and local police patrol the area on the lookout for intruders who can be arrested, fined for trespass, and escorted out of the county.

During the 19th century, the link between tuberculosis and alleged vampirism seems to have been a particularly strong one. Besides those mentioned previously, there are a number of other instances all across New England ranging in geographical location from Woodstock, Connecticut, to Barnstead, New Hampshire, all contributing to a fear of the returning consumptive dead whose intentions were to prey upon the living.

Despite all of our explanations, it has made us feel a little uneasy. And, indeed, who knows what might still be lurking in the darkness of the New England night?

New York

Between October 16th and 19th, 1924, the American horror writer H.P. Lovecraft penned a short story entitled "The Shunned House." The work, which was published in the October 1937 issue of the magazine *Weird Tales*, became something of a classic and is frequently reprinted in anthologies today. The tale deals with a strange, old, and abandoned house that fascinates the protagonist of the story and his uncle, largely because of the instances of illness and strange deaths that have taken place there throughout the previous hundred years. Peculiar weeds grow in the yard and there is a patch of strange and phosphorescent mold growing in the cellar. The place is permeated by a foul and unexplained smell. The investigators find an eerie yellow vapor emanating from what seems to be a moldy outline crouched in a fetal position. During the night, a foul "corpse light" bubbles up from the floor, in which a number of faces are clearly seen. The light takes over the narrator's uncle, turning him into a kind of monster with "black, decaying features," which causes the narrator to flee the house while his uncle dissolves and becomes one of the many faces within the yellow light. He later returns to the evil house armed with a gas mask and six carboys of sulfuric acid and begins to dig in the cellar. He eventually uncovers what looks like a white fungal-looking tube, bent in half and, realizing that he has found the elbow of some huge monster, scrambles out of the hole and dumps the acid into it. The Thing expires and an element of peace returns to the shunned house. There is a suggestion in the tale that the creature was vampiric, sucking the essence from all who live in the house in order to sustain itself and bringing illness and death to all there.

What is not generally known is that the writer based it on an actual building. Many Lovecraft scholars have suggested that the dwelling is based on a house that is still standing in Providence, Rhode Island, where Lovecraft spent most of his life. The house, located at 135 Benefit Street, was well known to Lovecraft; his Aunt Lillian lived there between 1919 and 1920. The house was built around 1763 by a merchant named Stephen Harris. At the time, because of the religious tolerance of the area, Providence had no common burying ground, so each family had a plot of land within their own property for the burial of their dead. After the Revolution, the street was widened and renamed in order to relieve the increase in traffic along Towne Street (now South Main). Many of the small family plots were dug up and the remains were relocated to the North Burying Ground. However, it's said that certain bodies were never recovered and still lie somewhere beneath the new street. According to legend, an elderly French Huguenot couple lived at what is now 135 and were buried within its grounds. Their bodies are alleged to have been among the ones who were missed.

Shortly after he had built the original house, Stephen Harris's luck began to change. Formerly, he had been a fairly prosperous merchant, but after the dwelling was erected, he began to suffer a series of calamities. Several of his vessels were lost at sea, which led to a series of financial problems for him. A number of his children, born within the house, were stillborn or died shortly after birth. Mrs. Harris began a gradual descent into madness and eventually had to be confined in an attic room where her wild screams from one of the upstairs windows often terrified other residents of the area. Some even say that she screamed in French—a language that she didn't know. This was an element that Lovecraft included in his story for *Weird Tales*: when the uncle is possessed by the Thing under the cellar, he babbles in French.

The house on Benefit Street would seem to satisfy all the inspirational criteria for the tale and, yet, other scholars have argued, using Lovecraft's own correspondence, that the actual source of the story may have partly lain elsewhere, probably in Elizabeth, New Jersey. In one of his rare periods outside Rhode Island, Lovecraft lived for a time in New York and then moved to New Jersey. Wandering through the New Jersey countryside, he visited Elizabeth on a couple of occasions and was struck by a peculiar building in the town. He wrote in a letter:

O n the northeast corner of Bridge Street and Elizabeth Avenue is a terrible old house—a hellish place where night-black deeds must have been done in the early 1700s—with a blackish unpainted surface, unnaturally steep roof and an outside flight of stairs leading to the second storey, suffocatingly embowered in a tangle of ivy so dense that one cannot but imagine it accursed or corpse-fed. It reminded me of the Babbit house on Benefit Street.... Later, its image came up again with renewed vividness, finally causing me to write a new horror story with its scene in Providence and with the Babbit house as its basis.

This particular house no longer exists, but there is no doubt that it proved at least some of the source for the story.

There is, however, a possible *third* source for the story (one that Lovecraft *may* have been aware of and that corresponds to the story perhaps more closely than the other sources), an account that appears in Charles M. Skinner's *Myths and Legends of Our Own Land* (published in 1896). In the cellar of a house on Green Street, Schenectady, New York, a queer, pale, white patch of mold in a human shape appeared from time to time. It was swept and scrubbed away on numerous occasions, but it continually reappeared no matter what form of detergent was used. It was a large figure in the shape of a recumbent man and seemed to be composed of a fluffy, fungus-like substance. Those who dwelt in the house frequently experienced a kind of lethargy and were subject to illnesses of various kinds. Some are even said to have died there.

The house stood on the site of an old Dutch burial ground, and speculation was raised as to what the curious outline might be. Some authorities suggested that this was the final resting place of some evil person who had been forced to flee from the Netherlands (or from some other American colony) and who was taking revenge on those who had trespassed on his grave. Others held that the site had been the location of some foul deed—a murder perhaps—and that a corpse had been hastily and shallowly buried and was troubling the inhabitants of the house that had been raised on the spot. But the most common suggestion was that the house had been built over the grave of a Dutch vampire that was continually trying to rise from its resting place, but was held in place by a virtuous spell that had been cast over the area. However, its malign influence extended far beyond the actual limits of its grave and into the house beyond, and it somehow managed to draw energy from those who were dwelling there in order to revive itself. But who was the person and was he or she really a vampire?

Schenectady is, of course, a very old city. In the mid-17th century, it was part of an area held by the Mohawk Nation, a part of the Iroquois Confederacy. Dutch settlers quickly established a small outpost in the Hudson Valley, which they named Fort Orange, but which the Mohawk named *Schau-naugh-ta-da* meaning "over the pine plains." The word became adopted by the Dutch, although the meaning was slightly different, referring to a bend in the Mohawk River on which the city now stands.

The Dutch initially established a colony there around 1661 as part of the settlement of the New Netherlands under the control of the Dutch West India Company. Its foundation is generally credited to Arent van Curler, who purchased a sizeable tract of land from the Mohawks and led a settlement there. In 1664, the English seized the colony as part of a war with the Netherlands, renaming the area New York in honor of the brother of King Charles II (James, Duke of York). But Dutch influence lingered on. It is said that in an attempt to eradicate it, the English destroyed Dutch-style buildings

and even built their own houses on former Dutch sites, some of which may
have included graveyards.

This fragmentary history of the area might serve to explain the circumstances in which the house was built on a graveyard, but what of the idea
that a vampire may have been buried beneath its foundations? It is perhaps
worth remembering that in the famous vampire novel *Dracula,* the Irish
author Bram Stoker makes his celebrated vampire-hunter, Abraham Van
Helsing, Dutch. Indeed, Van Helsing has become almost as famous as the
vampire count himself. Little is known about Van Helsing's past except that
he was formerly associated with one of the novel's other protagonists, Dr.
John Seward. It is worth noting that many of Van Helsing's expressions are
uttered in German, and it is thought that Stoker may have intended him
to be of German origin, which would perhaps give him a slightly greater
knowledge of vampires, as the creatures are not as prominent in the Netherlands as they are in some other parts of Europe. That is not to say, however,
that vampires do not feature in Dutch folklore.

In Dutch tradition, vampires are included in a generic group of night-
time horrors known as *nachtmerrie* (nightmares). These are creatures that
appear during the hours of darkness to create mischief and attack livestock—mostly horses—but that have sometimes been known to attack humans as well. The nachtmerrie can take a variety of shapes—sometimes as
skinny old women, their heads covered with dark shawls and with incredibly long arms, or as beautiful young girls. Sometimes, the being can take
on the form of a black creature, somewhere between a dog and a cat, which
can leap on the bed of a sleeper and create awful dreams while drawing
energy from him or her. The sleeper usually wakes in a sweat, exhausted
and feeling vaguely ill. It is no use locking the doors or windows, for they
can enter a building or a room through the smallest crack. They climb upon
a victim's chest and withdraw energy, blood, or vital fluids by sticking an
enormously long tongue into the person's open mouth. In some cases, the
nachtmerrie can strangle its victim by the force of its attack. If no measures
are taken against it, the creature will return and the victim will grow weaker
and weaker until he or she finally expires. In some parts of the Netherlands,
these creatures are also known as Waalridders and are said to be the embodiment of evil spirits who draw sustenance from the living. Nachtmerries

and Waalridders can sometimes be recognized by the fact that their eyebrows have grown together. It should also be pointed out that many of the nachtmerrie are not reanimated corpses, but rather living individuals who take this form after nightfall.

In many cases, the nachtmerrie can enter a room through a crack and perform its ghastly acts without really waking a sleeper. However, they will always signal their presence by giving the sleeper extremely bad or torrid dreams. To have one of these, say the Dutch, is a sure sign that the individual has been visited by these creatures or that it is trying to exert some form of influence over him or her. In order to create such restless dreams, the nachtmerrie does not even have to leave its house (or its grave), but can sometimes draw the good out of an individual from afar.

So what *was* the fungal outline on the cellar floor in Schenectady in the late 1800s? People living in the building experienced lethargy, vague nausea, and nightmares, coupled with disturbed sleep. Was their vitality being leeched off by some kind of vampiric being and, if so, what was it? Although there is no firm evidence, some rather vague speculation to its identity may be given.

As has already been stated, during medieval and early modern times there was a strong link in the minds of many Europeans between vampirism and witchcraft. The Dutch, however, do not seem all that preoccupied with their witches, so there were fewer major witchcraft trials in the Netherlands than in other surrounding countries. There were, however, some cases, several of which date from the time of Spanish influence in parts of the country. However, under the prevailing law the procedure of witch accusations and trials at this time was rather complicated. As in other parts of the world, many of the witchcraft accusations in the Netherlands were between people of the peasant classes and usually concerned everyday matters—the cursing of livestock or crops, the churning of butter or the making of cheese, or the loss of a valuable item, and so on. If an accusation was made, the victim could demand compensation from the alleged witch, and if that were paid or carried out, no formal trial would take place. The alleged witch might also start a formal slander against his or her accusers in which case no trial could take place. Many cases were thus settled without ever coming to court. Nevertheless, there were some witchcraft cases that do appear in official records. Although it is true that many of the instances of accusation are scattered throughout the years, there are certain periods when the courts seem rather busier in dealing with such claims.

Between 1522 and 1525, for example, there seems to have been a spate of cases that rose out of common disagreements and developed into full-blown witch accusations. This may have been the work of the Inquisition set up by the Holy Roman Emperor Charles V to hold back the advance of the Protestant religion in the country. In 1522, Trij van der Molen, a native of a small hamlet near the city of Roermond (southern Netherlands), was arrested and brought before the courts. She was accused of bothering some-one in the main street of her village, after which that person had experienced an illness and bad dreams. Trij was suspected of being a nachtmerrie and, under interrogation, she admitted to having made a pact with the Devil and to drawing off energies from some of her neighbors by supernatural means. She was burned at the stake. In 1525, two women were charged with magi-cally entering a neighbor's house and leaping on him as he slept, riding him through the countryside all night like a horse until he woke, sweating and exhausted. Others also came forward with similar claims and the women were submitted to questioning, during which they admitted a pact with the Devil and practicing evil rites.

In 1581, a woman named Kael Merrie, living along the Maas River, was accused of bewitching a young child and causing him bad dreams. She de-nied the charges, and because there was not enough evidence to bring her to trial, she was banished from her community. Even though there was little evidence against her, it was widely believed that she was a Waalridder and she was subsequently attacked by a group of vigilantes and mercenaries and was drowned in the Maas River. Two other women who were suspected of consorting with her were also captured by the group and also drowned. Although such activities were condemned, there was little that local justices could do to stop them.

In the period between 1583 and 1592, Dutch witchcraft trials flared again, this time in the south of Holland. These trials might have come about through the more widespread use of the celebrated *Malleus Malificarum* in places such as Germany, which lay just across the border, and also by a more rigorous use by the Dutch courts of the *Sachsenspiegel* (*Saxon Mirror*), a book of law compiled by the Saxon administrator Eike von Ripgow. The major accusation at this time centred on the town of Goedereede. Goedereede fell within the legal jurisdiction of Voorne and, in 1581, Pauwel Aertsz was Public Prosecutor there. Aertsz was a severe man, greatly influenced by Thomas Aquinas's *De Ketterhammer* (the 13th-century Heretic's Hammer), which dealt with demonology and considered the possibility of diabolic agents secretly living among God's people. Consequently, the authorities were always on the lookout for the possibility of witchcraft.

Things started off innocently enough when, in 1581, the prosecutor's sister lent her goat to a certain Leene Dimmensdr. When the goat was returned, its milk could not be churned in order to make butter, and the prosecutor suspected witchcraft. He decided to lay a trap for her. He asked her to churn some milk taken from the goat that her sister had loaned her. If it didn't churn, then it meant that she was innocent, but if it produced butter, there was a suspicion of witchcraft. Unsuspecting, Leene churned the butter and presented the results to the prosecutor. She was not prosecuted, but Aertsz noted the incident and marked the family down for special attention.

Shortly afterward, Leene's sister Nijinge was accused of sorcery. It was said that during a disagreement, she had cast a spell on a neighbor, Lenaert Jacobszoon Leerecop, causing him to be troubled with pains. He also suffered at night from troubled sleep and all sorts of wild nightmares. Again, there didn't appear to be sufficient evidence, and no formal charge was filed, but the sisters were now firmly on the prosecutor's radar.

The sisters were not at liberty for long. On the orders of the prosecutor they were picked up and taken to Voorne. Part of their witchcraft charge involved drawing the energies from their neighbors for their own benefit. The charge against Nijinge is dated July 10th, 1584, and was based on the testimony of Leunis Corneliszoon, then six years old, which had been given against Nijinge. He was also her grandson. The child stated that on several occasions he had seen his grandmother consort with a little old man dressed in red clothes who had given her a silver vial to drink from. The boy was sure that the little man had cloven feet and that what his grandmother had been drinking was blood. Strangely, even when faced with this evidence, the prosecutor didn't act immediately (perhaps because the boy was very young). However, on June 29th, 1585, Nijinge was arrested, along with neighbor Willemgen Jansdochter, on suspicion of witchcraft. The arrests came about because Lenaert Jacobszoon Leerecop had renewed his accusation in front of two prosecutor's assistants from Voorne. It was decided that, for administrative reasons, the trial would be held in Goedereede—the first time such a trial would be held in such a relatively minor town. The mayor and the local officials had no experience of dealing with such trials, so they hired a Flemish lawyer, Fransinus Zoetius, who had a great deal of experience in Belgian witch trials, as an advisor. His arrival placed a different emphasis on the case. He assisted the local magistrates at their questioning, and the woman denied everything. She denied cursing the neighbor and a number of other charges that were put to her. She did, however, admit to casting a spell against her own son and another relative, but later would retract the confession, saying that she had been confused.

The magistrates were still not satisfied and became even more alarmed when several other people came forward to say that they had experience disturbed sleep and had awoken exhausted and ill after dreaming of Nijinge during the night. They had no doubt that she was a Waalridder, and that they had been visited by her malicious spirit as they slept. The woman was a vampire of sorts and could torment them even without her physical body leaving her house. The advisor Zoetius now recommended that she be questioned under torture, an executioner was brought from Dordrecht to assist in the questioning. The torture involved both Nijinge and her sister being hoisted on a paleye. The women were also deprived of sleep. However, neither of them confessed.

More people came forward accusing Nijinge of being a vampire and a nachtmerrie. Nijinge's body was shaved and she was given loose clothing—the reason for this being that it was impossible for the Devil to stand next to her or to hold onto her. Because there had been little evidence against her, Leene had been released, but under intensified torture Nijinge confessed to witchcraft and implicated her as well; she was subsequently rearrested. On January 12th, 1586, Nijinge was subjected to more torture and confessed

to cursing certain neighbors. It is not known if she was questioned further. Her son Peter visited her shortly after she had been tortured on January 12th, but what passed between them in unknown. Nijinge Dimmensdr
and Willemgen Jansdochter were both burned at the stake for witchcraft on
January 22nd, 1586.

As for Leene, torture was once again threatened, but was not necessary, as Leene quickly and willingly confessed, stating that the Devil or his
representative had visited her roughly two years after her husband's death
and had proposed to her. He promised her great power over her neighbors,
saying that she could enjoy their health and energy as she saw fit. At first
she refused, but he returned the following month to see if she'd changed her
mind. Although greatly frightened, she didn't ask him to leave right away,
but asked him his name. He replied that his name was Jacob and that he
came from Sommelsdijk. After much discussion, they finally agreed that
they would live together, and the man drew a mark in blood on her forehead to seal the agreement. This scared her so much that she turned away
and asked him to leave. However, within the month, he returned and said
that he wished to sleep with her. She agreed to this. The following morning Jacob gave her a magic powder that she could use to gain access to her
neighbors' houses without their knowing and to turn herself into a cat.
Leene said that she had tried the powder several times and had entered
the houses of neighbors with whom she had a dispute and had drawn off
their energies. She had also gone around for eight weeks in the form of a cat
terrorizing them all. The confession was a damning one, and there was no
doubt in the magistrates' minds that she was a witch. The prospect of being
burnt scared Leene greatly, and before the sentence could be carried out,
she managed to escape from prison. Making her way to the harbor point in
Goedereede, she drowned herself in the water.

There was also a third sister. Although Eeuwoot Dimmens had only
been peripherally named in some of the accusations against the other two,
she was still under suspicion by the authorities. And once the suspicion had
been planted, there were soon other accusations directly concerning her,
although no evidence was ever presented. Nevertheless, in May 1592, when
Eeuwoot was 67 and crippled, she was arrested and charged with witchcraft,

coupled with an accusation of being a nachtmerrie. A judge arrived from Voorne on July 29th to conduct a preliminary trial and the accusations were named, one being that she had drawn the "goodness" from the house of her neighbor. The old lady replied that she was confused and that she couldn't really remember anything regarding the accusations. There was no firm evidence against her and she didn't confess, but she was put back in prison until the prosecutor could decide what to do. She remained in prison for four months and the confinement was having an effect on her rather fragile health.

The prosecutor now applied to use torture, but this was rejected because of her general physical condition (she might die before she was able to confess), and second on the lack of evidence against her. Even from her prison cell, a semblance of Eeuwoot had been able to torment some of her neighbors, appearing in their bedrooms at night in order to draw their energies from them and leave them exhausted in the morning. But the evidence was shaky and the authorities were not able to proceed to a full trial. Eeuwoot continued to languish in prison while the prosecutor looked around for more compelling evidence of witchcraft. Finally, on April 22nd, 1593, 11 months after she'd been first incarcerated, several more accusers were brought forward. There was no new evidence though, just accusations that were probably motivated by petty disagreements and dislike. Eeuwoot's husband, Marinus Faeszoon, now petitioned the authorities to have his wife released.

In his petition, Faeszoon stated that his wife had always been a quiet woman and that she had been a good mother and had raised a respectable family. There was no evidence against her except that of malicious gossip. The magistrates agreed, and said that if no evidence were produced, Eeuwoot should be freed. Sensing that the judiciary was moving against him, Prosecutor Aertsz renewed his application for torture, only this time he applied only to the local authorities. Eventually this was granted, and the executioner was brought once again. Before he subjected her to the rack, he kept her awake for nine days and nine nights and then she was questioned again. She did not, of course, divulge much information. However, she did admit to associating with the Devil or his agent. Nevertheless, there was not enough evidence to hold her, and with her husband applying once more for her release, she was freed.

Although Eeuwoot had been freed, Prosecutor Aertsz was not done with the family just yet. A half-sister named Joosgen Dircx Costers lived nearby and had been implicated in the alleged witchcraft and nocturnal vampirism of her relatives. The prosecutor now suspected her of being a witch as well. However, her husband was Adriaen Corniliszoon Clerck, an important man in the local community. As well as being a former mayor of Goedereede, he was also serving as the town clerk at the time the prosecutor made his accusations. As the number of stories about her alleged witchcraft and about her being a nachtmerrie began to grow, Joosgen became worried—after all, she had seen the fate of her two half-sisters. Like Eeuwoot, she appealed directly to Prince Mauritz, who directed that she be cleared of all the accusations against her. The prosecutor was, however, determined to press ahead and placed the accusations before the local authorities in Goedereede himself. They came to the conclusion that the accusations had no basis and that the defendant was innocent of all charges. Joosgen's good name was reinstated and the case against the family came to an end.

The case had important ramifications for witchcraft and nachtmerrie cases in the Netherlands. From late 1592 onward, it was almost impossible to get anyone convicted simply on the accusations of neighbors—the accused had to admit diabolic involvement freely and willingly (without the use of torture). This was the decision of Hof Van Holland, and it was perhaps in response to the petitions had been laid before it. It is worth noting that both Eeuwoot and Joosgen had husbands of some standing in the community who were able to plead for them, whereas Leene and Nijinge were both widows and fared less well in the face of accusations—even in places like the Netherlands survival depended on a male protector as far as witchcraft accusations were concerned. Also, there had been a recent witch trial in the town of Schiedem where torture had been used, leading to some questionable evidence, and Hof Van Holland didn't want a repeat of that. But just because the law had changed it didn't mean that people's perceptions were any different. They still believed in nachtmerrie and vampire kind and still took folkloric protections against them.

From 1613, the position concerning witch trials took on a new element in the Netherlands. As Protestantism began to spread, those who still practiced Catholicism or took a different view to the accepted line were counted as witches and night visitors. Their accusers were no longer their neighbors, but the authorities themselves.

We only know of the second major witch trial in the history of the Netherlands because of a pamphlet. All records of the proceedings have been lost. The trials took place in Roermond, a city that stands on the lower Roer and on the eastern bank of the Meuse River. In 1613, roughly 64 persons were arrested on suspicion of being witches and nachtmerrie. The first was Tryntjen van Zittaert, a local woman who, together with her daughter, had boasted that they could enter the bedrooms of several children and cause them to die by "drawing the breath" from them. The boasting took place at an unfortunate time—there had been a spate of bad harvest, blighted crops, diseases in animals and fish, human miscarriages, and widespread unemployment in the surrounding countryside. It was said that the miscarriages were the work of nachtmerrie, who had "drawn the good" out of unborn children. The boasting was initially done to some children with whom Tryntjen's daughter had been playing, and on hearing of it, the children's parents made a formal complaint to the church, who immediately raised the matter with the authorities. Charges were brought and the affair assumed the status of a full inquisition. Under questioning with torture, Tryntjen and her daughter made a full confession and began to implicate others in their witchcraft. More arrests quickly followed. It is possible that some of those arrested were of a slightly different religion than the growing Protestant faith, or of no religion at all, and that the arrests were religiously motivated. While in prison, Tryntjen's daughter (then 12 years old) allegedly made things, such as coins, appear from her mouth at will. There was little doubt that the child was skilled, but it was taken as evidence of witchcraft. When tortured, Tryntjen confessed to having killed at least 41 children and a number of adults by drawing the goodness from them as a nachtmerrie and of blighting a number of crops and animals as a witch. She also implicated several other people including a local doctor, Jan van Ool. While van Ool and 10 others were being arrested, Tryntjen and her daughter were brought to trial. Both were found guilty; the mother was burned, and the daughter locked in a convent for the rest of her life.

Jan van Ool was tortured and finally confessed to being a witch. He stated that he had killed his wife because she had refused to agree to a pact with Satan, and that he cut her up into small pieces and had thrown her down a well. He also claimed that he was forced by the Devil to extract the life out of one person for each 10 that he healed. In the years that he had practiced as a doctor, he had gradually drawn the goodness (and the life) out of 150 people in total. He was burnt alive, but not before he had accused at least 41 other witches and nachtmerrie. All of them were submitted to torture and every one of them confessed. They had inflicted disease and taken the good from many people, including their own families.

The witch hunt then moved slightly across the German border. In the municipality of Straelen in the district of Cleves, a woman named Entjen Gilles was arrested and confessed to having "drawn the good" from the unborn fetuses of pregnant woman, causing them to be stillborn. She had also magically damaged the wombs of many women, leaving them sterile. She was burnt alive.

In total, there were more than 63 witches and nachtmerrie brought to trial, all of them found guilty and condemned to death. At one point, two people were being burnt every day, as their cases were rushed through in the minimum amount time. It is said that more than 600 small and unborn children were destroyed by the nachtmerrie and that 400 adults and more than 6,000 animals were killed through witchcraft.

What brought about the end to the persecutions is largely unknown. Perhaps the social and economic climate changed; perhaps the Dutch judiciary took a wider view and limited the powers of the church and certain social authorities. But, like the accusations in Goedereede, their effect was devastating. Some of those who fled started to settle elsewhere, somewhere they were not known and could perhaps start a new life, far beyond the gaze of the authorities. Somewhere like the New Netherlands.

Ever since the English explorer Henry Hudson had reported to the Amsterdam authorities in 1609 that he had found fertile land on the East Coast of the New World, Dutch colonial interest there had been piqued. It was further stimulated by the publication of his report in 1612 by the Dutch Consul in London, Emanuel Van Meteren. Similar to many of his Dutch contemporaries, Van Meteren saw immense commercial and traditional opportunities in such an area, and the merchants of Amsterdam were determined to exploit these. Between 1611 and 1612, the Admiralty of Amsterdam sent two secret expeditions to what is now the New England coast in order to see if a way could be found to reach China by following some of the rivers. Between 1611 and 1614, the region between Maryland and Massachusetts had also been mapped and assessed by explorers such as Adriaen Block, Hendrick Christiaensen, and Cornelius Jacobsen Mey. However, the British were also showing an interest in what is now the American East Coast, and it was essential that the Dutch laid claim to the area and established settlements there as quickly as possible. Speedily, the Dutch West India Company assumed jurisdiction in the region and began shipping settlers there. Emigration to the New World was encouraged in the Netherlands, as Dutch merchants strove to formalize a trading presence there.

It has been noted elsewhere in this book that suspicious Dutch immigrants were still arriving in America as late as the 1800s. In the port of Charleston, South Carolina, the curious house occupied by the Black Constable, John Domingo, had formerly been owned by a Dutchman who had run a shop there. Both the man and the place had a sinister reputation, and it was rumored that the Dutchman had been forced to flee the Netherlands for some unspecified reason, perhaps religious persecution (although this description could cover a number of reasons). Might someone similar have been buried beneath the foundations of the house in Schenectady in an earlier time? Someone who might have been a witch and a nachtmerrie? All the symptoms that affected the people in the building—tiredness, evil dreams, illness, and loss of energy—would seem to correspond to those earlier cases detailed in the Netherlands.

There is no *exact* identification of a possible individual who might have been buried in the old Dutch graveyard on which the house had been built, but there are legends. It has to be said, however, that some of these tales may have been made up for various reasons. The British who took over the area may have wished to discredit the Dutch who had been buried there, and they may have been circulated by different landlords within the city who were competing for tenants. Nevertheless, the stories may have some validity and certainly assume a rather sinister tone.

The stories concern Zwarte Piet, also known as "Black Peter." Peter van Lind arrived in the area around New Amsterdam sometime during the Directorship of Willem Verhulst or of Peter Minuit when the Eighty Years War was at its height. He supposedly came from a village somewhere near Amsterdam and was supposed to have a dubious background. It is alleged that he was accused of witchcraft and of causing stillbirths. He was also accused of summoning and of consorting with demons over which he had dominion and which he sent to do evil against his neighbors. No one knows what profession he followed, but he was also known to have alchemical skills.

His evil ways did stop when he came to the New World, for he terrified the settlers with alleged magical practices. According to some accounts, he lived in one of the new Dutch villages along the Hudson Valley, while others say he lived in a small cabin well away from the settlement. It is also said that he worked as a hunter and traded among the local Indians and learned their ways.

Van Lind supposedly consorted with Lenape shamans, and from them he learned the secret of sending his dark spirit out for mischievous purposes (although some argue that he already knew how to do this). And he was supposed to be able to draw down old gods that the Indians had worshipped for his own benefit. It is said that he was almost a law unto himself in the developing colony, and that even the authorities there were fearful of him.

There are various accounts of how Peter van Lind met his end. Some say his body was found in the deep woods (it was said that he had been frequenting very ancient and pagan altars there) and that the body was marked with great slashes. Had he encountered something among the remote forest tracks that had torn at him with ravening talons, eventually killing him? Others say that he died in his cabin while trying to summon something using magical incantations. Others say that he died of perfectly natural causes.

No one can say exactly where he is buried, but it is widely believed that he was given a Christian burial. Could it be that he was buried in an unmarked plot in some ancient Dutch graveyard in what is now Schenectady? Certainly he was suspected of being a nachtmerrie and of drawing energies from some of the other colonists. Even after death, his influence may have been supernaturally felt in the immediate environs of his grave, and the fungal outline on the floor of the cellar may have identified his last resting place.

Although much of this is simply speculation, there may be *some* fragment of truth in the tales. And such people might have been nachtmerrie— a terror that the settlers brought with them from the Netherlands to the New World. The outline on the ground may have been the fungal form of one of these Dutch vampires who might have placed the whole house under its dark spell.

What finally became of the eerie shadow is unclear. Perhaps it did eventually succumb to the cleansing agents that were used against it. Maybe it faded away on its own. It could be still there, buried under earth and rubble in the cellar. The original house is, of course, believed to have been long pulled down, but the shadow might remain. And what of its influence— does it still try to draw the energies from those who happen to be in its vicinity? The area of Schenectady is still there and is still populous. Maybe the shadow is still there, waiting to break a holy spell that entraps it...waiting patiently.

MASSACHUSETTS

O ff Route 127, traveling toward the village of Annisquam in the city of Gloucester, and way up among the clumps of twisted trees and roots that cover the area, lies a scattering of stones and boulders with the outline of something that had once stood. Although there are car parks nearby, the area is still a wilderness, heavily forested, and just as it might have been in the 1600s. However, these stones and boulders—a number with inscriptions on them—are the last vestiges of the remarkable settlement of Dogtown, perhaps Massachusetts's most celebrated abandoned village.

The hills and valley of the New England coast are peppered with the fragments of many settlements that have come and gone throughout the years and in which the early settlers strove to make a living in a new and harsh environment. Some were incorporated into greater townships, others simply abandoned to the elements and environment. All have their own dark histories.

One such place is the settlement of Old Colony or Plymouth Colony, now long abandoned, which was almost wiped out by an epidemic of "consumption" (tuberculosis) around 1807. With the majority of the population of the village dead from the disease, the survivors became worried that they had fallen prey to a vampire. One family was suspected, even though they had fallen victim to the epidemic as well. They are unknown, but the family was a large one, certainly one of the oldest and most venerable in the district consisting of 14 children. However, in 1807, only a mother and one son remained; all the others died within one year of each other. When the boy began to cough and struggle for breath, several of the remaining inhabitants decided to test the theory of vampire intervention. It was thought that one of the family—the 13th girl, who had been one of the first to die at the age of 16, had been returning from the grave to attack her family and perhaps the wider community. Rumor was that the girl had been something of a strange character, greatly interested in ways of foretelling the future, which counted in the local mind as witchcraft. Consequently, it was decided that her body should be exhumed and examined for traces of vampirism. This was done in the presence of her mother and ailing brother. When the coffin was opened, the mother claimed she saw the visage of someone who had been a tenant of the silent grave, but lit up with the brilliancy of youthful health. The curls were thick and lustrous, the cheeks dimpled, and the eyes had lost none of their blue vibrancy. This was a corpse that should have been rotting! What sort of measures were taken is not recorded, but it is said that the boy in question was so shocked by what he saw that he lasted barely a year afterward, with the mother quickly following him to the grave. Others died too, and the settlement was abandoned some years after this. The story was later published in the *Old Colony Memorial and Plymouth County Advertiser* in 1820 as "a curiosity of former days," showing that the idea of the vampire stalking the tiny village families and community still hadn't gone away. It was still right there in the social memory.

But it was not only disease and vampires that troubled the communities around Gloucester and Cape Ann. During the 1700s, the waters around the Cape were a haven for pirates who often attacked shipping coming into the port of Gloucester. One of the most notorious buccaneers in the region was Captain John Phillips, who commanded the former British schooner *Revenge*, and who preyed on vessels along the Massachusetts coast between the years 1723 and 1724. Although not as flamboyant a rogue as Blackbeard, William Kidd, or Barbarossa, Phillips was greatly feared by the coastal communities.

Phillips had started his working life as a carpenter. While voyaging from England to Newfoundland in 1721, his ship was taken by pirates under the command of Thomas Anstis, who forced Phillips to join his crew. He served Anstis for a year as the ship's carpenter. In 1721, while off the island of Tobago, Anstis sent a number of his crew to careen a captured vessel; as they were doing so, a British warship showed up. Anstis took flight, abandoning Phillips, and the others took refuge by hiding in the woods. Phillips and his companions retuned to Bristol, England, where he tried to settle down again in his trade as carpenter. But piracy had got into his blood and he was soon off to sea again.

His decision was aided by the arrest and trial for piracy of some of his former comrades; in order to avoid capture, he took passage once again in 1723 for Newfoundland. There, he resolved to take a ship and return to the pirate life. With only four companions, he managed to capture a British schooner that had anchored in Petty Harbour in Maddox Cove, which he renamed the *Revenge*; with the stolen vessel, the four of them sailed south to Barbados, taking a number of fishing boats along the way and building up their crew. After attacking a couple of merchantmen, Phillips counted among his crew both the brutal John Rose Archer and a man named Pedro. After attacking and plundering several ships off Tobago (and killing most of their crew) Phillips and his men sailed for the American coast.

During 1723 and the early part of 1724, Phillips plundered the New England coast, attacking settlements there at will. It was not only booty that the pirates sought, but people as well. This was for two reasons: First, Phillips wanted to build up his crew (several of which had been killed in the taking of ships in the West Indies), and second to sell as slaves in the Caribbean. It is unclear how many persons he took before sailing north again for Cape Sable near Nova Scotia, where he captured a sloop. The vessel's commander was Captain Andrew Harradine, who conspired with several other prisoners to take the *Revenge* and kill Phillips. Harradine and his confederates attacked the ship's crew on April 18th, 1724, killing Phillips, the gunner, the boatswain, and the sailing master, and overpowering the associates. Then they sailed for Annisquam Harbor and later for Boston. Most of the pirates were hanged, although Archer was temporarily spared only to be executed later in Boston. Phillips had only been a pirate for eight months, but the terror he caused along the New England coast had been profound. And he was not the only one who raided in these waters. From time to time, bands of marauders raided the coastline, taking away captives that they could then sell in the plantations of Jamaica and Barbados. Pirate captains such as Henry Sturgis, William Fly, William White, and others found such raids fairly lucrative, so many of the coastal communities often lived in terror of pirate ships.

To avoid the attentions of the sea wolves, many communities moved further back into the hinterland and away from the immediate coast. Although they still maintained a connection with the ocean, their houses were well away from it and in high, rather inaccessible places that were easy to defend against any form of raid. It's possible that the settlement that would become known as Dogtown was one of these. Even today, the "lost village" of Dogtown is remote and difficult to get to.

Cape Ann was, nevertheless, a place with a rather ghostly reputation. Two miles inland from Gloucester's main settlement, in 1692, ghostly armies had been seen, late at night, traversing the difficult terrain; shouts and musket fire from an unseen battle were heard by a number of people living there. The times in this period were vastly unsettled; the wars going on in Europe touched American shores. Local English were fighting the French in what became known as King William's War, as England's William III took on the forces of the French King Louis XIV in Holland and Belgium. Natives threw themselves into the mix as well, fighting for whichever side paid the most or whomever they thought would be of the most benefit to them. By 1692, the wars had reached Cape Ann, and the town of Gloucester was extremely unsettled. Is it any wonder there were tales of phantom armies and spectral Indian raids among them? One prominent story in Gloucester told of an incident in 1675 during what was known as King Philip's War. This was a series of battles fought by the colonists against a local Wampanoag sachem (chieftain) named Metacom (who styled himself as King Philip), which is described as one of the bloodiest conflicts to be fought on American soil. One night during the conflict, a house was apparently set on fire and burned to the ground by a group of Indian raiders. A number of people saw the conflagration and the flames rising up into the night sky as the Indians whooped and displayed their hatchets, threatening to kill anyone who ran from the blaze.

The next morning, however, the house was there, not burned down, and the family who lived there had apparently been untroubled during the night. Yet many had seen the blaze for miles around. They spoke of an old grandmother staggering from the burning building with an Indian knife half in her body, and yet, there she was, alive and hearty as ever. In fact, when anxious relatives called, she was found eating breakfast! The occurrence was simply dismissed as a spectral vision.

However, about a week afterward, the area *was* attacked by a roving band of Wampanoag, and the house was indeed burned down and the old lady was killed. A detachment of local militia was sent to drive the Wampanoags back into the scrubby hinterland and into the woods. The original vision was dwelt upon as a premonition of things to come. Again, in 1692 (the same year as the celebrated witch trials in Bay Colony, further along the coast), Ebenezer Babson thought his own house was under attack. Returning home one evening, he claimed he saw two men run from the back of the building and into his corn patch. Convinced that his wife and family had been butchered, Babson burst into the house to find them enjoying a typical evening together. They had neither heard nor experienced anything, and a subsequent search of the immediate countryside revealed nothing. And yet, Babson was absolutely certain he had seen the men and had heard what they said. And his story was not untypical of the area. Stories of phantom armies and spectral Native American raids crossing and re-crossing Cape Ann were extremely common in these unsettled times. Perhaps it was actually *because* of the times that such legends flourished. They did, however, give an insight into the minds of the people living around the Cape and how they framed their world in terms of demons, ghosts, and visions. Incidents such as the burning house or Babson's vanishing raiders were not ascribed to delusion or mistake, or even to the internal pressures that the colonies were suffering (Native American attacks, wars, and difficult harvests), but to some supernatural origin that could threaten the colonists' existence. It was only to be expected that such tensions would spread to the witch trials in Salem.

The settlement that became known as Dogtown was established around 1693 between the colonies of Gloucester and Rockport (or Sandy Bay as it was known then), and was built on high rocky ground, well away from the coast, to protect against both pirate and Native American attack. By the early 1700s, much of Cape Ann had been thoroughly deforested in preparation for settlement and to discourage attacks (because they used the undergrowth for cover), so that the rocky surface of the town was fully exposed with scarcely a tree or bush to relieve the eye. This clearance had been turned into a rather profitable lumber business, and soon wood was being exported from Gloucester in rather large quantities—it would be later claimed that an entire fleet of the British Navy would be made from Cape Ann hardwoods. A large and important sawmill had been established on the very edge of the forest around 1642, and New England cordwood and other lumber flowed through the port of Gloucester at an impressive rate. While the woods had been cleared in the Gloucester/Rockport area, however, the land that had been left was possibly the worst type—rocky, infertile ground that would bear next to no crops. This did not overly worry the selectmen of Gloucester, who saw the future of the settlement not in farming or in agriculture, but in fishing and merchant shipping in and out of the ports. The cabins and houses of fishermen and trading men would take up much of the region, they believed. And, no matter how infertile and rocky the soil, these dwellings needed to be well away from the coastline to protect against pirate raids. Ships were still seen prowling the waters off the Cape, and whether they were or not, these were believed to be pirate craft or French privateers. The location of the new settlement—to be known as the Common Settlement or Common Town—also lay on a direct route between Sandy Bay and Gloucester. Only people of quality would live there, and it is estimated that by 1750, more than 100 respectable families had settled.

Around 1721, officials measured out 43 lots across the rough highland terrain, which would make the basis for the village. It was just over a minor river from Gloucester, which was sometimes no more than a stream, and was known locally as the Alewife Brook. It was also within walking distance of the Green, which was the town's gathering and social center, and where much of the commerce of the area took place. This also facilitated the use of the various mills in the area along the Mill River, into which the Alewife Brook flowed.

When planning the new village, the local selectmen had assumed that it would entice new families and settlers into the area and expand the local population. However, it was some of Gloucester's own families who began to colonize the cleared land, breaking up the boulders and hard rock that still remained. Those who came were a Godly group, steeped in Biblical tradition (as many Puritan families were), and well aware of the spiritual value of hard work. It served them well in this inhospitable landscape, and soon a thriving settlement was raised, ready for the families to put down roots. Some agriculture was attempted using seaweed—rich in nutrients—as a mulch to encourage growth, but while some crops thrived, the land was too rocky and too strewn with boulders (just as it is today) to entertain any serious farming. Nevertheless, it was a triumph of achievement against the terrain and, as a village, it would continue to thrive for many years until its decline was brought about by a man named Nathaniel Coit.

The disputes within the developing village began with the rebuilding and relocation of the area's First Parish Meeting House. In early New England, it is difficult to overestimate the importance of the Parish Meeting House. It combined much of the spiritual and practical aspects of communal life. They were places where the communities gathered both for religious and civic matters. Property sales, announcements regarding colonial law, and even marriage announcements were all posted there for locals to read. The heads and hides of predatory wolves and other threats to the population were placed on display, and the House was often used as a place for storing gunpowder and weaponry in case of Indian or French attack—which was still very much a possibility in those early days. Indeed, those attending religious services often brought firearms with them in case of a sudden attack. It was the center for everything. The Meeting House also preserved the status quo in most communities through its internal arrangements. Seating was set so that the leaders of the village were assigned seats at the front, and a gradual diminution in social status ran all the way to the back of the hall. The seating plan was not an arbitrary one—people could not just sit where they liked at public gatherings. Parish committees were even created to allocate the seating at public meetings based on a mix of lineage, wealth, and public service. Many of the community's elder statesmen were allocated the most prestigious seats, and this served to solidify their perceived social status. The Common Town Meeting House provided something of a problem in this respect—the building was old and drafty, and parts of it were not suited to some of the more venerable, but infirm, community elders. And there was a mix in the seating arrangements. Whereas some of the "incomers" were descendants of established Gloucester families, others were not, so the seating was being continually rearranged in order to satisfy local egos. Seats were allocated by the Parish Committee on the express understanding that there should be no grumbling, but this did not prevent quarrels and falling-outs. The 19th-century New England historian Alice Morse Earle tells of two sisters-in-law who, although allocated seats beside each other, continually fought over who had the more "dignified" one. The dispute became so heated that a special meeting of the town's selectmen had to be convened to resolve the matter. Some other disagreements were so severe that they were passed down for several generations.

In an attempt to both sort out the decaying building and establish a proper seating pattern, it was suggested that a new Meeting House be built and the congregation be relocated. However, this was not as simple as it first appeared. Many of the village's older inhabitants opposed any attempt to move the Meeting House to a different location, as a new Hall might change the seating arrangements among the more venerable, which had been carefully worked out through the years. Change, they argued, was not necessarily a good thing. Among those who took this view was Nathaniel Coit. Coit was a village elder, in his 70s, but with an extremely sharp mind, and as one of the more venerable community members, was well used to getting his own way. His only interest was in maintaining the status quo, the way that things had been done for many years.

Already in 1729, the year that the dispute broke out, change was underway in Gloucester. Up until then, the First Parish had served all of the Gloucester area, which was fine as long at the community remained small. From 1700 onward, however, the population of Cape Ann began to expand at an alarming rate—far too big for a single parish. From 1704 to 1755, the number of people grew from roughly 700 to 2,800. And this new population spread out through the Cape, increasing travel across difficult terrain to attend worship. At last, some congregation members in some of the outlying villages, tired of traveling, broke away, and formed parishes of their own. Even so, the numbers of people arriving in the Cape Ann settlements continued to grow, and as Gloucester developed as a port, many of these new "incomers" had a maritime background. The demographics of the community were beginning to subtly shift, as old families with a long-established pedigree in the area gave way to expanding newer ones with perhaps slightly more radical ideas.

The idea of a new Meeting House was first proposed in 1729 and was initially rejected without much discussion. Old families and venerable leaders saw little need for a new building in which some of the "incomers" might hold sway. Besides, there was a dangerous idea abroad: pews in the new establishment might actually be sold, allowing certain families to assume financial superiority over some of those who might be more established within the community. Thus, the notion of a new building was quickly shelved. Nevertheless, those favoring a new Meeting House were not so easily dismissed. In 1734, the First Parish members voted in favor of abandoning the old Meeting House by the Green and building a new one near the harbor, which was more than a mile away. And the proposal regarding the selling of seats was also put to vote and was only rejected on the slenderest of margins (by four votes). Of course, disputes wracked the community. The "incomers" vowed to push their idea concerning the sale of seats through by any means—wealth would be the sole determining factor in the community. The old families whose rank and status were determined by family lineage, spirituality, and service to their community suddenly found themselves increasingly marginalized. The issue was now being forced by wealthy merchants and leaders.

The old families, however, fought back, and as the new Meeting House rose beside the harbor, their opposition to it and all that it stood for centered round Nathaniel Coit. The idea of selling seats in the new House didn't really bother Coit all that much—he was one of the settlement's wealthier figures and could afford an expensive seat—but he had antagonized the harbor leaders by his stiff opposition to the building of the new Meeting House in the first place, and, when the building was finally constructed, an urging to people not to attend it. People heeded him, and for its first year the new House, twice the size of the old one, stood empty. The harbor leaders responded by bringing a suit against him; this meant that Coit would almost certainly be guaranteed one of the less favorable and less venerable seats in the new establishment.

Nathaniel Coit answered them by threatening to form a completely separate parish, one in which old values would be respected. However, in order to do this, he would have to petition the Massachusetts General Court and demonstrate that he had enough support to do so. This involved collecting a petition with sufficient signatures to make this major split possible. The harbor leaders wanted no split—such a rift might affect their power base in Gloucester and weaken their perceived political strength. They tried to stop him, but Coit went ahead with his petition. His own power base lay in the highlands in the Commons Settlement or Common Town. Here, the people were not all that financially well off by comparison to those who lived around the harbor area—their "wealth" lay in their good names, their established family traditions, and their work for the common good. They readily signed his petition because, under the new proposals, they could not afford to maintain their positions within the community and would almost certainly lose out to their wealthier neighbors. It also meant that the values of heredity, spirituality, and continuity would be maintained within the Gloucester settlement—something that had been long cherished among the colonists.

By November 1734, Nathaniel Coit had gathered more than 84 signatures for his petition. Many of those who had signed simply could not afford the new seats, and others were too old and infirm to make the journey down to the harbor. They were of a "different sort" to the wealthy inhabitants of the harbor area. In an attempt to block Coit's petition, they filed their own complaint, drawing attention to the number of seamen now living in what they called "the Upper Towne," who paid no taxes nor gave the ministers any support. They also tried to give the impression that the Commons Settlement was a den of vice and degeneracy. In their evidence to the General Court in reply to the petition, they openly said as much to the Court members.

In May 1739, after numerous representations and reconsiderations, Coit's petition was rejected, leading to various arguments all through the Cape. Parish meetings were disrupted, there was violence at some gatherings, and many of the meetings dragged on past candle-lighting time when the settlement's curfew began. "Nightwalking" after dusk was considered evil and was considered a punishable crime; the fact that many meetings went on after that time shows the severity of the subject to the colonists.

Undeterred by his failure, Coit filed a second petition. Again, the harbor leaders were hauled before the General Court to answer it. They claimed that additional and less-expensive seating had been added in the new meeting house, and if the people in the Upper Towne had difficulty in traveling to the new Meeting House, then they should move nearer to the harbor. The harbor leaders were shrewd enough to realize that Gloucester's future did not lie in the Upper Towne, the Green, or in the Common Settlement, but down on the shoreline where the town's economy was located.

Replying to Coit's second petition, the General Court called in a surveyor named Josiah Batchelder, who was sworn under oath, to calculate the distances between the Upper Towne and the Meeting House. Batchelder determined that it was a distance of 2 miles from the average Commons Settlement home to the Meeting House, and this extra mile constituted a legitimate complaint. This, of course, did not please the harbor leaders. They complained that those who had assisted Batchelder in carrying his surveyor's measuring chain had all been Upper Towners and had not been subject to the oath he had taken. Moreover, several of them had been friends and relatives of Nathaniel Coit. Tempers flared with the harbor leaders accusing the Upper Towners of all sorts of scandalous and degenerate behavior. The lines between the two were already being drawn and perceptions were being fixed.

In an attempt to reach a compromise, the Court ruled that the Upper Towners could hold services in their old Meeting House during the winter. This, of course, did not please everybody—the harbor leaders complained that this was "giving in" to Coit's intimidation, whereas some of the older people of the Commons Settlement complained that the old Hall was too cold and drafty during the winter months. Other compromises were offered, all were rejected. Frustrated beyond words, the court eventually granted Coit's petition and the first parish was formally split with a new parish retaining the old Meeting House. The wake of the split was wracked with argument and ill-feeling. Nathaniel Coit may have won the battle, but he had lost the war and dug a deep division in the community about which he claimed to care so passionately. The status quo that he had sought to maintain was already slipping away.

He did not enjoy his hollow victory for long. In 1743, and at the age of 84, Nathaniel Coit died, leaving behind a legacy of distrust and hatred within his community. It was customary for Puritan parents to allow their children to look into the open grave of a venerable elder to see a great person laid to rest, and also to be aware of their own mortality. So deep were the divisions that only a handful of parents allowed their children to do so at Coit's graveside. The gulf that was beginning to open up between the town and the Commons Settlement was extremely deep and bitter, and it would continue down the years.

In 1777, and with the American Revolution underway, one of Gloucester's wealthiest merchants, David Pearce, began building and fitting a warship for the defense of the Massachusetts coast. Ever since the beginning of the War, Cape Ann had been a target of the British Navy, being so fully exposed to attack as it was. One morning in August 1775, the people along Gloucester's harbor area were awakened to the sound of cannons blasting from the British warship—the *Falcon*—just off the Cape Ann promontory. Worse would have followed had not some of the Gloucester men managed to capture a British officer and several crewmen who were rowing ashore in the early morning to set fire to the town. Following the incident of the *Falcon,* protective earthen ramparts were raised and some of the town's men were pressed into service as a defense militia. On November 1st, the Massachusetts Legislature formally sanctioned ships to serve as American privateers to plunder English merchantmen coming to and from the port of Boston and elsewhere. This was, in fact, a licensed form of piracy, as the spoils taken from the vessels were often split among the crew before the authorities could get their hands on them. With trade and supplies decreasing because of the War, many places such as Gloucester turned to such robbery as a means of self-preservation. It seemed ironic that the inhabitants of a port, which, 50 years earlier, lived in fear of piracy, now turned to piracy themselves. In fact, privateering along the Massachusetts coastline became such a lucrative business that, before the end of the War of Independence, 13 other colonies had adopted the practice with the blessing of the Continental Congress.

On July 1st, 1777, Pearce's ship, named the *Gloucester,* was ready to sail. Many of her 130-strong crew had come from the Commons Town, the others coming from the Harbor Area or from further into Cape Ann. The townspeople cheered her off as she moved along the shoreline and out into the open sea. She would return, it was promised, with enough food and rations to see the colony through the long, hard days of winter.

About a month after the *Gloucester* had departed, the people around Cape Ann were alarmed when a small fleet of British warships appeared out of a fog along the coastline. Although described as a mighty armada, it is unclear just how many vessels there were. They contented themselves with firing several cannons at the town before vanishing into the fog again and presumably sailing further up the Massachusetts coast. However, their very presence alarmed many of the Gloucester inhabitants who were convinced that this navy was still in the area and could still attack them. There was much speculation as to the motives and destination of this fleet. Little, however, was heard of the *Gloucester*.

About two weeks later, however, hopes were raised when John McKean, who had been the former Commons watchman and a member of the *Gloucester's* crew, sailed into the harbor in command of a captured ship, *The Two Friends*, which carried a cargo of provisions—gum, balsam, licorice root, and a supply of badly needed salt. The ship had been captured by the *Gloucester* on the open ocean, east of New York. There was even greater rejoicing when another Commons man, Isaac Day, sailed the captured British cargo packet, *The Spark*, into Gloucester harbor, its hold laden with fish and even more salt. The vessel had been on its way to Newfoundland, but had been captured by the *Gloucester* off the Grand Banks and taken back to Cape Ann as a prize. On August 31st, Captain Fisk, commanding the American warship *Massachusetts* out of Boston, recorded that his vessel was the lead ship in a squadron of about four Massachusetts privateers making their way along the New England coast, one of which was the *Gloucester*. The ship seems to have swung north, raiding along the Newfoundland coast, but Fisk's entry was the last record of it.

Back in Commons Town, women waited patiently for news of their husbands and sweethearts. Lookouts were dispatched to high vantage points to keep an eye for the approaching sail of the returning ship. There was nothing. Newspapers were scanned fervently. Insurance companies were legally obliged to announce names of captured prizes, together with the name of the capturing vessel. After *The Two Friends* and *The Spark,* there was no mention of the *Gloucester*. The vessel had vanished just as surely as if she'd never existed.

Strange stories began to circulate in the Gloucester community concerning the supposed loss of the vessel—many with supernatural overtones. In one, a ball of light (known as a *corposant* in seafaring circles) had traveled among the houses of Commons Town, visiting the doorways of each house from which a crew member had gone, lingering for a time there before passing on to the next house and eventually vanishing. In another tale, the faces of several of the crewmen had been seen in the waters of a local well. All of this seemed to suggest that the *Gloucester* had somehow perished somewhere at sea. However, the Commons women continued to hang on, hopeful that the vessel would one day make a return to port.

As the War of Independence dragged on, it began to take a toll on the Commons community. With their men gone on the ship, the women were finding life difficult. Americans were not the only ones who had turned to privateering. During the course of the War, other privateering vessels, backed by the British, attacked boats coming to and from the coastal ports, seizing their cargoes and taking their crews prisoner. Gloucester was particularly badly hit. Cargo was taken and boats sunk, their crews drowned. By 1779, the town had lost well over half its fleet, leaving about a sixth of its inhabitants dependent on charity of one sort or another. Disease and illnesses took away many others, especially from among the Commons people.

Midday on May 19th, 1780, the sky suddenly darkened all along the Massachusetts coast. It continued to darken until it appeared as if it was midnight. Birds flew home to nest and flower petals closed. It was the famous Dark Day, and to the Puritan people, it was taken as a signal that the Great Day of Judgement could not be far away. Preachers spoke from their pulpits with a fiery missionary zeal, and congregations prayed earnestly for deliverance. For the people of Gloucester, it was an evil omen. Many thought it signaled the defeat of American forces, the collapse of their community, or that the War would continue without end. Even when the Dark Day passed, those doubts lingered, and they were, in part, well founded.

By October 1780, Cape Ann had been all but decimated, and its people reduced to beggary. The mysterious disappearance of the *Gloucester* had certainly contributed to the sense of foreboding and depression that hung over the place, but the unending and deeply rooted poverty that had been caused by the War was also a significant factor. The population of the Settlement was now living close to levels of utter destitution. It comprised a significant number of widows—out of around 3,000 souls, nearly 350 were widowed and dependant on at least some form of charity. This, of course, was true in many other New England settlements, but nearly all of them had the ability to bounce back.

The split that had been started by Nathaniel Coit back in the early 1700s was still there, and while harborside Gloucester slowly pulled itself together after the War, few deigned to help their struggling neighbors up in the highlands. Indeed, the land beyond the Alewife Brook was considered "suspicious territory" where witches would congregate. Gradually, the area deteriorated even further. Those who had money enough to leave did so. Others built houses down near the harbor, integrating into the developing Gloucester society. Some rented out their property, but failed to maintain it and allowed it to fall into neglect. Some had no other choice than to stay. The place began to acquire a rather sinister reputation, as more and more colorful characters moved in.

No one is exactly sure when the name "Dogtown" was first used in relation to the Commons Settlement, but it was probably used in a derogatory sense. Some have suggested that it originated from the numbers of feral canines who wandered around the area or from the fierce dogs that were kept by old widows for their own protection. Few of them had large numbers of canines within their precincts (although in a few instances some of them did). It might even have been that the name didn't refer to a town at all, but to some location such as a hog-wallow or hitching-post along the road, or even a lonely drinking house out in the wilderness. In most cases, however, the name had a seedy air to it, suggestive of run-down, low-life, working class, non-salubrious places. It might also refer to a location where unusual and seemingly disgusting practices might be carried out. For example, in California during the gold rush of the mid-19th century, the name was applied to a camp of Chinese miners who allegedly ate dogs as part of their diet. The name suggested both difference and derision and was almost, without doubt, an insult. Is it any wonder that the area attracted the rebellious, the eccentric, the insane, and the weird?

Some of those who lived in the declining settlement were the descendants of the old Commons people who had always lived there, several of whom could trace their ancestry back to the earliest foundations of the town in 1693. These were people like Joseph Stevens, who had once been a relatively prosperous farmer and who had even built a large yard with a high wall around his Commons home. He lived with his sister Molly on what became known as the Dogtown Road and they were considered a particularly unpleasant couple by their neighbors. Few took pity on him as his fortunes began to decline, and in the end, one of his descendants was forced to simply live in the cellar of what had once been the family home. A more popular person was James Whitham, a shepherd who owned some of his own sheep and also acted as a herder for Colonel William Pearce, who resided just beyond Dogtown and whose sizeable flock attracted British raiders during the War of 1812. It was against these interlopers that Whitham defended his master's animals, earning high praise from the Colonel. However, the shepherd was almost drowned in Granny Day's Bog, a notorious swamp, and had to be discharged from the Colonel's service. There was also Captain Samuel Riggs, a descendant of Thomas Riggs, who had been one of the founding fathers of the Commons Settlement and had owned land as far away as Rockport. The Riggs house, situated on the very edge of Dogtown, was considered to be one of the oldest buildings in the area, if not in all of Cape Ann. Further along, a blacksmith named Joseph Allen had set up a smithy in 1674 where he raised 17 children. This was not the only large family whose descendants spread throughout the village. Another was Nathaniel Day, who raised at least 18 children, including three sets of twins, with his wife Mary Davis, and whose enormous family continued to form a part of the backbone of the later settlement.

A much more eccentric character was Captain John Morgan Stanwood, who was the village cobbler during the 1800s. He worked out of a "boo," a small attachment to his own house on the Commons Road, which he had made out of slabs of turf and boulders set against the house frame. Although he claimed to be something of a naval hero during the War of Independence, it's not actually certain that Stanwood had ever been to sea, let alone done any fighting. He had, however, been somehow involved in some foreign trade around the port of Gloucester and, after the War of 1812, he had stayed on as a Commons resident. He was crippled, claiming that he had been injured in a naval exchange, but later became convinced that his legs were made of glass and refused to walk anywhere. He married the daughter of Peter Lurvey, another Commons resident and something of a local hero. Lurvey had been killed, together with Benjamin Rowe and the minister's pet hog, during the War of Independence, when the British frigate *Falcon* had opened fire on the town in August 1775. It had been Lurvey who had attempted to organize the Gloucester militia against attack from the vessel, and who had saved the town from being fired. His wife continued to live in Dogtown, reaching the imperious age of 104, although not in good health and with her mind wandering. Captain Stanwood, of course, never failed to trade on his father-in-law's reputation, and besides being the cobbler, also set himself up as a kind of doctor, curing ailments in those who came to him.

Just as eccentric as the Captain was a freed slave named Old Ruth, who frequently dressed as a man and sometimes went by the name of John Woodman. She was employed around Dogtown as a builder and was well known for her hearty manner and hard work. Old Ruth also had certain curious physical characteristics, in that she had several long teeth. As far as vampire teeth go, both written fiction and Hollywood have led us to believe that these are either the canine teeth or the lateral incisors, thus allowing the vampire to maintain its supposedly good looks and not differentiate it too much from ordinary humans. However, within Westernized folklore, if the creature has long teeth at all, it can sink them into the body of its victim. Some German "shroudeaters," for example, had two long and prominent front teeth, which they used to tear through their grave liniments in order to break free from the grave. Other vampires were said to have at least three or four teeth with which they can attack their victims. It was supposed that "Old Ruth" probably had the long, tusk-like teeth of the former kind, which perhaps set her apart from some (though not all) of the other inhabitants of Dogtown.

Although she had a hearty way about her and was regarded as a good worker into her latter years, Old Ruth was often regarded with some suspicion outside of the settlement. Her cross-dressing and the use of a masculine name would certainly have marked her out as something of a witch and perhaps as a vampire as well. In parts of Albania, for example, transvestism is often taken as a sign that the person will become a *sampiro* (an Albanian vampire) upon death. Indeed, male sampiro often appear to have feminine characteristics, and the creature goes about making kissing noises as it passes. Any form of deviation from the accepted social and sexual norms would result in the person concerned becoming one of the Undead. Therefore, Old Ruth, with her long, fang-like teeth, and her supposedly strange ways, might have been taken as a vampire. As far as Dogtown was concerned, the freed slave's rather sinister aspects were somewhat moderated in that she lived on the upper story of a house. By Dogtown standards, she was reasonably wealthy, owning cattle, oxen, and several sheep. She made a living cooking meals for those less fortunate than herself. Her specialty was boiled cabbage.

Even so, there were some uncertainties about the strange woman. It was said, for instance, that she could travel the length of the Cape Ann coastline in the form of a great black crow or bat, doing harm against some of those that she encountered. In the end, Old Ruth was taken to the Gloucester Poorhouse where she was finally forced to wear skirts and adopt more feminine dress.

But Old Ruth was not the only person with strange teeth around Dogtown. At various times in the village's history, there have been at least three or four individuals with unusual dental phenomenon living there. There was, for instance, Judy Rhines (born 1771), who was regarded as something of a witch and a prostitute, who had large incisors. At one time she lived with another lady, Molly Jacobs, and together they were said to "ply their trade" with fishermen and some of the crews who came on the ships sailing into Gloucester harbor. They and another lady of the night—Liz Tucker— made up a kind of "red light district" in Dogtown, but while the others were despised, Judy Rhines was feared. Local legend claimed she had supernatural powers and could make potions and salves for many cures and other purposes. The basis of many of these unguents was barberries, which she picked around the village. She made them into potions and candles by mixing them with other ingredients, one of which was rumored to be human blood. It was said that when one of the "special candles" was lit, things that had been lost were mysteriously found. However, it was also said that Judy Rhines traveled each night from Dogtown in order to acquire the blood of sleeping Gloucester folk in order to make her enchanted lights. It was also said that she drank blood and that she slept in the dark of a potato pit during the day.

Also sporting long fangs was another freed slave, Cornelius Finson, also known as Black Neil, one of the last people living in the village during the severe winter of 1830. He had served as the village hog slaughterer, but he had also had some minor clerking experience in Gloucester and Annisquam. He lived with Molly Jacobs, believing that there was a great treasure, buried by the celebrated pirate Captain William Kidd, hidden in her cellar. He dug several pits, but found nothing and, abandoning his former partner, went to live with Judy Rhines. The thought of two dentally abnormal people living together added to the sinister speculation regarding Dogtown. Some even suggested that it had become a nest of vampiric beings. At some point, Judy seems to have left Black Neil and the roof of her house appears to have fallen in. Neil moved into the cellar, where he lived for long periods. It's thought that he was looked after in this latter time by Sammy Stanley, grandson of the enigmatic Mrs. Stanley, who lived at 25 Wharf Road in a house owned by the late Pater Lurvey. Although a boy, Sammy had been brought up as a girl and dressed as such, preferring to call himself "Sally" from time to time. He/she worked as a "washerwoman" around the area and was good to Black Neil, not particularly frightened by tales of the former slave's vampirism. However, there seems to have been a falling out between them, and Black Neil was once again left to his own devices. During a severe winter in 1830, he was found huddled in the corner of the cellar, almost covered in snow and with his feet badly frostbitten. He was taken to the Gloucester poorhouse, but died a week later. However, his ghost, with its long teeth, was believed to hang about the ruins of his former dwelling in Dogtown for several years afterward. There were stories that it might attack those who came about the place, very much like a vampire.

But the person who terrified people the most and who was most strongly associated with witchcraft and vampirism (and who also had odd teeth) was Tamzin or Thomasine Younger. Known as Tammy Younger, or "the Queen of the Dogtown Witches," she lived with her aunt, Luce George, at Fox Hill on the very edge of Dogtown. Luce George, reputedly a nasty old harridan with a foul tongue, had enjoyed a formidable reputation both as a healer and as a witch. The term *witch* (as was the term *vampire*) was a rather flexible one. In a number of fairly localized communities around Cape Ann and beyond, healing was primarily the preserve of a number of women who acted pretty much as the first port of call in instances of illness or injury. In the Puritan mind, however, there was not much to choose between such activity and witchcraft, so many of these healers were believed to be witches. And there is no doubt that at least some such women used their "arcane knowledge" or alleged powers to cast curses or prepare potions that were not altogether savory in nature. Whether or not they worked is another matter, but the perception was certainly there. Luce George belonged to

the latter class of women and reveled in the idea that she was a witch. She told fortunes and prepared "healing medicines," but she was also said to make love charms and other philtres, which had no good purpose. She also wandered the Gloucester harbor, threatening the fishermen there that she would cause storms, which would sink their boats if they didn't give her a share of their catch—which most usually did. She also claimed that with Tammy, she could bewitch her neighbor's oxen on the hillside unless some sort of protection was paid. Among the colorful eccentrics who inhabited Dogtown, she represented the darker side of things.

And Tammy was just like her and certainly enjoyed a similar, if not greater, reputation than her sinister aunt. A short, rather stout woman, she had a mean way about her and was widely disliked by many of the inhabitants of Dogtown. She churned butter, which she sold, as well as baskets of berries, which she gathered in the surrounding countryside. Both women were incredibly foul-mouthed and were well known for their colorful and intricate curses. Their house stood at the end of the bridge, which spanned the Alewife Brook and actually marked the entrance to Dogtown. Consequently, anyone who entered the village—carters, tradesmen, or ordinary travelers—had to pass by their front door. As soon as she heard a sound on the bridge, Tammy would open a small hatch in the doorway, secured by a piece of string, in order to see who it was. If it was someone she didn't really like (or even if it wasn't) she would hurl a string of obscene imprecations at them as they passed by. Some of these curses also contained threats, for example, that ill-luck would befall them or that Tammy would visit them in some form during the dark hours of the night. It was this latter threat that alarmed many and gave rise to the vampire myth around her, for Tammy had two long tusk-like teeth. In fact, many people who traveled into Dogtown and who fell under her curses were terrified that Tammy would indeed visit them at night and attack them with these fangs, drawing blood and consuming flesh as they slept. Realizing this, Tammy (and Luce George) used such threats as a form of extortion, charging a kind of "toll" on all those who passed into Dogtown and beyond to Rockport. Many carters and other travelers who passed across the bridge paid this awful toll and were supposedly spared Tammy's nightly visitations. Even so, the fact that she had made such threats and the fact that she had long and malformed teeth led to the rumors that she was, in fact, a vampiric being.

Tammy's teeth must have been uncomfortable when she ate, for at some point she approached Captain John Morgan Stanwood, the village cobbler, who was also an amateur dentist. He took a pair of pliers and attempted to extract them, but without much success. Despite a lot of pulling and straining, he only managed to pull them a little further out, and in the process, he caused Tammy a great deal of pain, much to the delight of those whom she had terrified. Now, with her hideous teeth even more prominent, the vampire stories concerning Tammy spread even further, and passers-by became even more terrified of the strange-looking little woman. Her threats became even more vicious and her reputation both as a witch and a vampire grew, extending beyond the borders of Dogtown and into the Gloucester area and beyond. Stories of her traveling across Cape Ann in various guises—a bat, a crow, a black dog—were legion. And when Luce George died, she became a figure of terror all through the community. Few dared cross her and there were tales of those who had met an untimely end through Tammy's nocturnal "visitations."

At the time of Tammy's death in 1829, her name had become so notorious throughout the Cape that it was difficult to actually find anyone who would bury her. Eventually, a cabinet maker named Hodgkins made her a coffin, but because he was convinced that her spirit still hovered around it and would attack anyone who interfered with it, both he and his family refused to have it in their shop and it was left out in a yard. There were many who said that Tammy had not died at all, but continued to live on as an immortal vampire. Some even claimed to have seen her figure walking around Fox Hill, long after she was dead. The vampire hadn't really gone away, as far as some people were concerned!

In many ways, it had become something of an embarrassment to the respectable citizenry of Gloucester and many of them were anxious to forget its history of poverty and degradation, witchcraft, and vampirism. Any reference to it is notably absent from many official records. John Babson's celebrated *History of Gloucester* (written in 1860), for instance, barely mentions Dogtown. A map, however, drawn by Major John Mason in 1831, identifies an area on the highlands, which it names "Dogtowne." It is also mentioned in a book entitled *Around Cape Ann*, which was a kind of walking gazetteer for the Cape and published in 1885, although here it is described as a residential area for some of Gloucester's more prominent and prosperous citizens and is dated from 1740. No mention is made of witches and vampires.

Although the famous author and historian Henry David Thoreau visited the now-abandoned village in 1858 and wrote about his experience there, most of our information concerning Dogtown comes from the work of Charles Mann, who in 1896, published a booklet entitled *The Heart of Cape Ann: The History of Dogtown*, which proved an invaluable source of material about the place. Mann interviewed a number of people who had been born in Dogtown or who remembered the location and recorded their memories before they passed into history. In 1901, new maps of the village were drawn up by the Cape Ann Historical Society, which conducted a walking expedition of the area, led by an old man named Eben Day. However, the result was a confused mish-mash of drawings with several important streets, locations, and houses omitted. The village also lives on in the paintings of the artist Marsden Hartley, who visited the region in the 1920s, and was inspired by many of the stories that he'd heard there. In 1931, he devoted an entire summer to producing a series of stunning oils coupled with poetry based around the site. Many of his paintings on the subject now hang in art galleries and museums.

In 1984, the old Dogtown area became the scene of the brutal murder of a local schoolteacher named Anne Natti. She had been walking her small dog in the area of the vanished village when she was attacked from behind with a massive rock. Not quite dead, she was then stripped in a nearby copse. She was left facedown in the mud and allowed to suffocate slowly. Her murderer was a local boy, Peter Hodgkins, who was a local dockworker and drop-out, and was regarded as something of an oddity by folks around Gloucester. He had several convictions for exposing himself to women and small children, and had been bullied as a child because of his long and rather strange teeth. Hodgkins confessed and then tried to commit suicide three times (once in the bathroom of the court) before his conviction. Although some writers have tried, it is difficult to overemphasize the emotional impact caused by this particularly horrific crime on Gloucester. Traditions and memories relating to Dogtown seem to have run deep within the community. Maybe the idea of Tammy Younger and her hideous teeth had not fully erased themselves from the communal mind.

Where do the roots of the connection between vampirism and Dogtown lie? Perhaps the idea was first formed when Nathaniel Coit initially split the Gloucester community in two over the location of the Meeting House. This created a "separateness" in the area that was to become known as Dogtown and the rest of the Gloucester folk, and allowed myth and exaggerated story to develop in the gap between the two. The ordinary, God-fearing people of the Gloucester port were ready and willing to believe all manner of things relating to "the other sort" in the run-down, embarrassing Dogtown community. And of course, there was a strong connection between vampirism and witchcraft. The old women—many of them widows of the men who had sailed on the vanished *Gloucester*—made a living by telling fortunes and preparing potions of various kinds, which in the eyes of godly people was tantamount to sorcery. Unlike the wholesome Gloucester harbor area, Dogtown was a place where both witches and vampiric beings dwelt. Some of them even had hideously malformed teeth and everyone knew that witchcraft and vampirism were closely connected. So it was believed that certain individuals from Dogtown could go about in spirit form, attacking those respectable people as they slept. And, indeed, the colorful and often downright bizarre characters that inhabited the village only leant weight to this perception. Like witches, vampires were never far away in the area.

Today, what was once Dogtown is something of a wilderness. Trees and large boulders—some inscribed with the names of Dogtown residents and information—litter the area. Although the area is beautiful, a palpable sense of desolation and menace hangs over it like a funereal pall. So, on a day when the cloud drifts low over Cape Ann and the sunlight dims just a little, maybe old ghosts of the eerie former inhabitants of the vanished settlement—the alleged witches and vampires who once gathered there—aren't really all that far away.

OHIO

Vampires are not always the suave, handsome European noblemen or beautiful ladies that we sometimes see in films or on television. Nor are they troubled, but essentially good-looking teenagers—this is the stuff of young adult fiction, television, and cinema, and has very little to do with the folkloric vampire. Here, many of the vampire creatures that infest myth and legend are often hideous and misshapen monsters. The *tikoloshi* of South African history, for example, is a grotesque dwarf with twisted limbs that can sometimes grow to the height of a giant in order to ensnare its victims. In its original state, it will climb onto a victim's bed and attack him or her by drawing blood from the crook of his or her arm. It is so terrifying that the very sight of it can drive a person insane. The Brazilian *jaracaca* or *lobishomen* is a small, monkey-like vampire that actually does not drink all that much blood, but can drain a sleeper of his or her energies, simply by squatting on their chest. It has a wrinkled, malignant face that can disturb or unsettle anyone who wakes long enough to see it. The *sampiro* of Albania is another truly frightening apparition. A tall and menacing figure swathed in winding sheets, its eyes are big and glowing like car headlights and it has terrible rending claws. It moves along on what seem to be high

heels, making an eerie sound along the stony roads through the countryside. Many *sampiro* appear to be associated with individuals of Turkish origin, probably reflecting the antipathy between Albanians and Turks. Other vampire creatures, for example, in parts of Romania and Bulgaria, are little more than decaying animated corpses that do not venture too far from their graves. These are ghastly, terrifying things, often in an apparent state of decomposition, which seem all the more frightening along the darkened country roads.

We have been lulled into a false sense of security by Hollywood and television, as we expect our vampires to be handsome, striking, or beautiful in appearance. Vampires in the cultures and legends of many countries are grotesque and monstrous to look at, and this often adds to their sense of menace. Historically, evil was always associated with the bizarre and unusual, particularly within the human form. Dark people, such as the monstrous mass murderer Gilles de Rais, or the American psycho Ed Gein, have sometimes been portrayed as physically twisted or ugly to look at—a fact that only emphasizes their malignancy. And the same seems to apply to the Undead in European belief. What may be the earliest recorded vampire in the Western tradition—Abhartach, the 5th-century "red drinker" of Celtic lore—is often described as small and deformed (possibly a hunchback). Thus, we tend to characterize out worst nightmares with twisted shapes and grotesque features, which seem to set them firmly in our minds.

From the earliest times, "abnormal" people have been regarded with suspicion. This, coupled with strange behavior, makes them appear threatening. In the ancient and medieval worlds, physical deformities were considered to be either a prognostication of evil times or a mark of the Devil. Newborn babies who carried some kind of disfigurement were often slain in an attempt to ward off evil, which might befall a community.

An 8 year-old boy, for example, was burnt around 1580 near the town of Shrewsbury, England, because he was born deformed. Both his feet were cloven, as was his right hand. This was taken as evidence of a grievous sin between his father and a sheep. In order to ward off possible Divine retribution, the community destroyed the child. A similar event occurred in 1674 in the village of Birdham, England. Here, a child was nailed to a church door and was bludgeoned to death; its body was then burned. The reason given was the same as before: an unnatural liaison between humans and animals. The child had to be killed in order to avoid God's vengeance on the entire community. The body had been nailed to the church door to remind churchgoers of the awful results of bestiality. In the Brocken area of Germany in 1684, according to Johannes Mayer in his *Tuefelbushen* (published in 1690), a woman was publicly stoned to death for giving birth to a deformed child. The birth was allegedly the result of having sexual congress with a horse, although no evidence was offered for this allegation. In 1692, in the same region, a woman gave birth to a casket of iron nails, and for this, she was killed.

Deformed births and grotesque people were often seen as signals portending the End of Days. In a rural area of Bavaria in 1702, a number of strange and misshapen infants born in one year panicked the population, inspiring religious revivals in a number of villages (accompanied by several deaths of the deformed children). In Alsace, France, similar births caused widespread alarm around 1708. All of these were considered to be signs of great evil and of approaching menace. Thus, some deformed people living within communities were strongly associated with the forces of darkness.

In fact, such an idea had become so ingrained into the psyche of most societies that traces of it could sometimes still be found in communities during the 20th century. However, as medical science progressed, such abnormalities came to be explained—and yet some of the old uncertainties remained. It was all very well to say that such people were the result of perhaps a congenital problem or that the disfigurement came from a recognized medical condition, but their appearance still sent collective shudders down society's spine.

One of the most notable of all the conditions, and one that sometimes caused the most fear among ordinary people was that of hydrocephalus. Known as "water on the brain," the physical characteristics of the deformity were rather striking. The condition is created by an abnormal accumulation of cerebrospinal fluid in the ventricles or cavities of the brain, causing the head to swell to an unusual size. Besides this progressive cranial enlargement, symptoms include convulsions, tunnel vision, and often mental retardation. It can also cause death. It has been known since around 2,500 BC where it appears in ancient Egyptian medical records. The Greek physician Hippocrates also mentioned it in his works around the 4th century BC, although its effects were more accurately described by the Roman Galen around the 2nd century BC. Throughout the Middle Ages, hydrocephalics were regarded both with fear and suspicion, and their condition was said to be an outward sign of inward evil. There was no cure. Even today, the medical response to the condition is both fairly limited and complicated. It involves a series of what are called "cerebral shunts," using a ventricular catheter in which some of the fluid is drained off into other areas of the body. This can be a difficult process, and is not always successful. Large-headed individuals have existed (and still exist) in many parts of the world.

As late as the 1950s, the idea that deviant sexual practices were some-how connected to the existence of large-headed individuals (Melon Heads or Weeble Heads) was still quite common. In her *Folklore of Herefordshire* (1955), folklorist Mary Letherbarrow makes reference to an entire family of large-headed people living in the village of Risbury in Herefordshire. They had large and well-rounded heads, which was the result of system-atic inbreeding. They took very little to do with their neighbors and many locals shunned them as being "odd and dangerous." They were still living in Risbury at the time Letherbarrow was writing in the mid-1950s. Writing slightly later, the anthropologist Hannah Williams also makes reference to the Risbury "Melon Heads" (which she calls "Weeble Heads") and sug-gests that their family tree was rather complicated. The name of the family concerned is not disclosed, but she suggests that inbreeding and abnormal sexual practices might have been a contributing factor to its general condi-tion. At the time when Williams was writing, the family was still living in Risbury. So what became of the Melon Head family? They seem to have vanished, although in 2009, there was a report of one of them living some-where close to the Sandpits Estate, west of Leominster in Herefordshire, but sightings of this individual were rare.

Aside from the Risbury instances, there is anecdotal evidence from other parts of England and indeed from other areas of the world. In 1969, folklorist Jane Davis claimed that there were "Wobble Heads"—individual members of a hill family—living in a remote area of Snowdonia in Wales. The family dwelt on a remote farm and were generally avoided because there were a number of unhealthy and frightening stories about them—one of these being that they would drink the blood of sheep, which had been left out to graze on the mountain slopes. It was even thought that they might attack humans who ventured too near to where they lived. A similar story from the 1920s comes from the Forest of Dean, where a family of danger-ous Wobble Heads dwelt. Little is known about them, except that they had both cannibalistic and vampiric tendencies, and were said to attack travel-ers through the Forest at various times. As before, stories concerning them may have been inspired by their strange appearance.

England and Wales were not the only places for these disfigured people. A family of Melon Heads lived near the village of Konzenburg in Bavaria in the mid-1800s. Several local murders were laid at their door, but noth-ing could be proved. Like the Risbury Melon Heads, they were extremely aggressive if approached. In the context of local folklore, some even drank blood. Again, in the Black Forest area of Baden-Württemberg in Germany, there were other dangerous Melon Heads who still attacked travelers.

The idea that Melon Heads were both cannibalistic and vampiric was a common one in many areas and was firmly rooted in their curious ap-pearance. They were also linked in the popular mind with both sin and evil. Such a concept was so deeply imbedded in the human psyche that it trav-eled with many European peoples wherever they went—most notably to the New World. And so the legend of the Melon Heads entered the world of American folklore and urban myth. Many were said to exist in remote rural areas where some of the early European settlers had put down roots. Such people were often hardy and rather reclusive—preferring to stick to their own societies—and gave rise to whispers and gossip in the more settled ar-eas. Stories began to circulate in areas of Kentucky and Tennessee of Melon Heads living in almost inaccessible areas such as the Rutherford Mountain region on the border of the two states during the 1940s and 50s. In Arkansas, there were also tales of such people dwelling in isolated areas of the Boston Mountains in the north of the state. And in Louisiana, rather frightening stories of cannibalistic Melon Heads living deep within the bayou country were common in the 1920s and 1930s. The remoteness and inaccessibility of such areas often added to the actual horror of the accounts.

Around the time of World War II, another element began to creep into such tales. Previously, the existence of the Melon Heads was attributed to inbreeding or to sexual perversion (as in the Risbury and German cases), but now some of this was also attributed to surreptitious scientific or medical experimentation. This widened the scope of the legend from "hillbilly inbreeding" into a broader context. These might be personal or even government research, using humans as guinea pigs. Such a notion was just as horrible as imagining that the Melon Heads were the results of sin or of sexual deviance. It further widened the geographical scope of the myth—no longer were such tales confined to the remote hill country, but now they might be in areas of more urban population. Although clandestine, such experimentation might be conducted on the very outskirts of towns or cities. And they were not the sole province of unlettered mountaineers, but rather of educated, though suspect, medical minds. Indeed, during World War II, it was believed that the military conducted experiments in the creation of a "super soldier" who could fight in any theater of war and who had enhanced intelligence with which to fight the enemy. Even after the war, the idea of the "mad scientist" still persisted—a crazed figure totally obsessed by a scientific ideal, the execution of which superseded all moral and ethical constraints.

Throughout time, the myth of the crazed scientist expanded and developed. He was working for the military or the government on some ultra-secret project about which the general public could not be told. Or he was some sort of insane individual who was crazily planning some sort of national domination. He preyed on the most vulnerable of society—the old and, more particularly, children—as the subjects of his horrific experiments. And because they had been in some way altered, this myth merged with stories of feral children roaming the remote woods and created a tableau of horror and fear. Discarded results of fiendish experimentation were now roaming freely in certain areas and, like Frankenstein's monster, might put "normal people" at risk. Such creatures might even eat human flesh or drink human blood. The idea of a failed experiment seemed, perhaps, even more terrifying than the offspring of carnal sin. Indeed, it was assumed that some of these awful creations did drink blood, making them vampires in the literal sense. And they prowled around urban areas, often just beyond the glow of the streetlights. The scientific idea of urban menace actually gave these alleged horrors a greater imminence. They were out there in the shadows just beyond the light's comforting glow—or so the myth said.

Among these unquestioned scientific creatures were the Melon Heads. These were no longer the product of folkloric evil, but were the results of questionable experimental practices. Perhaps they were the offspring of some genetic manipulation (either by a crazed individual or scientific facility—maybe even a government agency) to enhance human intelligence or strength. What had been created were monsters. The idea that the Melon Heads were the products of a failed government experiment gained much ground in a number of states and they had been seen all across America from Michigan to Massachusetts to Texas. Such sightings were often incorporated into the local folklore of the area.

The state in which the Melon Heads feature strongly in urban myth and legend, however, is Ohio, particularly in Cleveland. The Kirtland suburb of the city has achieved a notoriety all of its own concerning the Melon Heads centering on a specific section known as the Gore Orphanage Road. The area borders on some dense woodland in which groups of strangely headed humanoids—the results of terrible genetic experiments—are still said to dwell. The name *Gore* allegedly derives from a Dr. Gore who ran an orphanage and conducted terrible (and illegal) experiments on the children who were inmates there. In a bid to raise their intelligence, he created a number of Melon Heads, who eventually turned on him and killed him before escaping into the surrounding woodlands. Their presence there has supposedly been recorded since around World War II, but even before that, the place already had a sinister reputation. This stemmed from the macabre history of a place known locally as Swift's Hollow.

The Hollow takes its name from Joseph Swift, a property developer and landowner who moved there from Massachusetts around the mid-1820s with his wife Eliza. A reasonably wealthy man, Swift built a grand house on the banks of the Vermillion River, which soon became known as "Swift's Mansion." According to contemporary accounts, it was a grand and ostentatious dwelling, the likes of which had never been seen anywhere around and probably in all Ohio. Was it any wonder that such an elaborate building took on the name of its builder? Although the house was officially known as "Rosedale," it was always called "Swift's Mansion" and the area as Swift's Hollow.

Soon after they settled in the Hollow, bad luck hit Joseph Swift and his family. In 1831, Swift's 5-year-old daughter Tymphenia died from a mysterious illness; in 1841, his 24-year-old son Herman also died from a peculiar illness. Around the time of his son's death, Swift made a series of particularly bad investments, including one on a proposed railroad that had been scheduled for development. The whole scheme suddenly and unexpectedly fell through, leaving him almost bankrupt. The Civil War completed his financial decline, and he was forced to sell his grand house in 1865 and move away.

The man to whom he sold the house, Nicholas Wilber, had a curious reputation. This was an era when Spiritualism was taking hold in some parts of America and Wilber was both interested in and associated with the movement. He began to organize spiritual experiments and séances in the house. There were various attempts to communicate with and to raise both ghosts and demons, all of which haunted the mansion and the surrounding Hollow long after Wilber had gone.

Although he was obsessed with supernatural entities and powers, Wilber's sojourn in Swift's Hollow did neither him nor his family any good. Like Joseph Swift before him, his family was hit by a series of unfortunate and tragic illnesses. He and his wife lost four children to diphtheria—Jesse (age 11), May (age 9), and the twins Roy and Ruby (age 2). All of them died within six days of each other as the terrible illness swept through the mansion between January 13th and January 19th, 1893. Wilber then began to suffer from a strange wheezy and wasting disease, which might have been related to diphtheria. His wife died there in 1899 and Wilber followed her in February 1901.

The grand house now lay abandoned and the notion of such a mansion lying derelict out in the woods, especially one that had been the focus of Spiritualist activity, prompted many local stories of ghosts and the walking dead throughout the surrounding community. Special attention was drawn to the abandoned and overgrown children's graves in the woody undergrowth, and the crumbling mansion was generally regarded as being haunted by a number of ghosts, some of whom Wilber had summoned during his experiments.

The story of the Melon Heads is a much later addition, but it is also strongly connected with Swift's Hollow. At the end of 1903, the mansion was bought by the Reverend Johann Sprunger, a Lutheran minister who had the idea of starting a self-sustaining Christian community there. His intention was to provide work in the local area, but also to provide a refuge for neglected or abused children from the surrounding district. He hoped to teach boys and girls the benefits of a virtuous life, as well as husbandry and farming techniques, thus contributing toward the local economy.

The institution was not really an orphanage in the conventional sense; although Sprunger constructed dormitories in the house, these were mainly used by the Christian workers while the neglected boys were billeted in specially constructed accommodations at the nearby Hughes farm and the girls at the neighboring Heywood property. Sprunger viewed this entire complex as a community, which he named "The Light and Hope Orphanage."

At this time, Gore Orphanage Road was simply called Gore Road. According to many people, the roadway took its name from a sinister custodian of the orphanage who had mistreated those in his charge. However, the name probably comes from the shape of the road itself, which resembled the outline of the hem of a skirt. A gored skirt is made from a triangular piece of material that is narrow at the waist, but wider and more comfortable at the bottom. This type of skirt was quite popular in Ohio, and the edge of it may have given the road its name. The word *orphanage* may have been added later to facilitate the institution that the Reverend Sprunger had established there.

As time went on, rather disquieting stories began to circulate in the locality about the Reverend Johann Sprunger. For example, he and his wife Katherina had moved to Ohio from New Berne, Indiana, where they had run a more conventional orphanage. This establishment had been destroyed by a mysterious fire in which three small children had died. Although no official blame had been attached to him, rumor said that the Reverend Sprunger had been somehow responsible for the blaze. But there were even more unwholesome stories. There were hints that Katherina was actually Johann Sprunger's sister with whom he was having an incestuous relationship. Of course, there may have been nothing to the rumors, but they certainly created an unsavory and suspicious atmosphere about the old place. The whiff of incest now hung about the place like a tangible pall and sparked other stories about the couple there.

Soon, vague fragments of gossip began to turn into darker tales of neglect, child labor, and abuse. In order to keep the food bills down, the Reverend Sprunger bought sick and dying animals from neighboring farms at knockdown prices and made the children eat the diseased flesh. Porridge was boiled up for breakfast in the same pot that was used to wash soiled underwear. There were tales of beatings and other maltreatments. The reality of these stories became exposed when several children ran away from the community and turned up in Vermillion on the other side of the river, bringing with them alarming tales of a regime bordering on outright torture. In 1909, Ohio conducted a formal investigation into the running of the home. Surprisingly, the Reverend Sprunger and his wife readily admitted all the charges that were laid against them, but because the state had no real laws or framework for dealing with orphanages at the time—and because the inmates were a mix of orphans and children whose parents were still alive—no real action was taken to improve the condition of the children. The Sprungers were, however, cautioned and the matter was laid to rest.

Previous to that, however, just as the investigation was getting underway in 1908, a tragic and horrific incident occurred 40 miles east in the settlement of Collinwood. More than 176 children at an elementary school were either burned or trampled to death as a fire gutted the building. The blaze had been deliberately started by the school janitor—a German-American named Herter (even though he lost four of his own children in the blaze and was injured in trying to save several others), and he was briefly arrested and detained. The main deaths were of children on the second floor of the building who tried to descend a flight of stairs in order to escape as soon as the fire alarm sounded. However, the fire was already taking hold at the foot of the staircase and some of the children turned to make their way back up to the classrooms that they'd left. Those who were coming down shoved them into the flames below. When they reached the rear exits, the fleeing children found them locked (this was taken as proof that the janitor must have been somehow involved in the blaze) and when rescuers tried to open the doors from the outside, they found that they opened inward and that the crush of bodies on the other side prevented anyone from getting through to safety. The fire spread quickly through the trapped children, setting their dresses and hair alight.

It was a horrific incident, and one that burned itself into the minds of both survivors and rescuers alike. The disaster actually meant the end of Collinwood as a community, as many of the families, fearful at the lack of fire control there, moved away to places like Vermillion, bringing their memories of the horror with them. This horror somehow transferred itself in the popular imagination to the Light and Hope Orphanage and to Gore Road.

The Reverend Sprunger died in 1911, two years after the state investigation, and the orphanage finally closed in 1916 in a welter of financial problems and unpaid bills. Pelham Hooker Blossom of Cleveland bought the property and began to lease the land out to local farmers while allowing the great house to fall to rot. Finally, there were a number of fires within the old Swift Mansion—perhaps deliberately started by locals—and the buildings were partly destroyed and then pulled down.

Stories began to circulate that, before the house had been destroyed, it had been owned by an "old man Gore," who had also run it as an orphanage. He had given his name to the road and reputedly mistreated the children who were in his care. There was another, more sinister story as well. Apparently, Gore had been a medical doctor and had been employed either by the government or by some private foundation to conduct experiments on the children, all of whom had nobody to fight for their rights. In the end, the children had turned on him and it had been *they* who started the fire that had burned down Swift's Mansion. Before starting the blaze, they had killed Gore and had drank his blood. They then escaped into the surrounding woodlands in order to continue with their vampiric activities. The story might originate from a confused memory of the Collinwood fire a number of miles away, and might have nothing to do with Swift's Hollow.

However, there is an intriguing story concerning a mysterious Dr. Crow, who reputedly took over the building after it closed. This shadowy figure spells his name Crow, Crowe, Krohe, Kroh, and even Khune, and he was allegedly a scientist employed in the area by the government on some secret project. This apparently involved the collection of blood; it was said that Dr. Crow was some sort of "blood specialist" who was also involved in genetics. He is believed to have adopted some very unorthodox methods for his research, some of which involved the kidnapping of children from the surrounding countryside. No date is give for these activities, but it was around the late 1800s/early 1900s, although some place them around the time of World War I, claiming that Crow's activities were part of the war effort. The purpose of the experiments, however, is unknown, but they were said to involve the collection of blood and the injections of certain fluids into children. This turned them into blood-drinking monsters, increased their strength, and caused their heads to swell in a grotesque way. Whatever they were injected with also increased their ferocity, and they became almost savage and animal-like in their ways. Eventually, according to the legend, they turned on Crow and killed him, setting fire to the old Swift Mansion in the process. As in the other stories, they fled out into the woods around Kirtland where they still wait. From time to time, they will attack people with the express purpose of drinking their blood or eating their flesh, for these children are cannibalistic. They will also spirit away other small children for some unknown purpose deep in the woodlands. Perhaps they take them for food! And late at night, some people living in the edge of the woods claim to have seen huge swollen heads with luminous eyes peering in at their windows after dark. The Melon Heads, they say, are on the prowl!

Researcher Ryan Orvis, citing the *West Geauga Sun* as his source (Geauga County is near to Kirtland) found evidence of a Dr. Kroh who was allegedly in the area around World War II. Kroh was an unlicensed doctor, but a follower of the Austrian priest and geneticist, Johann Gregor Mendel, who conducted experiments in cross-plant hybridization. Kroh, it was claimed, attempted to alter the genetics of children by injecting them with various substances. One of his experiments allegedly increased the size of their heads in an attempt to increase their intelligence. It also gave them a taste for human blood. However, the experiments failed, and in a fit of pique, Dr. Kroh bundled all the deformed results of his experiments into the back of a car and released them around the area of the Chagrin River in Kirtland. There, they fled into the woods. In some of the newspaper's accounts, the doctor treated the children with radiation, so the Melon Heads were also radioactive. Subsequent newspaper articles have pointed to the strangely large number of child graves in the nearby King's Memorial Road, and have suggested that these might be from Kroh's failed experiments.

Since the end of World War II, there have allegedly been a number of sightings of the Melon Heads—both as children and as fully-grown adults—along the Gore Orphanage Road and Wisner Roads in the Kirtland suburbs. Many of these sightings come from passing tourists or from local schoolchildren who have been exploring the woods. But there is a strange conformity about the descriptions even though they come from people who don't know each other: a humanoid with an abnormally large head, dressed in a kind of "institutional" clothing, which is torn and often bloodstained (white shirt and brown, ragged, button-up trousers). There is a distinctly feral quality about such figures, which disappear into the woods again almost as soon as they are seen. Maybe this has more to do with human imagination rather than the stories of the orphanage at Swift's Hollow. Worse, it's also said that animals—dogs, cats, and others—have been found in the same place with their blood drained. This has led to even further tales of vampire activity in the vicinity of Gore Orphanage Road, all of which is attributed to the Melon Heads in the forest. There are also tales of people who have disappeared into the woodlands for one reason or another and, like some of the children, have never been seen since.

And yet, for all of Ryan Orvis's research, there is nothing truly concrete to connect the Kirtland area with abnormal genetic experiments. Of course, it has been argued that such genetic manipulation by Dr. Kroh was conducted in secret, but even so, there would have been *some* trace of such activity. And all the newspaper accounts that have been offered up appear to be very vague when it comes to specific detail. But that's not to say that such things didn't happen or that there might be something out there in the Kirtland woods.

The strange stories of the cursed family of Joseph Swift, the Spiritualism of Nicholas Wilber, and the utter weirdness of the Light and Hope Orphanage of the Reverend Sprunger and his curious sister have all combined to create an aura of creepiness around the area. The region can certainly be a spooky one, and several other eerie legends have grown up around it; for example, there's a Cry Baby Bridge on Wisner Road, just north of Kirtland's Chardon Road. The ghostly child who weeps there is said to have been an inmate of the old Gore Orphanage. It might be easy to dismiss the Melon Heads as a fantasy or urban myth that has been dreamed up by gullible teenagers and tourists, but what if there is something more to it? Many of the accounts show a curious uniformity and nearly all the descriptions of the beings coincide in an eerie and alarming way. And there are similar accounts from some other nearby states.

In Michigan, the story of the Melon Heads is connected with the old Felt Mansion near Laketown. Local legends say that they are the descendants of hydrocephalic inmates of the nearby Junction Hospital for the Insane, and that they have been living in the woodlands around Laketown for many years. As the result of abuse (and perhaps experimentation) by a number of doctors at the hospital, these inmates broke out and fled into the nearby woods. There they found the decaying Felt Mansion, which they used as a base, prowling out into the surrounding countryside to attack humans and perhaps even drink their blood. The flaw in the story is that such an asylum never existed in the area. There certainly was a Junction Hospital, but the Allegan County records simply list it as a regular hospital with no mental facility attached to it. Nevertheless, a local newspaper, *The Holland Sentinel*, carried stories of beings seen in the woods and some people's recollections of the Weeble Heads. According to some of the printed stories, several of the doctors who conducted the experiments were killed by the Melon Heads, and their bloodless, chewed remains lie buried in unmarked graves not far from where the old Felt Mansion once stood. A spectral sight of one of the doctors being killed is frequently seen through the old mansion's doorway. And it is said that anyone who sees this phantom vision will be pursued by the Melon Heads, who will attempt to drink their blood.

In Connecticut, the legend appears to take on an even darker tone, with origins that supposedly date back to Colonial times. In Fairfield County, it's said that a certain family settled in the Trumbull area after having been driven out of Massachusetts for witchcraft and cannibalism. This family was supposedly comprised of vampires. Faced with local hostility, they retreated into the neighboring woods where their descendants continue to live, some of them as Melon Heads, until today. The legend has been amended to include the now-obligatory insane asylum and the customary riot by some of its malformed inmates. There seems to have been a hospital at Grant Wood in Fairfield, which did indeed experience a serious fire in the 1960s. A number of the patients were evacuated, and according to local folklore, some disappeared and were never found (there is absolutely no evidence for this assertion)—these are said to be the ancestors of the present-day Melon Heads, which are to be found in the area. In Trumbull, they supposedly haunt the area around Velvet Street (which is also known locally as "Dracula Dive" on account of their alleged blood-drinking), and in Shelton it is Saw Mill City Road. Velvet Street is still an unpaved dirt road running through deep woodlands, and several people have reputedly disappeared along its length. Such disappearances have, of course, been attributed to the Melon Heads, and this seems to have been borne out by the finding of a number of dead domestic animals in the area, which allegedly appear to have been drained of their blood.

Back at Swift's Hollow in Ohio, nothing remains of Rosedale except for a few old graffiti-covered sandstone blocks and a similarly decorated entrance column. Those who visit the Hollow claim, like the workmen in Connecticut, that they have the sensation of someone watching them from somewhere close by. And they too hear unexplained calls and noises in the surrounding woodlands.

It is not surprising then that such a remote and unfrequented area gave rise to legends of the Melon Heads. Many of the families in this region were interrelated, and of course this gave rise to stories about incest and of queer-resulting births. Much of this must be regarded as prejudice and storytelling by people who regarded themselves as "more civilized" and who wished to portray the barbaric hillbilly as something short of an animal, committing incest and sexual deviation at will. In a sense, the Rutherford hillbilly followed on from the medieval sinner in former European times in terms of deviance and promiscuity. It was to be expected that some of these allegedly inbred children would exhibit signs of deformity, such as being Melon Heads. And there were tales of such individuals living in the very remote regions of Rutherford. For example, in the far reaches of Hat Hollow, Kentucky, there were tales of such things as "man-bats," creatures with huge heads and vampire features (sometimes even covered in a kind of fur), which prowled the rocky courses of tiny creeks and the thick woods, killing anyone or anything that they came across and drinking their blood. It is said that the wooded gullies and ravines around Hat Hollow echoed with their eerie cries as they called to one another. Similarly, loggers working on a sawmill up in Buffalo Lick Hollow, Tennessee, claim to have glimpsed figures in a remote wallow with large and malformed heads crossing a small creek. These beings are generally taken to be offspring of local families who have been thrown out into the wilds and left to fend for themselves.

Are the stories of Melon Heads in both Ohio and elsewhere true, or are they mainly urban (or even rural) myths? If they are true, are such beings the results of failed clandestine genetic experiments carried out by the government, or by covert organizations and individuals? As night closes in on the forests of America, strange shadows move in the half-light and strange sounds are heard. Are there really things lurking out in the woodland night—waiting, perhaps, to drink your blood?

MISSOURI

In May 1673, a Jesuit priest named Father Jacques Marquet and a French trader named Louis Jolliet traveled down the Mississippi River in a couple of canoes, mapping and exploring the river banks. On the rough maps that Marquet made, he marked a region known as *Missouri,* taking the name from an Illinois Indian word *ouempssourita* (pronounced *wimhsoorita*) meaning "those who have dug-out canoes." In doing so, he not only named an indigenous tribe and a tributary river, but also an area of land that would one day become a state. Father Marquet claimed the area for France, although the French never really referred to the area as Missouri, preferring to call it Illinois Country. In 1682, Rene-Robert Chevelier, the Sieur de la Salle, made a successful journey to the mouth of the Mississippi and passed through the area once again, reinforcing the French claim. The French authorities took little interest in "Missouri," however, and simply established a line of trading posts there to facilitate commerce with local native tribes. Perhaps Chevelier had plans for a wider commercial enterprise in the area but, if he had, he died before they could be completed.

There is an old tale that says when Father Marquet arrived in Missouri, and was standing on the banks of the Mississippi, local tribes showed him some low hills and told him that strange lights were seen there—lights that would draw the energies from anyone who ventured too close to them. The Father told the Native Americans that there were evil spirits that had been sent by the Devil to torment them, and that they were to pray for deliverance from them. Only God could drive such things away. The Devil, they were warned, was everywhere, and was seeking to subvert all of God's creatures. For the priests who followed the French traders, the area known as Missouri was an earthly place in which the Evil One and his agents would make themselves manifest.

Father Gabriel Marest, who established a mission station on the west bank of the Mississippi in 1700, was particularly exercised about the presence of evil in the surrounding countryside. His station comprised French settlers and groups of Kaskaskia peoples who had fled into the Illinois Country to avoid raids on their villages by marauding bands of Iroquois. This angered the Sioux, who held lands around the Des Peres River where the Kaskaskia were settling. In 1703, they forced Marest to move his mission south and strengthen his links with the Kaskaskia. In learning the language of these people, the good Father also learned some of their lore and beliefs. He learned of moving lights that danced and bobbed, and sometimes drew the energies of travelers into themselves, leaving those whom they encountered weak and tired. He believed, as did the Kaskaskia, that these were witches and evil spirits who had been sent by the Enemy of Mankind to do harm to God's people. He recorded his thoughts in a journal, stressing the sense of growing evil, which the Kaskaskia conveyed to him. Some of the natives thought that they might be the spirits of the dead, seeking a way back into the world or trying to do the living harm, and some of the French priests in Marest's mission tended to agree with them. Unexplained lights, and the strange noises and sensations that accompanied them, were undeniably the work of devils. Through the years, other tribes began to drift into the area, brought there by hunting or driven there by enemies—the Missouri and the Osage were prominent groups who settled the region. The Missouri were reasonably well settled along the Mississippi, and became allies of the French. They too had their folktales about strange and moving lights, which sapped the energies of those who saw them or who got too close to them.

To the south, Louisiana was developing rapidly as a French colony, and gradually entrepreneurs and speculators began to see the wisdom of developing a trading trail from the Great Lakes to the new French lands. This would mean the growth of the settlements in the Illinois Country and, in 1717, the French king Louis XV accepted the offer of a Scottish economist and financier named John Law to set up a company to manage such a development. Law's company was given a monopoly on all trade, ownership of all mines, and use of all military posts in the region, and agreed to encourage the settlement of 6,000 white settlers and 3,000 black slaves in the territory. Included in this agreement was the Illinois Country and the Company of the West quickly went about its business, appointing Pierre Dugue de Boisbriand as governor of the area. He set up his headquarters at Fort de Chartres about 18 miles north of Kaskaskia Settlement and began to develop the region, initially through mining. This eventually led to the establishment of Madison, St. Francoise, and Washington Counties.

Despite all of this developmental and economic activity, the old Indian stories did not go away. Miners and engineers throughout the region still heard tales of moving lights that had vampiric properties, and gradually these began to incorporate themselves into local white legend as well. The French explorer, Philip Francois Renault, took mining land in the region in 1719 and brought over five black slaves to work in his own mines—the first black slaves to work in Missouri. The tales, however, frightened the workers, as did hostility among indigenous tribes and bad weather. In 1742, spurred on by hant stories and devil tales, Renault was forced to sell his lands, having made little profit.

Spanish settlers were now entering the Missouri area, and both France and Spain made an agreement against the English, who were also attempting to expand into the midwest. However, Native Americans wars and a war against the British further north were going badly for the French, and they pursued peace. In order to get their Spanish allies to sign a peace treaty, the

French now transferred parts of Louisiana and part of Illinois Country into Spanish hands under the Treaty of Fontainebleau in 1762. Under the complicated terms of the Treaty, the Eastern bank of the Mississippi and a part of Louisiana was ceded to the English, and this included part of the country known as "Missouri." French settlers living in this area were concerned about living under British rule and, as the implementation of the Treaty of Fontainebleau proved slow (its terms were not fully revealed until 1764), many decamped for what is now the state of Missouri, the British portion forming what is now largely the state of Illinois. Indeed, the new Spanish overlords encouraged them to do so in order to limit the influence of British traders who were finding their way into the area.

Large numbers of English Protestants were now arriving in the Northwest Territories (of which neighboring Illinois was a part) and the Catholic inhabitants of Missouri believed to be threatened. They strengthened their fortifications and encouraged more missions into the area. Tensions increased when, in the late 1770s, the Spanish settlers began aiding the American rebels in their war against the British (the War of Independence). Spanish officials in the two major towns in Missouri, St. Genevieve, and St. Louis, actively sent militia forces to aid the revolutionaries in their struggle. In June 1779, England declared war on Spain, and Spanish settlers in Missouri felt an even greater threat. In May 1780, the British attacked St. Louis and, although the town was saved, the loss of life was severe.

Following the American Revolution, a set of completed treaties was drawn up between the European powers to determine the land acquisition. The Spanish managed to retain much of Louisiana and part of Missouri Territory, but were forced to accept a large number of American Protestants crossing the Mississippi River to settle. In order to deal with the Catholics, Spanish authorities asked an American military officer, Colonel George Morgan, to set up a fort from which he could control the new Missouri territory on their behalf. Morgan set up a colony known as New Madrid, but rapidly fell out with the Spanish governor of Louisiana, Esteban Rodriguez Miro, and the colony was quickly abandoned. Nevertheless, the heavy influx of American Protestant settlers continued, and despite Spanish efforts to the contrary, it grew. In the end, the Spanish realized that the new settlers were not interested in converting the Catholic inhabitants, nor were they particularly loyal to Spain—they tolerated them because of their contribution to the area. But the American influx was having a profound effect on the territory, changing both the language and demographic make-up.

And yet underneath the changing social position, there was an undercurrent of superstition and mystery. In Missouri, religion—particularly the Catholic religion—had been a strong element of the early cultural and social life before the arrival of the Protestant settlers. After all, the area had been first mapped by a Jesuit, and French Jesuits had certainly played an important part in the formation of the territory. However, in 1763, the Jesuits were expelled from the region by the French authorities, mainly because of their wealth and power and their willingness to meddle in political and military affairs. With the Jesuits gone, there was a shortage of Catholic priests all through Missouri Territory, as under Church laws, French priests from other administrative Catholic areas were forbidden to preach in the region, so the Spanish served the religious needs there by a succession of priests from Louisiana and from the southwest. It was not until the mid-to-late 1780s that St. Genevieve and St. Louis received permanent clerics. The Church was also alarmed by the number of Protestants who were crossing the Mississippi and, though the civil authorities tolerated them for economic purposes, the Catholic bishops were fearful that they might try to convert the indigenous inhabitants.

The temporary priests saw value in reinvigorating old beliefs and old fears. Coming from the southwestern areas, they had heard stories there of witches and demons that traveled as balls of light and who sometimes carried out evil in that form.

During the late 16th and early 17th centuries, there had been a spate of high-profile exorcisms and other supernatural activities carried on by the Catholic Church in both France and England. Faced with a rise in Protestantism (particularly that of the Huguenots), the French Catholic Church began to resort to miracles and exorcisms in order to reassert its authority. The Devil was everywhere, seeking to subvert God's people, and the only refuge lay in the offices of the Catholic Church and its priests. And if the Evil One had been active in early modern Europe, he was also powerfully present in the unknown territories of a new continent. Faced with the rising tide of Protestantism flooding into the new area, the Church resurrected old tales of ancient horrors lurking in the Missouri region that could threaten the settlers there.

And they had ready-made demons lurking there. When Father Marquet had first arrived in the area, the natives had told him stories about strange lights that came and went of their own accord, which could sometimes draw the energies from those who witnessed them. These, the Father (and those who came after him) had decided, were the instruments of Satan. Although not exactly describing them as such (because that would have given credence to old Native Americans beliefs), the Church hinted that these lights might be agents of the devil or manifestations of the souls of evil folk. Curiously enough, this perspective was also accepted by many of the incoming Protestant settlers. The Protestant religion also accepted the imminence of the Devil, and anything strange or unexplained was often interpreted as a concrete manifestation of evil and the workings of the Evil One. The idea of evil, flickering lights were gradually incorporated into Missouri folklore by all sides.

The notion of unexplained lights being some form of supernatural manifestation is an old one that appears in many cultures and one that existed long before Father Marquet had heard it from the Native Americans along the banks of the Mississippi River. Stories concerning them had already appeared in European traditions—all of them associated in some way with death—and this perhaps aided the assimilation of the idea into the folklore of both Catholic and Protestant settlers in Missouri.

In Ireland, England, Wales, and parts of France, strange lights often seen at a distance were said to either be the souls of the dead making their way through the world, or a prediction of imminent death in a community. This belief was strengthened by noting that some of these lights primarily appeared in old churchyards or burial grounds. In Cornwall and Wales they are known as "corpse candles" and were said to look like the flame of a candle that moved of its own volition. They often appear as balls or columns of pale blue light that travel along certain tracks and pathways, although, according to the Reverend Edmund Jones in his *A Relation of Apparitions of Spirits in the Principality of Wales* (1780), some have seen the appearance of a skeleton-like figure carrying a candle. He recounts the testimony of Mr. Joshua Coslet ("a man of sense and knowledge"), who had seen such a light, carried by a dark man in the parish of Llandeilo Fawr in Carmarthenshire. The spectre had his hand over his face, but the Reverend Jones is convinced that this being was Death himself. Some even claimed they saw faces in the flame of the light, revealing those who were about to die. The Reverend Elias Owen in his *Welsh Folklore* (1896) simply describes them as a flickering light that travels along old roads and cart-tracks where funerals have taken place, usually following the path of the cortege. W.Y. Evans-Wentz, while researching his *Fairy Faith in Celtic Countries* (1911), spoke with an old lady in Pembrokeshire who told him that a corpse candle had simply appeared right in the middle of the room where she was sitting. She described it as a great luminous mass, pale blue in color. It swelled up and filled a greater part of the room of her small cottage, which incidentally lay only a little way from one of Wales's most ancient monuments, the Pendre Ifan Cromlech. Suddenly, it seemed to burst or fall in upon itself and vanish. Shortly afterward, one of her relatives died.

In parts of Yorkshire, the phenomenon is described as "hobby lights," and is referred to as such in the Denham Tracts written between 1848 and 1856 by Michael Denham. These are collections of folklore and ghostlore in 54 pamphlets and notes concerning beliefs and superstitions among rural folk. There are several references to the "hobby lights" in the Tracts, each one signifying them as dangerous phenomena.

To approach or try to tamper with these lights was to invite disaster. An old tale from England tells of how a drunken sailor attempted to light his pipe from one of the flickering lights. He was struck by a fearful blow and left with a peculiar black mark on his face, which became poisonous and eventually killed him. According to some traditions, others have approached these lights and have been forcibly struck or something terrible has happened to them. In some cases, interlopers have experienced all the energy being drawn from them, leaving them weak and unable to pursue the light when it moves.

In Eastern Europe, such lights are said to mark a place where great wealth is buried, but can often only be seen on St. George's Eve (April 22nd) when, at midnight, all the evil things in creation hold sway from midnight until daybreak on the 23rd. To approach such lights at this time is highly dangerous, as they can draw the life from the individual or deliver such a blow as to do harm. The terror and superstition of St. George's Eve is mentioned, interestingly enough, in the first chapter of Bram Stoker's classic vampire novel *Dracula.*

Although these English, Welsh, Irish, and East European encounters are obviously distressing, in South America the flickering light takes on a much more sinister and more deadly dimension. Here, the corpse light also exists, and is sometimes known as *fugo fatuo* (fake fire) in countries such as Brazil. Regionally, it is called the *batata* or *Mbae-Tata* (taking its name from the Old Tupi language of Brazil), and can refer to a large serpent that can form out of light and smoke. It has eyes made from fire, and by day it is almost blind, but at night it can see everything in the world. Legend says that this was one of the creatures that was left after the Great Flood swamped the world, and that it survives by drawing the "goodness" (energy and wholesomeness) from anyone who approaches its lair. It is supposedly a version of the cave anaconda.

Dangerous though this is, it is not considered to be as deadly as the *Luz Mala* (evil light) of Argentina and parts of Uruguay. This is not a great smoky snake, but a ball of light that travels around the back roads of the country searching for victims. It is greatly feared, and often Argentinean people will take long detours to avoid roads on which it has been seen. The light appears in two colors: white (in which case it represents a soul in great torment; whoever sees it is asked to pray for them and to give an offering at the church), and red (which is the most dangerous, and the person who sees it should run, because red equals the presence of the Devil). The origin of the *Luz Mala* is unknown, but it is generally thought to be the soul of an evil person or of a person who has not been properly buried according to Christian custom. As such, it will seek to harm the living who it believes are responsible for its condition. It is certainly under the control of the Evil One. In some parts of Argentina, particularly the northeast of the country, such phenomenon is known as Mandinga Lanterns (*Mandinga* being a regional name denoting the Devil in human form). Tradition says that such lights are especially bright on August 24th—the feast of St. Bartholomew—and when they appear, they will show the position of buried treasure. However, one must be incredibly careful, because St. Bartholomew's day is the one day of the year when Satan is free from the supervision of the angels and will try to lure greedy mortals to their doom with promises of wealth. The way to drive these demons off is to take a knife with an iron blade (over which the Rosary has been said at least three times), and to strike at the light with it. The evil light will then retreat, but any treasure that it has been "guarding" will also disappear. Similar to a poltergeist, this phenomenon can generate unearthly sounds, like a person screaming or the clanking of chains; similar to a vampire, it can draw off energy from all those who approach it, unprotected by the Church or by holy ritual. Such lights are also usually associated in the popular mind with witches and evil beings, and are certainly under the control of the Devil.

The idea that the lights pertained to something evil also translated itself into the myths of the Native Americans further North. The Makah of Washington State, for example, believed that the lights—especially the Aurora Borealis, which they sometimes saw—were the fires of evil dwarves who captured and ate travelers through their country, cooking them on a spit over a roaring blaze. The Mandan of North Dakota explained these lights as the fires of gigantic wizards and medicine men, who cooked their enemies in great stew pots and then ate them, while the Menominee of Wisconsin believed that these flashes of brilliance, often seen in the dark, were the lights of torches held by unfriendly gigantic cannibal creatures who were hunting for victims. The Fox Indians of Wisconsin took a view that was more in line with early European traditions. For them, the lights were an omen of pestilence and misfortune—they were the souls of dark sorcerers and medicine men who were hostile toward them.

This rich tapestry concerning lights and strange brilliances, both European and Native American, was taken up by the settlers as they came into places such as Missouri, and incorporated into their own folklore. They began to spread out across the new Territory, placing more and more demands on the Spanish administration, largely based in Louisiana. In the late 1790s, the Spanish began to realize that the area was too large and diverse for them to effectively manage, especially with dwindling reserves and, so, in 1800, a treaty was negotiated for the return of Missouri to French jurisdiction. This transfer was codified in the Third Treaty of San Ildefonso, which remained secret for a short time.

After Louisiana became a state in 1812, the remaining area became known as Missouri Territory. By 1810, however, the influx of European settlers of varying religions flooding into the area had more or less overwhelmed the indigenous French-speaking element and had pushed the Native American peoples back further West. The land was of a particularly good quality and farmers were anxious to put down roots and form the foundations of statehood. During the War of 1812, the territory was a frontier area with an American military base—Fort Bellefontaine—established near St. Louis. From the early years of the 1800s, more and more settlers poured in, changing the demographics of the region, but laying solid social and political foundations. In 1818, the territorial administration submitted a request for statehood to the United States Congress. The application became mired in controversy, as it had submitted the request on the grounds that it become a slave-holding state (perhaps because of the number of southerners who were now living there and who owned slaves). However, in 1820, the Missouri Compromise cleared the way for statehood and, in 1821, Missouri became the 24th state.

During the late 1820s, there was a rush of farmers into Missouri from parts of Kentucky, anxious to avail themselves of the new land. Generally, faiths other than Catholicism were tolerated, if not sometimes encouraged. Apart from the Mormon War of 1838, when Governor Lilburn Boggs issued the Missouri Executive Order 44, calling for the expulsion and extirpation of all Mormons in the northeast of the state, Missouri tended to be fairly lenient toward all creeds.

Although the demographics within the new state were changing, there was still an underlying Catholic ethos, which had been established under both the French and Spanish. The new settlers often incorporated or linked these underlying beliefs with events that had occurred within various communities or to perceptions that they had about the world. For example, at Wolf Hollow near Excelsior Springs, there is an old abandoned house at the end of an overgrown road in which a strange light is said to appear. The place was used by the Ku Klux Klan in the years following the Civil War, and many freed slaves and people of African origin or descent were tortured and killed there. The evil light was supposed to spring up as a direct result of such activities, and is dangerous to those who sometimes venture close to the building. People claim they have heard demonic laughter from the place as soon as the lights are seen, and some state that they have experienced a feeling of weakness when approaching the old house. Is there something dwelling within those crumbling walls that manifests itself in an eerie light and can draw the energy from passers-by?

Nor is the house in Wolf Hollow the only such building in the area. Back in the woods near Excelsior is an old village of about eight small houses. Rumor says that this was an old slave camp, others that it is what is left of an old hotel. All these houses have had their windows boarded up and have been left to rot, and it is simply considered to be an abandoned village. The place, however, has an evil reputation, and is avoided by most local residents. Strange lights are said to move among the old houses, sometimes like candle flames and sometimes like balls of fire, traveling at an incredible speed. There are sometimes sounds, too, such as the clank of chains or children and women weeping. Coupled with these sounds, a fearful lethargy seems to creep over any who hear them or indeed see the lights. It is almost as if the lights and ghostly sounds are drawing energy from all living things nearby; tradition states that they are somehow associated with the slaves who dwelt here, although nobody is sure quite how.

Strange lights are also associated with an old churchyard at Elk Creek Presbyterian Church, near West Plains. On certain nights of the year, some of the graves are said to glow. According to tradition, an epidemic swept through the community and carried away certain people who were buried there. Those who see the lights on the grave will often become sick and die from plague-like symptoms, fitting in with the idea of vampires spreading disease and pestilence. Nearby and slightly to the north of the town, while crossing a low bridge, motorists have often reported feeling slightly unwell and have seen a strange light bobbing at the end of the bridge. Some travelers have even suggested that the light forms itself into the shape of a child's head; others claim that the light takes the form of a young girl.

Strangely, a similar story comes from Livingston County. Unlike the other tale, this is part of a piece of local folklore with an evil tradition attached to it, which also involves the Slagle Cemetery within the county. The name Joseph Slagle can still send a chill along spines in both Livingston and Caldwell Counties.

According to a history of Livingston and Caldwell counties (published in 1886), Joseph Slagle was a settler who arrived from West Virginia around 1830. It is not altogether clear if Joseph was his actual name, but he was born around 1810 in Augusta County, Virginia, one of 12 children. He studied for the ministry for a time, attending Charlottesville College. Slagle was living in the general area of Medicine Creek around 1839 when he sold goods at Cox's Mill, the only water-mill in northwestern Missouri. He prospered and became a local justice of the peace and was elected to the County Bench in 1846. He was soon one of the biggest landholders in the region, owning properties totaling more than 1,400 acres. However, there were some factors about him that raised eyebrows. One was that in a settled community with strong and conservative notions, Joseph Slagle had been married five times. Indeed, he seemed to have an unfortunate way with women and none of his wives survived for very long. His first wife, whom he had married in 1832, was Catherine Long, a native of Ohio who had borne him a son, Columbus Genoa. She died unexpectedly in 1841 when it was whispered that Joseph Slagle was "courting" someone else. In November 1843, Joseph married again, this time to Catherine Stone from West Virginia, who died unexpectedly in August 1844. Wasting no time, Joseph married again in May 1845, this time to Sarah Littlepage. She died unexpectedly in September 1846, leaving a daughter, Susan Catherine. In 1848, Joseph Slagle took yet another wife, Elizabeth Crawford from Illinois, who died without warning early in 1849. By now, tongues were wagging, and suspicions were sometimes being openly voiced; this forced Joseph to wait until 1869 before taking another bride, Miss Lottie P. Ellis of Indiana, who bore him another son, Joseph Lee Slagle.

With such a number of wives, Joseph Slagle was understandably the subject of much gossip and speculation. Indeed, there were stories that Slagle had murdered some of these unfortunate women in order to obtain monies and properties, but nothing could be proved. However, among some of the families of the dead women, things were slightly different.

It was Joseph's marriage to Elizabeth Crawford that brought matters to a head. At the time, a curious rumor was circulating saying that he had been expelled from his ministerial studies for his strange views and beliefs, that he had given himself over to Devil worship, and that he was actively sacrificing his wives to the Evil One in unholy ceremonies. All of these rumors gave Joseph something of a sinister reputation, which circulated far and wide, and in some ways took away from his status as a leading citizen. They also reached the ears of some of Elizabeth's relatives.

Elizabeth Crawford's half-brother, Benjamin Collins, lived in Quincy, Illinois. He was something of a disreputable character, widely regarded as a drunk. He was described as a nasty and malicious character, possessed of a ready and fearsome temper. When he heard of Elizabeth's marriage to Joseph Slagle, he allegedly flew into a vile frenzy and began to recall some of the sinister rumors about the man. He also drew attention to the fact that Elizabeth was a young woman, whereas Joseph was quite old. He declared that he would set out for Missouri and that he would kill Slagle—no sister of his was going to be sacrificed to the Devil.

He arrived in Chillicothe in mid-April and took rooms in a boarding house there. He struck up a friendship with a man named Thomas Gilkison, and together the two of them began to frequent some of the drinking establishments. During these expeditions, Collins repeated many of the old rumors concerning Slagle and his intention to kill him.

On the morning of the April 19th, Collins and Gilkison set out on their usual round of drinking. Collins was unarmed. At about the same time, Joseph Slagle left home to look for a lost cow, taking a rifle with him. When Joseph Slagle met up with the men, Collins bid him good morning. Slagle returned the greeting and Collins then asked him how he was keeping. Slagle replied that his life had been at stake long enough, whereupon he raised the rifle and shot Collins dead. As the first shot did not completely kill Benjamin Collins, Slagle fired again, this time killing him instantly. Afterward, according to Gilkison, Joseph Slagle seemed greatly distressed. He went and surrendered himself for murder and was indicted by a grand jury. When the case eventually came to trial, Joseph Slagle was acquitted, the jury being of the mind that he had killed Collins for reasons that were altogether proper and just. It's thought, however, that the trial had been rigged in Slagle's favor.

In order to resolve a discrepancy with dates around the murder, it has been suggested that Elizabeth Crawford, who was Collin's half-sister, was not Joseph Slagle's fifth wife, but rather another lady of the same name that he had also married—if this is the case, he married six times. The murder (even though he was acquitted) and the multiple marriages gave Joseph a rather strange reputation, and some people wondered if there was not something in the old stories of Devil worship that had concerned him. It may have been that people were jealous of him (he was a relatively wealthy man in the community) or frightened of him. Not even the threats made against him by such a drunk as Benjamin Collins seemed to provide any motive for his murderous actions, and gradually the incident metamorphosed into wider tales of supernatural activity. Slagle died in 1895, but the legends about him still continued.

The churchyard where Joseph Slagle, his wives, and his offspring were laid to rest became known locally as "the Old Slagle Cemetery" and it gained something of a sinister reputation. The cemetery is supposedly haunted by a glowing light that sometimes approaches passers-by and leaves them feeling terrified and drained of all energy. Sometimes, the lights are said to change into the semblance of Joseph Slagle's face. Not only this, but close to the cemetery an old bridge used to stand, which was also said to be very badly haunted. A light was said to drift along the bridge on certain nights of the year. Those who sometimes crossed this bridge experienced a fearful lethargy, which did not dissipate until several hours afterward. A number of stories have grown up around the place throughout the years, adding to its mystery. Recently, the owners of the property had the bridge demolished, though the lights around the area are said to still be active. The place where the mill stood is said to be haunted by the lights, and people claim to have heard whisperings and mutterings around the actual area where the building was located.

Similar stories are told of another abandoned mill at Clinton. Here, peculiar noises are heard that resemble whisperings and moanings, and curious lights are seen moving between the windows of the old building. Again, people who approach the building experience a peculiar sense of weariness, which can leave them inexplicably physically drained. There are numerous stories about the old place (none of which would appear to be true), concerning murders and suicides within its walls, and this has probably fed the vampiric ghostlore that surrounds it.

Unexplained lights (not always vampiric) are also seen in woodlands and along old country roads, hinting back at some of the old tales that are brought from other parts of the world and into Missouri. At Fort Leonard Wood in Pulaski County, for instance, lights are seen in the woods, sometimes around the Thayer Elementary School, and by the perimeter of the Army base, and it is said to be extremely dangerous to approach them. Near Sullivan, along a stretch of roadway in Franklin County known as the Glaser Road, a strange luminous mist is said to appear at certain times. This strange phenomenon was at the height of its appearances during the late

1950s and throughout the 1960s (although it was seen infrequently during the 1940s), but has appeared a number of times since. It is always seen during a full moon. Observers state that it can change color and, from a much more sinister perspective, is also said to be able to follow people, as if possessed of some form of intelligence. It can also change direction if need be, as though aware of its surroundings or being guided by some outside agent. Reports of the size of the misty light may vary. Sometimes, it is said to be a small ball, traveling at great speed; other times it is a large bubble-like phenomenon, moving very slowly and deliberately, as if seeking something out. Again, those who see it are sometimes gripped by a terrible weariness. Another ball of luminous mist has been seen down by the state park further along, and this behaves in exactly the same way.

Just outside Jefferson City is a stretch of old and nearly abandoned highway, along which a vampiric light is said to pass. The roadway is bounded on either side by cornfields, and the light or a glowing mist travels through these fields alongside travelers on the road for a distance of about 4 to 5 miles. Sometimes these travelers complain of an energy loss and severe headaches, as well as pains in all of their joints and muscles. Down this road is another old bridge—a second bridge along the stretch around which eerie lights sometimes flicker. It is said that during the Civil War, a local family was taken down to the bridge and hanged. Those killed included very young children. The horror of this event left its mark on the area, and the spirits of the dead now form the basis of the evil lights, which moved around (and under) the bridge. This is sometimes confused with the Wainwright Bridge just outside Jefferson City, where strange noises and eerie lights are often seen around the hour of midnight. Some accounts state that the sounds actually come from under the bridge and consist mainly of wailing cries and that this is the area from where the lights and glowing mists seem to issue. Curiously, no less than four farmer's bodies have allegedly been found under the bridge, mysteriously drained of blood.

It's not just old stretches of roadway and dangerous-looking bridges that are haunted by such things. Blood-drinking and energy-sapping lights are often seen around old cemeteries, such as those at Jericho Springs. It is said that lights are often seen moving of their own volition within the cemetery confines, and that these odd brilliances may have the power to draw energy from the viewer. Some are said to be associated with the graves of local families, but opinions in the area tend to vary as to exactly who these families might be. Again, descriptions of the lights vary from large-glowing masses to small balls of what appears to be burning fire. All of them, however, create fear and apprehension among those who see them. Few of them are seen outside the cemetery surroundings.

The most famous of all the "Missouri lights," however, are the Hornet Spooklights, which are often seen near Joplin and on roads along the Missouri-Oklahoma border. Opinion regarding this phenomenon is divided—it is often referred to as a "spook light," suggesting that it is no more than some form of ghost; other accounts state that it is much more dangerous and may have energy-sapping properties if approached by the unwary. It is, however, a peculiar and inexplicable occurrence.

Roughly about 12 miles south of Joplin, a small and unpaved back road runs through a lonely stretch of countryside. Nearby is the border village of Hornet (about 6 miles southwest of Joplin), which is a very small community. The stretch of road, though only about 4 miles long, has acquired a certain sinister notoriety and, in keeping with the influence of the Evil One, which is said to be paramount in the area, is widely known as The Devil's Promenade. Along this stretch of road, a light is said to travel and has been witnessed by many people through the years. Although it is said that the light has never harmed anyone, many are very wary of it and there are stories around Hornet—some undoubtedly for the benefit of passing tourists—that suggest that it might be very dangerous to go near.

No one knows what the light might be or what its origins are. Some legends say that it has been there for centuries and was witnessed by both the Quapaw and Osage Indians who hunted in the region. Father Marquet had also heard of the "devil lights" by local Native Americans when he first came to the Missouri Territory in the 1670s. However, accounts of the phenomenon have certainly existed since Civil War times, around the 1860s. As far as is known, however, the first formal report of the light appeared in 1936 in the *Kansas City Star*, and this was taken up by the noted folklore writer Vance Randolph in his seminal 1947 book *Ozark Superstitions*. Randolph drew on a number of oral legends concerning the origins of the glow from lost children to beheaded Native Americans. There are also tales of the spirits of evil Native American medicine men returning in the form of the lights. Some locals have attempted to interfere with the Light.

There are, of course, a number of more scientific theories used to explain the lights along The Devil's Promenade. One states that it is a kind of luminescence that comes from rotting trees and that it is no more than a sign of decay. The light, it is pointed out, has been seen in both damp and marshy areas, and is probably no more than the emission of gasses in that region. However, this does not explain its appearance along the actual path of the Promenade, which is neither damp nor marshy in nature. Another explanation is that the misty brilliance is caused by minerals in the soil. This does not account for the fact that the light appears to move along the section of road, and that it sometimes vanishes only to reappear a mile or so away. Other suggestions assert that it might be caused by some form of electrical or atmospheric conditions, which are caused by shifts in the ground. There have certainly been earthquakes in the region around the mid-1800s and it is significant that the moving lights were first formally reported around this time. And yet, this does not completely account for the feelings of lethargy experienced by some people who have tried to follow the path of the brilliance. Nor do any of these explanations account for the fact that the spook lights seem to move of their own volition and perhaps with a seeming intelligence, which is not usually given to natural phenomena.

In the late 1950s through the 1960s, there was a Spook Light Museum based in Hornet and run by Leslie W. Robertson. This contained numerous photos of the lights with a number of encounters with them. It also had a viewing platform with a telescope through which visitors could observe the mysterious phenomena without having to go too near it. Some of those who had observed it in this way declared that it was not a single light at all, but a major brilliance with a number of other smaller lights around it. They all moved very closely together, weaving and darting like fireflies. The central brilliance, they said, was like a candle flame.

There have been several attempts to investigate the mysterious light—one of the most celebrated by the author Raymond Bayless in 1963. He visited the site and allegedly saw the phenomenon, but did not approach it. Accounts concerning it seem to go back a long time; in fact, one of those whom Bayless interviewed, Mr. Arthur Holbrook, was an elderly local resident and a person who had been interested in the phenomenon for many years. He stated that he had first observed the light in 1905. He also stated that the light could be dangerous if one got too close. Holbrook dismissed the claim that it might be an atmospheric anomaly created by car headlights on a nearby roadway, as there had been no automobiles around then and The Devil's Promenade had been only a stretch of dirt road. Others told Bayless that the light was a very ancient phenomenon—"an old Indian thing"—and that it represented some force that resided in the area and had since time immemorial. It was also dangerous to humans.

Nevertheless, the spook light has proved something of a tourist attraction for the Joplin area. So great is its fame that each year thousands of curious individuals turn up in the hopes of seeing it. Even the Army has taken an interest and has monitored the light on a couple of occasions, but their conclusions are no more definite than those of the general public.

There are other instances of strange lights—some of them allegedly vampiric, others not—all across Missouri. And as night falls over Missouri, lights flicker on the edges of town and along rural roads, but not the lights that one might expect—they are not the wholesome lights of windows and streetlamps. These are more ancient lights with perhaps a long history dating back to Indian times. Do they actually represent primal forces that are somehow locked in the landscape? Or are they mysterious beings that have coexisted alongside mankind for centuries? And are they things that intend to do humans harm, either by drinking their blood or sapping their energies? Be careful of the seemingly welcoming brilliance along the roadway or among the trees, because what awaits you there may not be what you might expect!

Arizona/New Mexico

Take a closer look at your neighbor. Are you sure that you know them? That it *is* them? It might be somebody or *something* else. It might be a skinwalker, and it just might be there to drink your blood. Especially if you live in a place such as Arizona or New Mexico!

Vampirism in the American southwest tends to be a little bit different from vampirism in the New England states such as Rhode Island or Vermont. It is just as dangerous, of course, but there are certain distinctions. For example, it is strongly linked with witchcraft, and the vampire does not actually have to be dead to become one of these creatures. Through witchcraft they can often take on other shapes—both animal and human—and can actually remove their skin in the style of South Carolina's boo-daddies. However, when the skin is removed, the vampire is no more than a ball of hellish red or yellow-red light, which can often travel from place to place at amazing speeds. In the southwestern states, distinctions between vampirism, werewolfery, and witchcraft also often tend to be blurred and are usually interchanged at will. Vampires in the American southwest are therefore known as "skinwalkers," a term that combines vampiric entity, werewolf, and evil magician.

The idea may come from a number of traditions that have been prevalent in the area throughout the years. At its most basic, it derives from the Navajo culture, in which the original skinwalkers may have been shamans within a Native American tribe. In the Navajo language, the name for skinwalker is *yee-naaldlooshii*, which is also the term for an evil witch. It can also mean "one who wears a skin," and may refer to the idea that perhaps the early shamans wore some sort of animal skin covering in order to disguise themselves. This, of course, is not unique to the Navajo or Native American culture in general, as in many early cultures, shamanistic practitioners may have dressed in such skins in order to perform their ceremonial duties (in fact, this may have been the origins of the werewolf legend). In Navajo tradition, however, certain skins may not be used for ceremonial purposes, because they often carry evil connotations. These are bear, coyote, wolf, and cougar pelts, which should not be worn. If any human dons them, he or she will be seized by the evil in the pelt and might become a witch, vampire, or skinwalker. Sheepskin and buckskin are two of the few hides used by the Navajo and the Zuni, the latter used mainly for ceremonial purposes. There is an old Navajo legend says that if a skinwalker is wrapped in a buckskin cloak, the evil will leave him or her, and he or she can return to conventional society. However, the individual would be forever tainted and might even revert to being a skinwalker or vampire at some future date unless specific remedies known only to certain shamans were carried out.

In many parts of Western Europe, a vampire is not created through the bite of another of its kind (as Hollywood and a number of writers of such fiction would have us believe), but by an individual breaking a social or cultural taboo. (Indeed, the wearing of, say, a coyote pelt is sometimes still considered to violate a social taboo in Navajo society.) Thus, those who committed incest, were homosexuals, or who engaged in forms of anti-social behavior might be destined to become werewolves in life, but almost certainly would become vampires while still alive or after death. As far as women were concerned, it was also considered in a number of cultures (including that of the Navajo) that childless women would almost certainly become witches and vampires. Barrenness in women was considered to be a sign of their evil, and it was generally assumed that those who became vampires were evil already and that the vampirism was simply the outward manifestation of that evil. Similarly, harboring dark thoughts against one's neighbors for a long period of time might also be enough to turn a person into a vampire. Thus, the vampires were often someone who was an outsider or who didn't fit in terribly well with those around him or her.

Even so, many believed that vampires lived among them. In late medieval Europe, the 1486 publication of the *Malleus Maleficarum* (*The Hammer of the Witch*), by the Inquisitors Heinrich Kramer and Jacob Sprenger, clearly placed witches and evil-doers as members of the community. From this position, they worked from within to corrupt God's children and lead them into wickedness, working almost like the Devil's secret agents. For many people, the most important aspect of Sprenger and Kramer's work was to locate the evil being at the very center of the community and to define someone who was "a bit odd" or who acted slightly outside the conventional norms of society as an enemy of God. In fact, this idea formed the basis of many of the European witch persecutions of the later medieval period and early modern times. The Inquisitors tapped into a perception that had existed for countless years previously and that was even found within tribal societies. The person who did not act in the ways in which others did, who did not obey agreed communal norms, or who had exhibited either knowledge or sensibilities that were beyond those that others may have held, was always viewed with suspicion by the community. In this sense, Native American societies were little different from those of the villages of medieval Europe. The person who displayed shamanistic qualities was often viewed as someone who was "ambivalent"—someone who could help individual members of the community, but who could also turn against them in terrifying ways.

Thus, the skinwalker could take not only an animal form if it so chose, but also a human one, as a member of the community. And it may take on the appearance of someone who is already familiar to that community—a central figure such as a local healer or somebody who is on society's periphery and whose ways are known to be anti-social—investing them with evil and vampiric powers. It is not exactly clear how a person becomes a skinwalker. In some versions of the belief, it is done by performing a certain ceremony that draws down a spirit like a ball of light, which then possesses the individual, imbuing them with witchcraft knowledge and vampiric powers. Such ritual involves a perverted song and "unclean acts," for the spirit that is invoked is unutterably evil. This gives the individual the power to "steal" the body of a companion (usually that of a living person) and to use it for wicked ways. The Navajo also believe that if a normal person locks eyes with a skinwalker and that gaze is held for too long, the skinwalker will have the power to drain all the good from the person's body and perhaps even assume his or her identity. The only way anyone can tell if a person has been "consumed" by a skinwalker is that their eyes may glow in the darkness. Their breath is also foul and reeks of carrion, giving away their true identity to others. Despite being abroad in their communities during the day, like conventional European vampires, many skinwalkers strike against their neighbors during the hours of darkness.

Navajos and members of other tribes are incredibly hesitant, even reluctant, to speak of their nocturnal skinwalker experiences. Perhaps this is because of a belief that even talking about such things will invite them back to torment the individual. Gradually, however, some stories emerge, each containing themes that concern the skinwalker. Many of these, of course, are vague and sometimes confused, but they give a picture of the fear in which the creature is held. Sometimes the creature will attack a house in a village, banging on the walls and rattling the windows with its force. It will even sometimes climb onto the roof and roar down the chimney, terrifying those within the building. If it should climb up secretly and remove its skin high on the rooftop, then a ball of light might drift down into the room and attack the family when they are asleep. Sometimes, a strange, animal-like figure is glimpsed near the house around twilight or as the light starts to fade, and the family within knows that a skinwalker is close by. Sometimes, so legends state, the animal will venture close to the house and will try to peer in through the windows. At other times, the creature will appear in the guise of someone who is known to the family or as some member of the community. In this case, it will encourage the family to open their door and admit it. It then has them at its mercy.

Among the Zuni Indians of western New Mexico there is a belief that the skinwalkers can sometimes enter a house by using the discarded hair, the spit, or even the shoes of the people within the place. This is done in the form of a spell, and once again links skinwalking and vampirism with the idea of malefic witchcraft. Neither Zuni nor Navajo will leave their shoes outside their doors, lest they fall into the clutches of a passing skinwalker, nor will they spit in case this is gathered up by witches and used in spells to enter their houses. Similarly, great care is taken to burn all discarded hair and nail clippings, so that these too are not used in a spell to come into the house when they are asleep. Exactly the same precautions were taken with old clothes, which had been close to a person's body, and if children urinate outside the house, they are advised to kick dirt all over it to avoid it being drawn up and used in a spell or curse.

In the Native American cultures of the southwest, the belief exists that many of the skinwalkers deliberately follow what is known as "the witchery way." According to their lore, the "witchery way" has existed almost since the dawn of time and is part of a story concerning the first people on Earth who were known as "witch people." They were able to perform all sorts of feats, which today would be seen as magic, but then were simply part of their culture. Such traditions were passed down orally from generation to generation. However, in these early times, the ways of the people were very different; they were permitted to drink blood and eat the dead flesh of corpses—things that would not be allowed today. The witches among them were mainly male, but old and childless women could also be sorcerers.

As time progressed, other peoples settled in the plains and valleys of the American southwest and the witch people became fewer and fewer. Soon, only a few remained, most of them living in remote hills and valleys; those who did preyed on their new neighbors, becoming skinwalkers and attacking them late at night and usually to drink blood. There were also certain rites that a person could go through in order to follow their traditions and gain the powers of the original "witch people." For instance, some can be "baptized" by using a certain dust made from ground-up corpses. The best are usually the bodies of small children or twins (especially potent) and the ceremony at which the skinwalker is "anointed" with such dust has been described as resembling a Native American version of the European Black Mass at which old gods are evoked. The central ritual of such a ceremony is something known as "the witches sing," which is a calling on the ancient spirits to come down and take possession of the adherents, changing them into blood-drinking skinwalkers and giving them power to change their shape.

Among Christian Native Americans, there is a slightly different story and origin to the skinwalker belief. In the beginning, all people were created so that they could change their shape in order to protect themselves from the other animals that inhabited the earth. They were God's special creation, and he gave them this ability in order to survive on the savage Earth. Through the years, mankind gradually began to lose that ability (they had less and less need for it), although some still managed to retain it. However, those who were still able to manipulate their shape had strayed from the path that God had laid down for mankind and used their powers for evil. They practiced things that were abominable—for example, they drank blood and performed acts of witchcraft. In some versions of the belief, God asked for the gift of transformation back again, as it was no longer needed, and although most of mankind did indeed give it back, others wanted to hold onto it for their own selfish reasons and have retained and maintained that power down throughout years. Some may have retained the power by deliberately committing evil deeds or breaking taboos in order to distance themselves from God. In fact, says the legend, they are still among us today. And they are still evil by nature, trying to do mischief against those who live around them. And, they may still drink the blood of innocents when the mood is upon them. It is during the hours of darkness, according to the Christian Native Americans, that the evil nature of such people is at its height, because God has turned his face away and allowed evil its freedom. At this time, the skinwalkers go about making various noises, the most favored being that of a baby crying. This is to lure God-fearing people from their houses (as they think that a child has been abandoned) to a place where the skinwalker can pounce upon them and drink their blood.

The skinwalker is usually described in Navajo, Ute, and Zuni folklore as being naked, albeit wrapped in a coyote skin or in the pelt of some other animal. In other legends, it is often described as a mutated version of the animal in question. However, the skin may be shed—being little more than a covering or mask that is simply worn during "the witches sing"—when the skinwalker feeds. The central core of the skinwalker's being is, of course, the ball of shining light, the glow of which often surrounds the skin-wrapped being or the mutated beast just before it pounces.

In many Navajo folktales, there is the common story of the hunter who shoots a strange and frightening beast that he encounters in the forest, which then escapes, wounded. The hunter follows a trail of blood, sometimes deeper into the forest, but in most cases back to his own village. There, he finds a human being who is known to him and who sports a wound, which is in a similar place to that which he inflicted on the curious beast. The implication is clear—the beast and the person are one and the same (the person is, in fact, a skinwalker, who took the beast form in order to do harm or to break taboos). This is, of course, very much in keeping with shapeshifting folktales from other countries (for example, Celtic folklore abounds with such stories) and reiterates one of the central tenets of the *Malleus* that something evil was living among communities in an everyday guise and possibly largely undetected.

Similar to European vampires, in Native American lore, the skinwalker has the ability to spread sickness and disease wherever it goes. Epidemics among Native American communities are sometimes still attributed to the wandering skinwalkers, who send out and spread such illnesses as a form of malice. In this respect, their sole objective is to do harm to their neighbors and is a testimony to their evil intent.

"Skinwalkers are purely evil in intent," says Las Vegas anthropologist Dan Benyshek in an interview in Dr. Colm A. Kelleher's book *Hunt for the Skinwalker* in 2004. "I'm no expert on it, but the general view is that skinwalkers do all sorts of terrible things—they make people sick, they commit murder, they are grave robbers and necrophiliacs, They are greedy and evil people who must kill a sibling or other relative to be initiated as a skinwalker. They are supposed to turn into wereanimals and can travel in supernatural ways." To this, other anthropologists add that they can also drink blood or leech away the energy of, say, a sleeping person. While not accepting the truth of such folk myths, Benyshek says they are important because sometimes they can manifest themselves in very real ways within Native American society. "Anthropologists," he says, "have conducted scientific investigations into the beliefs in Native American witchcraft because of the effects of such beliefs on human health."

Another anthropologist, David Zimmerman, worked with the Navajo Nation Historic Preservation Department and suggests that skinwalkers may be the flipside of the Native American shamans who deal with healing and spiritual harmony. He says some medicine men may also have been trained in the "witchery way," the dark side of the Native American supernatural, and may use this teaching to great effect in some instances. Witches and vampires are viewed with some fear, but also some great distaste amongst the tribes. Perhaps, they might even command less fear than they do in Europe. Journalist A. Lynn Allison seems to bear this out by drawing attention to the Navajo Witch Purge of 1878.

In that year, more than 40 witches and skinwalkers were killed or "purged" in a clash of Native cultures with the U.S. government-backed economic and social realignment. This realignment began in 1864 with the "Long Walk" (resettlement) of the Navajos from Fort Wingate and Fort Canby to Bosque Redondo (Fort Sumner), which was already occupied by the Mescalero Apache. The Bosque Redondo settlement was a miserable failure and, in 1868, the government permitted the surviving Navajo to return to their lands. However, it failed to make adequate provision for them to do so. Those who returned were destitute and hungry. They made do as best they could, but in such dire circumstances, the stage was set for the return of old superstitions and traditional ways and remedies.

In the summer of 1878, tensions began to expand and burst into flame. Some of the Navajo, who had returned from Bosque Redondo, had become slightly wealthier than others, mainly through stealing and warfare (which had always been endemic within Navajo culture) and gradually a social differentiation had opened up within tribal society. In a charged social atmosphere, deaths of livestock and unexplained sicknesses (and deaths) of tribal members raised suspicions, along with accusations of witchcraft and skinwalking. Feuds opened up between certain families and evidence of cursing was found buried in remote places, suggesting a skinwalking activity. Accusations began to fly. Because no Navajo could go and retrieve the curse items that had been found, a white trader Charles Hubbell was hired to go and get them where they were buried. He went up to Ganado Lake where the items had been hidden. According to Navajo legend, what Hubbell found was a spell written on a piece of paper (some variants of the story say that it was actually the agreement between the Navajo and the U.S. government), buried in a shallow grave. Shortly after this, the Purge began.

The killing of witches and skinwalkers was traditionally accepted as part of Navajo culture. The tradition was similar to the killing of witches and the destruction of vampires in Europe (the main difference being that the latter were already deemed to be dead). And as with European witch accusations and slayings, it was motivated by petty jealousies and animosities. Some of the skinwalkers survived the Purge, but had to leave the Navajo settlements, never to return.

It is commonly said that the first witch/skinwalker to be killed as part of the Purge was murdered right in front of Hubbell's trading post. The murder later necessitated the removal of the post to a different location at Ganado Lake. While it is unclear exactly who was killed and exactly where, it is clear that the slaying was brutal and that there was a lot of blood. It was also vicious enough to frighten Charles Hubbell himself. There was a widespread belief in a form of Navajo, Ute, and Zuni witchcraft known as antiih, in which spirits were evoked by spilled blood and violence, and would bring misfortune wherever they were drawn. Whether or not Hubbell believed in this, he moved to Ganado Lake. It is probable that none of the local Navajos would now use his post, because of the murder connotations and the fear of the dark and malicious spirits, which the spilled blood had drawn to it.

On May 31st, 1878, Charles Hubbell wrote a frantic letter addressed to "W.B. Leonard, Fort Defiance, Arizona Territory, Yavapai County." In it, he pleaded for ammunition and rifles to be sent urgently as he expected "a big row" among the Native Americans and he feared that large bands of them would arrive from "Canon de Chelle" (Canon de Chelly, Arizona) in order to create trouble. He feared that all whites in the area were in danger, and that his store and its contents would be destroyed. In a second letter written that same day, Hubbell stated that an informant named Ganio had told him that the Native Americans were arming themselves and that his own life was in danger. He appealed for soldiers from Fort Defiance to come and protect them. The restlessness had been caused by the slaying of a Navajo named Hastiin Biwosi, who had been murdered as skinwalker by a group of his own people. It is estimated that there were about 50 of his own community who hunted him down with horses and guns, eventually finding the place where he was hiding. He was dragged out at gunpoint and was taken before Totsohnii Hastiin, who was a *naataani* (a kind of informal but highly respected leader); he pronounced him as a skinwalker and witch. One of Biwosi's relatives, Ganado Mucho, spoke up for him, telling the others that the spirit of a skinwalker could return from the dead and cause them harm. But others were determined that the creature that was Biwosi should be killed. In the end, Totsohnii Hastlin threw up his hands and said, "Do what you want," whereupon they dragged Biwosi out, shot him, and then stoned his dead body.

For many days afterward, the tension remained. Ganado Mucho was particularly fearful, as he had committed a grievous act in being party to the killing of a close relative. And it was assumed that if a skinwalker had been malignant when alive, he or she would be doubly so when dead. Two witches had been killed, but they could certainly return and wreak vengeance on the community. A few days later, another *naataani*, a healer named Manuelito, arrived at Fort Wingate with a letter, which he dictated to J.L. Hubbell—who was Charles's brother—reporting that the Navajos had taken six medicine men prisoner under the suspicion that they were skinwalkers and that they intended to kill them all. He asked for military intervention to prevent this from happening. His request was answered. No less than 10 "witches and skinwalkers" were brought before Lieutenant D.D. Mitchell, who had arrived from Fort Wingate (and who had previously given a stern speech condemning the killing of such people by their own families) and all of them survived.

For a number of months afterward, there were isolated killings of alleged witches and skinwalkers throughout the area, but not on the scale of the Purge. Leaders such as Manuelito and Ganado Mucho assumed the roles of local *naataani* and helped to defuse much off the tension that still existed. Nevertheless, the fear of the skinwalkers remained, and their influence would be felt all through the region for many years after. The Purge had simply been a physical explosion of that fear. In this respect, the Navajo had been no different than the European communities of the medieval and early modern periods, who had been just as terrified of vampires, witches, and night wanderers.

During the Navajo Witch Purges, there was one secondary feature (after the curses of the witches themselves) among the instances of witchcraft that struck terror into the native population. This is the phenomenon of cattle mutilation and it stems from the widely held belief that if a skinwalker cannot attack a living individual or family, it will attack and injure his/her livestock. The belief was common in many parts of Europe as well. Unable to enter houses, European vampires often turned to the nearest form of sustenance, which usually happened to be the communal livestock, and many medieval and early modern farmers often lived in fear of losing either cattle or sheep to the wandering dead.

One of the most frequent livestock killings are what are known as "cattle mutilations" (bovine excision), which were quite common during the Purge. Although the term refers largely to cattle, it should be pointed out that the term is often used in a "catch-all" sense and that the cattle can also refer to sheep and horses. One of the striking features of such attacks (in modern times at least) is the deliberate nature of the injuries involved. Further, such slayings are often characterized by the loss of blood on the part of the animal, even though there is little spilled blood in evidence. This has led to suggestions that the killings are the work of vampiric creatures that have drained the cattle of their blood.

In the southwest, such stories (or indeed mutilations) are not new, but stretch all the way back to the time of the Spaniards. Late in 1540, the army of Francisco Vasquez de Coronado came through the area on its way to seek out the Native American cities of gold, which were supposed to exist in the region. They were following a trail that had been laid out for them by the monk Fray Marcos de Niza, who assured them that great wealth lay somewhere in the southwestern region. With them, the army brought herds of cattle that could be slaughtered along the way, in order to sustain them. At night, as the conquistadores and their men slept, the cattle were corralled in large pens on the edge of their camp. One night, well into the expedition, the cattle were attacked. The attackers were "little gray men" with hard and spiky skins, which set upon the animals in order to draw their blood and consume some of their internal organs. They were only driven away by fire—the men held lighted torches to push them back. Local natives later told the Spaniards that these were *chupacabra* (goatsuckers) and that they lived in the surrounding hills. They were cannibals who drank blood, and, if confronted they would attack humans as well as animals. It was said that they only came out at night. Coronado's generals sent a number of small expeditions out into the nearby hills, but found nothing. Locals, however, told them that the beings were certainly there and had lived there for a very long time, attacking their goats and cattle and sometimes themselves, and that there were some among them who could change shape, taking on the guise of a bird or a coyote. Many of Coronado's livestock had been severely mutilated and completely drained of blood. The great general marched his army through the region quickly, leaving the dangerous hills and their strange shapeshifting creatures well behind him. Other Spaniards in the area told similar stories of the chupacabra and of beings that could change their shape at will, all of which drank blood or devoured internal organs.

During the governorship of Ponce de Leon, there are a number of stories concerning cattle mutilations, chupacabras, and skinwalkers. There is a legend that a conquistador named Ferdinand Cubero led an expedition against chupacabra somewhere to the west of the present-day city of Albuquerque (although some variations say the vampire colony was based along the Santa Cruz River). Cubero was attacked several times during the hours of darkness by "little gray men" and sometimes by creatures that took the form of dogs and even the guise of some of his own men in order to create confusion in the poor light. The creatures seemed to have scant respect for the church, for among those slain were two friars who accompanied the expedition and their blood was drained from their bodies. Terrified that the powers of the Holy Orders did not seem to be able to protect them, Cubero ordered his men to pull back, but the creatures appeared to follow them for a time and several more men were killed.

After the establishment of Albuquerque as *Ranchos de Albuquerque* with a presidio (military garrison) in 1706, stories of skinwalkers and chupacabra still persisted in the farming communities throughout the area. The place was a military outpost and a number of patrols were sent out to investigate, but encountered very little. There were stories of soldiers finding the creatures sleeping in holes in the ground or in abandoned pueblos and killing them with both fire and sword.

Other stories concerning chupacabra and skinwalkers come from neighboring Arizona. Many of these tales also have their roots in the time of Spanish occupation there. The Jesuit Italian explorer, Father Eusebio Franscisco Kino, explored the area of what is now southwestern Arizona (then known as the Pimeria Alta) in the early 1700s and recorded a number of local tales concerning the skinwalkers. Following him, Jose Romo de Vivar ran cattle in the Huachuca Mountains, an area in which some of these creatures were said to live. De Vivar complained frequently to the authorities that his cattle were disappearing and were later found slaughtered and drained of blood. Locals said that the Huachuca were full of chupacabra and it was probably these that were creating the mischief. The Spaniards did not venture forth into the mountains, as it was suggested that they might encounter the likeness of walking men who could suddenly change into the semblance of animals or balls of light that could attack and kill them. Presumably what Spanish there were in the area were superstitious enough to keep well within their pueblos at night, so de Vivar's complaints probably went unheeded.

As more Spanish colonists trickled into the area, the authorities considered establishing a mission in the region and invited the Italian Jesuit and missionary Father Kino to do so. Father Kino had already established a number of missions around Sonora and Nogales, and he gladly accepted the invitation and founded the Mission San Xavier del Bac, just south of present-day Tucson. Local natives told the early missionaries of witch things that dwelt in ancient pueblos nearby, which would attempt to infiltrate and destroy the missions if they could. Such being could take on the guises of many things including *penitentes* (local Christian Native Americans seeking absolution from the fathers). According to legend, some of the early missionaries in the area encountered some of these beings and, although it is claimed that they were driven back to their abandoned and ruined pueblos by the impressive power of the Christian Cross, some variations of the tale leave out the Christian symbolism and speak of fire, musket, and cold steel. However, perhaps a more pressing threat than any supernatural witch came from the groups of marauding Apaches in the locality who frequently attacked the Sonora missions. These finally destroyed San Xavier around 1770.

In 1767 Charles III, King of Spain, banned all Jesuits from the mission lands in the Americas due to his vast mistrust of the order. He placed the missions in the hands of much more easily manipulated and "responsible" Franciscans. Once again, local natives complained to the fathers who set up in the rebuilt mission of attacks on their cattle by supernatural creatures. Away to the west in the wilderness, the Tohono O'odham told them there were evil men who had "turned their backs on God" and lived in crumbling pueblos where they practiced something that resembled the "witchery way." This turned them into great magicians and enabled them to take the form of owls and coyotes and other things in order to attack God's children. There are tales that the Franciscans (like the Jesuits before them) went out into the waste armed with crucifixes and Latin Bibles. Whether this was successful or not is debateable, for it is thought that the cattle mutilations in the area still continued despite the priests' intervention.

Indeed, such mutilations continued unabated for many years. The present mission church was begun in 1783 and completed in 1797. It was built under the guidance and direction of two Franciscan friars, Father Juan Bautista Velderrain and Father Juan Bautista Llorenz working mainly with native labor. A garrison had been established further downriver at Presidio San Augustin de Tucson to protect the building from any further Apache raids, but even this could not really protect the area around from the supernatural evil, which appeared to be stalking the region. Even at this time, stories of chupacabra and skinwalkers were still prevalent. Many local farmers said that they had seen their cattle attacked by what looked like small balls of light, which appeared to draw off the good (and blood) from the animals in question. The locals said this could only be vampire beings intent on doing mischief in the district. Although the good fathers investigated, it is thought that there was little trace of the supernatural threat to be found. A military expedition from the presidio and led by both the Fathers is said to have ventured out into the wasteland and even visited several of the abandoned and ruined mud pueblos there, but if they found anything, it is not recorded. They may have found a few native hermits living there, but probably little else. If this was the case, what became of these men? Were they put to death by the soldiers under the direction of the priests? Maybe they were skinwalkers after all. The expeditions returned to the mission, but allegedly, the cattle mutilations continued. All throughout the 19th and 20th centuries, farmers in Arizona, New Mexico, and parts of Utah have recorded sporadic instances of cattle mutilation. Although sometimes separated by many years, the mutilations are strikingly similar. Almost all involve the loss of blood and some internal organs. Local Native American groups attribute the activity to that of skinwalkers who could not attack humans.

Although such mutilations tend to be in "cluster groups" sometimes years apart, there have been some that have been particularly frequent and especially brutal. In 1999, for example, a spate of mutilations at Ash Fork, an area west of Flagstaff, Arizona, was so bad that the authorities decided to investigate. A team from the United States Department of Agriculture arrived in Phoenix. This time it was not cattle that they had come to investigate. Since 1998, more than 19 horses and a mule had been mutilated, and much of their blood was gone. The teams arrived at Ash Fork to determine whether these animals had been the victims of "an infectious agent" (that is, some disease), which had caused them to die in this manner. Two pathologists and an epidemiologist accompanied the groups and carried out extensive work on the dead animal bodies. Their conclusion was that "no infectious agent" was present at Ash Fork. Samples were sent for testing to the labs at the University of Arizona in Tucson, but the results of this investigation were never made public. Of course, when they arrived in the area, the teams heard many stories about chupacabra-like creatures and skinwalkers, and the cattle mutilations were often directly attributed to the activities of local witches. Balls of curious light—some of them behaving in peculiar ways or traveling at great speeds—were frequently seen in the Ash Fork area, and this was a sure indication that skinwalkers were present. Other tales told of uncanny creatures that were not altogether human, moving about under cover of darkness, and they were taken to be witches who had discarded their human skins and were now appearing in their true form for the purposes of attacking their neighbors' livestock. The teams, however, seem to have disregarded such stories and concentrated on the path of toxicology. Or did they, as some suggest, find other things, which is why their report has never been made fully public?

An even more extensive investigation, however, was carried on in New Mexico in the mid-to-late 1970s by the FBI. Between 1975 and 1980, more than 100 mysterious cattle deaths were reported in New Mexico with many more going unreported. It is thought that the total number may have been nearly 1,000. In most cases, the cattle were found, completely drained of blood, and with deliberate and precise cuts on their carcasses. In many cases, they were also swollen up with various organs (including sexual organs) removed. Once again, the old theories about the skinwalkers resurfaced, although this time they were accompanied by theories about UFOs and about clandestine criminal or even government activities. As with the Melon Heads in Ohio, it was thought that the military was conducting secret experiments somewhere in the wilderness that had somehow gone awry. However, the idea of skinwalkers was certainly very prevalent. Indeed, so frequent were these stories that the FBI were compelled to investigate as a response to the urging of local Senator Harrison Schmitt. The Senator wrote to the then-U.S. Attorney General Griffin Bell, demanding an investigation into what he believed was "organized interstate criminal activity." Bell responded the following month, stating that what Schmitt had described was "...one of the strangest phenomena in (his) memory." The FBI were therefore sent to Phoenix to investigate the mutilations and immediately heard the stories of skinwalkers and vampires in the region.

Initially, the Bureau was very reluctant to investigate the incident, and this reluctance remained throughout. Several times they tried to pull out of the investigation, but were directed to continue by the U.S. Department of Justice. They commenced in March 1979, but with the agreement that the scope of the investigated should be restricted to New Mexico's Native American lands, which lay in federal jurisdiction. The Bureau collected a file filled with memos and newspaper clippings from the area. FBI laboratories analyzed flakes of an unknown substance taken from the roof of a pick-up truck, the driver of which had encountered balls of light on a road near Taos. The determination of the tests was inconclusive, but agents determined that they were probably a type of house paint. At least that is the result of a report signed by now-retired agent Kenneth Rommel, one of the lead agents in the investigation. Local people begged to differ—they insisted it was the blood of a skinwalker and proof of supernatural activity. Others claimed it had come from a UFO.

Gradually, FBI involvement in the case began to fade away and slowly petered out. The Albuquerque office finally placed a "closed status" sticker on it and there the matter rests. The cattle mutilations attributed to the skinwalkers are deemed to stem from the activities of natural predators and scavengers. Although the FBI were aware of old Native American tales—and this is evident from their files—they largely discounted them. About 90 percent of the mutilations were explained in this way. This left 10 percent unexplained by conventional means and the FBI appears to have drawn a line under these and proceeded no further. What information they did release about their investigations was counted as "too glib" and "too superficial" by those who believed in other explanations. Notions of the skinwalkers still persisted, although, as time went on, a straightforward supernatural explanation gave way to ideas concerning UFOs and government cover-ups. Were the skinwalkers actually from outer space? Was the U.S. military actually using genetic technology found in a crashed spacecraft at Roswell, New Mexico, to create new forms of life, some of which had run amok and attacked the livestock? Many who saw the strange ball-shaped lights, origi-nally equated with Native American witches, now linked them with UFOs and extraterrestrials. There was even a theory that speculated that an orga-nization named Majestic-12 was operating in the area in clandestine genetic experimentation on some of the lonely ranches. Majestic-12 is allegedly the code name for a secret governmental committee made up of scientists, mili-tary, and politicians, which was set up in the wake of the Roswell Incident in 1947. According to tradition, the Committee was initiated by President Harry S. Truman and was first chaired by Gordon Grey, who was an offi-cial in the administrations of both Presidents Truman and Eisenhower. The purpose of Majestic-12, or MJ-12, was thought to be to investigate UFO contacts and other phenomena and to assess the possible use of UFO tech-nology in terrestrial scientific projects. Although it had been long suspected that such a group existed, it was finally confirmed in 1984 when a set of documents emerged showing the establishment of Majestic-12 by President Truman following the recommendations of senior science administrator Vannevar Bush, and James Forrestal, the U.S. Secretary of Defense. The im-petus for setting up such a committee was to investigate and possibly utilize both scientific and genetic material that had been found in the wreckage of the crashed alien spacecraft near Roswell. MJ-12 maintained links with other clandestine U.S. organizations such as the ultra-secretive NSC 5412/2 Special Group and the CIA's Office of National Estimates. It was suppos-edly something that was connected with Majestic-12, which had caused the cattle mutilations; whatever it was, it appeared to be something that the U.S. Government was secretly working on out in the New Mexico deserts. Since the 1980s, purported Majestic-12 documents have surfaced from time to time detailing covert meetings, but it has to be pointed out that nearly all of this documentation is of questionable provenance and has materialized in unusual circumstances. Indeed, the FBI has investigated and found the documentary origin to be suspicious. So, although there have been alleged reports relating to the creation of hybrid beings created from both human and alien DNA under the aegis of Majestic-12—perhaps, some argue, the true origin of the skinwalker—the hard evidence remains hazy and speculative. That is not to say, however, that *something* isn't going on out in the New Mexico/Arizona deserts—something that might not necessarily be of this world and that indeed might be being manipulated by clandestine sectors of the United States government.

The emphasis for the skinwalker legend seemed to move from the realm of the supernatural toward the secretly scientific. It seemed to have more to do with UFOs and mad scientists than it did with witches and demons. All the same, the old Native American folklore beliefs still persisted.

The two theories concerning extra-terrestrials and the supernatural came together in what has become known as "the Skinwalker Ranch." The Ranch is also known as the Sherman Ranch, and lies to the southeast of Ballard, Utah. The property is made up of roughly 480 acres. Although the ranch had been the focus of Native American folklore, the site was brought to popular attention by the *Salt Lake City, Utah Desert News* and later the *Las Vegas Mercury*, which is a publication for what it calls "the alternative society." The articles for the *Mercury* were written by George Knapp, who subsequently went on to write a book with Colm Kelleher in which they state that the ranch was acquired by the National Institute for Discovery Science (a privately-funded Las Vegas organization set up to study paranormal phenomena) for the purpose of investigating curious phenomena that allegedly occurred there. They particularly focused on the experiences of Tom Gorman, who had owned the ranch in the 1990s.

The ranch lies on the very edge of Uintah County, bordering the Ute Indian Reservation. The Utes have a story about a very ancient pueblo that once existed there, which had become home to a band of "witchy people."

However, Knapp and Kellaher seemed to be more interested in UFO activity, and the site was quickly dubbed "the UFO ranch." However, even with a more "alien-based" approach, not even *they* could ignore the tribal traditions of the Utes. For example, they mention a place not far from the ranch called Dark Canyon, where there were extremely ancient petroglyphs on the rock face, which was believed to show a skinwalker. To this place, skinwalkers could be summoned by Ute and Navajo magicians.

Experiments were conducted on the ranch to hunt down the skinwalkers (either supernatural or extraterrestrial) in 1996, and there was still some interest in the ranch (with surveillance cameras still rolling) in 2004. However, even Knapp admitted that very little had occurred. He left the National Institute of Discovery Science in 2004, and the investigators were forced to admit that, although there had been certain unexplained phenomena throughout the years, there were difficulties in obtaining evidence consistent with scientific publication. The skinwalkers, whether they came from an ancient pueblo, from the Dark Canyon, or from outer space, just hadn't shown themselves.

So what lies out there in the Arizona/New Mexico deserts? Something older than time? Something created by Native American witchcraft? A creature secretly created by the American government for some sinister purpose? Something from beyond the stars? Even today, the mysterious skinwalker proves as elusive as ever.

CALIFORNIA

People say said that the dead can often return from the grave for a number of reasons. The medieval church, for example, explicitly suggested that they came back to warn, admonish, and punish for these reasons only. They were not permitted to engage in excess physical harm to those whom they encountered, largely because they were the Blessed Dead, those whom God allowed back into the world for a limited time in order to complete what they left undone or to benefit their descendants in some way. Earlier tales, however, spoke of cadavers returning to be troublesome, stealing drink and food, and to inflict physical harm on the living. Some stories even said that the dead actually hated the living and would do them harm if and when they could. There was also the idea that the dead, having lain in the cold earth for a period of time, would leech heat and vitality off the living, making them like a parasite. In some texts, the dead are compared to ivy, which attaches itself to a healthy tree and draws off the good from it.

The comparison with the plant or vegetable worlds is not simply a coincidental one, for in some cultures, the dead can physically attach themselves to living humans (a bit like leeches) and draw off the good from them in

the way that a parasite might do. For example, in Czech folklore, such creatures—it is not clear whether they are the dead or simply some demonic
form of life—can often be found clinging to the interiors of old and perhaps
abandoned houses. Such creatures are often known as Ipeni Duse (clinging
souls), and are considered to be extremely dangerous. Descriptions of them
vary; some depict them as tiny monkey-like things, hanging on the inside
of the roofs of falling buildings, others as a massive shadowy insect, like a
gigantic armor-plated wasp, others still as some gelatinous being oozing
along a high overhang the building. When anyone enters the ruin, the Thing
drops down, connecting with the person's body by means of a stinger-like
spike or by suckers on the ends of its fingers. Once it is attached, there is
little chance of it being removed, and it will cling on, drawing all the vitality
from its host. In some cases, it will seize the victim about the neck and upper torso, clinging on while it leeches off vitality through its toes. This sce-
nario is often represented in the sea-faring Greek myth of the Old Man of
the Sea. In this tale, a sailor is called upon to carry an old man onto his back
across an obstacle such as a fast-flowing river or inlet on a beach. No sooner
has he hoisted the old fellow on to his back than the Old Man is revealed
to be a minor demon, which forces the sailor to carry him about while the
creature leeches all the man's energy from him. Thus, his good deed turns
into a living nightmare. Just exactly what the creature is—whether it is one
of the dead or a being of the Underworld—is not clear, but it is vampiric and
incredibly dangerous.

The idea of the clinging soul is found in a number of other cultures
besides the Czechs and Greeks. Even as far away as Tibet and Sikkim, these
beings often cling to the shadowy places on the insides of remote lamaser-
ies, feeding off the bad thoughts of the lamas, which float upward. These are
thought to be the souls of evil men in the area of the monastery who have
gravitated as evil entities toward its walls. In India, such beings are thought
to dwell in damp, dark caves and will attack any trespasser who seeks to rest
there. They are also known in some mountain areas of Germany and Italy,
particularly in the Brocken and Hertz areas of northern Germany where
they are considered to be especially active. And they are even known in

some of the remoter areas of the Ozark Mountains in America. It is even said that in these places, they were known to the Native Americans, long before the coming of the white man, but that the mountaineers also know of them and are wary of them. They are sometimes equated with mighty insects such as *Ulagu* (the name is a Cherokee word for "boss" or "leader") that are said to dwell in the darkness of the deepest recesses of the Nantahala Gorge in the remote areas of western North Carolina. These are indeed giant insect species that defy any classification and are said to be vampiric in nature. In some legends, they are said to be the souls (or the "clinging souls") of people who died in ancient times and who cannot reach the afterlife. Instead, they remain in this one, preying on the living and drawing energy and sustenance from them.

Sometimes, these "clinging souls" can enter a house undetected, find some shadowy place, and simply draw the good from everything and from the people who live there. In this respect, it might closely resemble the shadow things to be found in New York. In the Ozarks, they are considered to be "hants" and "gatherers" and sometimes "old timey things," which sometime drift down from the mountain graveyards and into the cabins of some of the mountain people. There they lie in the dark in some remote place and draw the good of the house into them. Either that, or they can attack the inhabitants of the cabin as they lie and sleep, enveloping them like some great mass of shadow and drawing whatever vitality they have from them. There is little that the mountain people can do to drive these things away, although certain "granny women" and "goomer men" living in the high mountains sometimes have power over them and can keep them at bay simply by burning herbs. If they are left unchecked, they grow stronger—feeding off living people. There are stories from Ireland, from times long ago, of such creatures that entered the cottages of the peasantry and were difficult to cast out—even by a priest. A story from the village of Blacklion in County Cavan, Ireland, tells of one of these things, mistakenly invited in by one of the daughters of the house, which creates terrible mayhem and draws the vitality from the family. In desperation, the man of the house seeks out a retired priest who lives nearby and who knows about exorcism.

This priest is able to finally drive the thing out, but only after a ferocious struggle, and he told the family that it is right that they contacted him when they did. If they had left it any longer, he revealed, it would have taken nine priests and nine bishops to get rid of the entity. This was how quickly such things took root in a dwelling. Although the being is usually dismissed as a poltergeist, some variants of the story attest that the family within the cottage experienced an intense lethargy—it may have been a form of "clinging soul" or "gatherer," which came from an old iron-age earthworks nearby.

In the previous Irish example above, the idea of the plant world is used once more. The priest in the story spoke of the entity "taking root," like a weed or something similar. And in some parts of the world, vampiric entities may have been viewed in such a way. They were sometimes equated with a form of *genius loci*—a particular spirit that attached itself to a place. In other sections of this book, we explore how certain forces might be identified with wells and hollows, and this once again reiterated that idea. The spirit was native to the area in which it was found—indeed, it seemed to *grow* in that particular place. And of course, such spirits were often hostile toward the human interlopers who came into their area. Therefore, one had to be careful if he or she slept in certain places, such as old mounds or to ancient stones or certain trees in case such localities contained such a spirit. Such things may have been ghosts of a sort, or they may have been ancient forces that had existed there since earliest times. And, although not all of them were vampiric, some were and could sometimes draw either blood or energies from those who slept near to them. Indeed, because such entities were the spirits of the place, they became in the popular mind, the *actual* place itself. They lived within (and as part of) the standing stones, the old mounds, or the trees that stood or grew within the area or upon the very site. This gave all of these largely inanimate objects a kind of virulent life of their own and those who ventured too close to them risked much. Those who settled close by or who perhaps camped near to them might fall under the baleful influence, for like the "clinging souls" they were often both hostile and greedy toward human beings. Like the animals that prowled about

the landscape (especially in earlier and perhaps more dangerous times), they sometimes viewed weak and largely vulnerable humans as their prey.

The linkage in perception between these ancient spirits and the world of growth and nature is important. In many ancient cultures, such forces were actually *thought of* as part of the natural world and were spoken about in such terms. We have already mentioned that it was sometimes as if the spirit was actually *rooted* in such a place, that it emerged or *grew* out of the landscape itself. This irrevocably linked it to the stones, trees, and plants of the land all around it. So, it is not uncommon in some parts of the world to find that the very rocks and plants themselves are connected to hostile intelligences that were inimical toward humans.

In *A Frontier Land*, which is a description of British military service in Northern India during the early 1900s, R.B. Gilbertson, describes a trek along the edge of the Himalayan foothills. During the course of their march they came to a small, dark valley along a mountain trail, where the track dipped down to a gloomy river many feet below. The valley was very shadowy and had an "uneasy feel" to it, according to Gilbertson, and even as it sent something of a chill through his being. What was particularly unsettling, however, was a large and twisted tree growing out of the rockface just above the track. Although the growth appeared to be dead, Gilbertson notes that there seemed to be a feeling of malignant life emanating from it—even a kind of *intelligence,* as if the Thing was *aware* of their approach. Logic told him, of course, that this couldn't be true, and yet he *sensed* its almost evil intent. Some of the stick-like branches stretched down from the rock face and onto the dusty trail along which they had to pass, but most of it hung from a rocky ledge, just above the height of a man, like some great bird's nest. The whole growth practically *oozed* menace. The bearers with the party stalled and refused to go any further—refusing to pass beneath the Thing and urging the British soldiers with them not to do so, either. This was a bad spirit, they explained, the essence of which pervaded the entire valley beyond and kept it dark and gloomy. There were no animals that lived in the valley, because the dark spirit had drank the life force from them; Gilbertson did notice that although they had been observing (and sometimes shooting) buzzards for a few days previously, none wheeled in the valley nor did he see any obvious traces of animal life. If they passed by the Thing, the bearers assured him, something terrible would befall them all and they would die—the goodness sucked from their bodies by the strange plant on the ledge. And looking at it, Gilbertson said that he could readily believe them. In the end, the expedition went by another route, high up into the foothills and by-passing that particular valley. Whether this was indeed a kind of vampire or, at the very least, the dark spirit of the place, Gilbertson had no way of knowing, but its memory stayed with him for many years afterward. It might initially appear strange as to why a simple leafless bush should make such an impression on a British military officer, but perhaps Gilbertson responded to the sight of the eerie growth at some deep, almost subconscious level and that it affected him in this way.

The idea of such ancient evil growths is not confined to any borders, however. Some of these appear in legends that come from the Spanish West of the continent and are associated with some of the early Spanish explorations along the coast of California.

From the 1600s onward, Spain took an intense interest in the Western Coast of America. Initially, the Spanish had concerned themselves with areas slightly further south in Mexico and Peru, but gradually, as they grew more confident of their power along these coasts, they began to sail along what is now the Western American coastline, although many of them did not land there. Those who did heard wonderful stories from local natives of mines further inland where pure gold was extracted, and of cities, the streets of which were lined with precious stones. They also heard horror stories of strange tree-gods who lived deep in the jungles—trees that could move of their own volition and that could eat men or draw their energies from them until they were dead. However, it was the idea of fabulously rich gold mines and jewelled cities that intrigued the Spaniards and drew them to the western coast of the continent. They dismissed the stories of the demon tree-creatures as legends—God would protect them against such unholy things if they had to venture into the interior! However, the coastal area with its hilly grasslands and deep, wooded canyons and valleys had few natural ports that would attract colonists or provide a base for an expedition further inland. Therefore, such expeditions tended to be limited until roughly the beginning of the 18th century. Even so, tales of strange forces that dwelt in the interior had percolated down from the 16th, and these included some accounts of certain vampiric growths.

During the expedition to the California coast, led by the conquistador Sebastian Vizcaino in 1602, one of his commanders split off from the main expedition and ventured inland. Legend says that somewhere in the Californian interior, they encountered a group of Native Americans who worshipped a monstrous vine-wrapped tree, tucked away in a cave-like cleft in the rock. This was said to be an ancient god that had existed in the region since before the coming of man, and which required sacrifice every so often. The thing drank the blood of those who were offered to it by wrapping their bodies in its rope-like vines through which it drank, in the same way that a spider might wrap its victim. Once it had it had a grasp on the unfortunate, it drew blood and energy from his or her body, leaving it a wasted husk. The Spaniards were taken to the cavern-like home of the thing where it was said that human bones, bleaching in the sun, were stacked as high as a man's waist. It is even said that several of the men fell foul of this awful thing and that they had been drained of both their blood and vitality. What became of this "god" is unknown, but although subsequent English expeditions heard stories of it, none actually saw it. The creature now seemed only to exist in legend, although the memory of it was still extant. However, there was no longer any mention of (or evidence of) continued worship. And similar legends persist, stretching down from early Spanish times until almost the present day. In these earliest times, the stories of pagan vegetative "gods" were spread by the coming to California by Catholic Christianity and the arrival of Spanish monks.

The real period of the Spanish missions in California, however, lay between 1769 and 1823, and were designed to spread the Christian (Catholic) faith among the Native American tribes. The missions were a mixture of religious and military outposts, and were actually the first real attempt to colonize the Pacific Coast on behalf of a European power. The fathers who arrived brought with them a formidable faith, but they also brought their own superstitions and an absolute abhorrence of "pagan evil."

There had already been a chain of Jesuit missions along the Californian coast stretching down as far as New Spain (Baja, California, and Mexico), but in January 1767, the Spanish king Charles III, expelled them and handed total authority to the Viceroy of New Spain, Jose de Galvez. De Galvez moved swiftly to install the Franciscans as the main missionaries in the region. They were led by Fray Junipero Serra, who arrived from Mexico to take charge of the missions on March 12th, 1768. The *padres* who traveled with him either closed or consolidated most of the existing former Jesuit missions and established the mission of San Fernando Rey de Espana de Velicata and the nearby Visita de Presentacion in 1769. Fray Junipero and Governor Gaspar de la Portola arrived from Mexico City to found the missions at San Diego and the presidio (a Spanish fortified base) at Monterey respectively, with Fray Junipero taking effective control of the missions. He immediately issued orders for the Christianization of the local Indian tribes, and during this period, the Spanish fathers heard many horrific stories of pagan rituals and gods in the interior of the country. Some of these were undoubtedly exaggerated and were told to shock and alarm the fathers, but some were said to have an element of truth and have made their way down to the present day in the form of Californian legends.

One of the stories that Fray Junipero heard was that of a great blood-drinking, man-eating flower, which sometimes spread itself like a carpet across the valley floors, concealed among the greases in order to trap the unwary traveler. Attached to the center of this flower were long, and rope-like vines that could restrain the victim if he or she attempted to escape. The vines themselves may have had the power to leech blood from the prisoner as they drew him or her back toward the hungry center of the great flower. Such deadly and vampiric growths lay in the shadows of rocky overhangs or under trees or in the deep woodlands. They were flowers of the dark, lurking in the shadows and waiting for blood. Perhaps such stories contained echoes of the old god plants worshipped by the Native Americans. Perhaps they were something else. Maybe somewhere out there in the Californian hinterland there really *was* something that perhaps had the attributes of, say, a huge Venus Flytrap, and could consume both animals and men with a deadly ease. The Indians claimed to have lost horses and cattle to the plant and showed Fray Junipero pieces of desiccated skin, which they claimed were from animals that the plant-thing had devoured. They even offered to show him a remote valley in which one of these plants was said to have thrived, but the holy man refused to go. Did he believe the Indians' stories, or did he know something that perhaps many of us don't? If the plants existed back in the mid-1700s, they do not seem to exist any more.

Fray Junipero also heard tales of another type of plant like creature from the Native Americans—a creature which also had vampiric qualities. This growth existed in the dark of a large cave high up in the mountains and was apparently like a giant mushroom of a great fungus ball, lurking in the shadows, waiting for victims. Again, it was considered by the local Native Americans to be some sort of pagan god. Such a creature, said the Native American legends, was a being that had been left over from the very foundation of the world, and had existed in the cathedral-like cavern since before the memory of man. It may very well have been the last of its kind, for at one time what is now the Eastern American seaboard was covered by them, and they grew in large forests there. This one, however, kept to the shadows. No Native American dared approach it, for, like the giant open flowers under their rocky overhangs, it had large tendrils, and thick whips, with which it could capture its prey and draw it in. The creature, Fray Junipero was told, fed in this fashion, absorbing its prey and digesting it at will, drawing the blood from it first. However, like many vampiric entities, such a creature feared the light, for the skies had been slightly different when it thrived on earth in the primal time. Therefore, it could be driven back by Native Americans bearing flaming torches, although few had tried. As with the giant Venus Flytrap-like blossom, the Natives offered to take Fray Junipero up into the mountains and show him the cave of the creature. Once again, the holy man refused. The reason that he gave was that he would not dignify such a pagan thing with his presence by going to see it. Although the Native Americans told Fray Junipero the location of the cavern in the mountains, it has since been lost. Even the name of the mountain range where the cavern was located has been forgotten, although there are some who say that the cavern lay somewhere in the Santa Cruz Mountains near Monterey. There are also tales that rock falls in these mountains blocked off a number of caves and caverns and that may include the one to which the Native Americans offered to take Junipero. The thing may still wait down there in the dark beneath tons of fallen rock.

In fact, tales of *something* living in a mountain cave, obscured by a rock fall, continued long after the Spanish fathers and conquistadores were long gone from California. There were other legends—namely that there were gold and silver mines located somewhere in the hills and mountains of southern California. These were said to be the workings of Native Americans and of the Spanish and there were rich lodes of precious metals that had been mined in places such as the Santa Susanna Mountains. These rumors were prevalent enough to have mining companies scour the area into the early 1900s, more than 50 years after the great California Gold Rush. As late as the 1890s, company agents and mining experts were showing up in places such as Stockton and Sacramento, intent on looking for claims (and lost mines) in the hills. Spurious maps began to circulate in a number of mining towns showing the locations of such whispered lodes—places such as a fabulous mine in the Pico Blanco Mountain country around Little Sur where in former times both Native Americans and Spanish settlers had led their burros up into the hills along winding trails to return with the animals laden down with precious metals.

But if tales of vanished mines were prevalent, so were stories of strange and lightless places, far underground where perhaps old things survived from some former time. In the late 1800s, a story was told in Stockton concerning two half–Native American prospectors, Henry Chee and Jacob Cahee, who had been hunting for gold in the Cascade Range of Northern California. They had accidentally stumbled into a vast cave system and, trying to find their way out again, they had encountered, on the shores of a vast sub-terranean lake, something they initially thought was a huge monster, rising out of the water. However, upon closer inspection, it turned out to be the dragon prow of a large Viking ship (perhaps a war-ship), which had become lodged in the rock. The men wished to investigate further, but the air in the caves was bad and they were already starting to feel unwell. They managed to find their way back into Stockton where the news of their strange and eerie find quickly spread. How had a Viking ship got there? Its existence, if it were to be proved, would be one of the archaeological finds of the century, and would shed new light on the early days of America. However, neither prospector had kept any record as to where the cave might have been, and subsequent searches of the area of its possible location proved completely fruitless. The tale was simply dismissed as another tall story from the Cas-cades, but was it? Maybe somewhere far below the mountain lies a strange interior world in which lies a wrecked Viking ship from centuries ago. Such cave systems do exist, some of which have been used by pirates such as Hip-polyte de Bouchard, who attacked and burned the Alta Californian capital of Monterey in November 1818. During his piracy, Bouchard was continu-ally harassed by both American and Spanish warships and had several hide-outs along the coast, some of which were large caves that stretched far back into the landscape. Some of these were used as storehouses for weaponry and supplies. In an account allegedly given by one of Bouchard's men, the pirate had used a massive cave system near a set of low hills close to the coast to store weapons and cannons for a proposed attack on the fortress at El Castillo and the isolated inland missions of San Juan Bautista and San Antonio. While looking for a way overland to attack El Castillo, Bouchard and his men came on the entrance to a great cavern that seemed to stretch back into the hills through a series of connecting tunnels, which linked a massive cave system. And, it seemed to stretch *downward* toward the very core of the Earth. The pirates decided to use the upper part of the cavern as a storehouse while they searched for the overland route. However, even the great Bouchard was frightened to venture any further down into the dark-ness of the lower levels, for there seemed to be movement down there in the shadows. There were sounds, such as the rustlings of dead leaves and the buccaneers were convinced that *something* down there was aware of them and meant them no good. Many of the tunnels were choked with weed and rock and the pirates did not wish to clear them. Using the stored weaponry, Bouchard captured the fortress by using a stratagem. However, the eerie sensations of the great coastal cavern remained with the pirates for many years afterward. The notion of an *intelligence* coupled with the leafy rustling sound down there in the dark was enough to send distinct shivers along the spines of even the most hardened of seafarers.

Similar stories have come from various parts of California, one of the more famous being the tale of Alfred K. Clark (known locally as "Uncle Al") in the 1930s. Around 1910, Clark—a veteran of the Civil War—headed West, greatly fascinated with tales of lost Spanish gold and the hidden mines of California. Backed by a local doctor, Clarence H. Pearce, he began prospecting in the Big Sur area, traveling as far as Pico Blanco. He befriended the Little Sur Indians, who told him of a fantastic realm far below the earth where terrible things dwelt. Guided by some Native Americans, Clarke was taken in confidence to the supposed entrance to this awful underground world. It had been blocked off by a major rock fall, and was all but impassable. This was where Dr. Pearce came in. Clark convinced the doctor that a vast lode of silver lay down there, and if only the rock could be cleared away, he could get at it. Pearce provided men and equipment, but after several months of back-breaking labor, nothing was found. There were more falls further down in the tunnel and these had to be cleared away. Furthermore, the workmen—mainly Native Americans—were getting jittery, claiming something was watching them as they worked. There was a disagreement between Pearce and Clark and, disillusioned, the Doctor pulled out of the enterprise. The workmen packed up and left, but Clark continued to work in the remote place, becoming something of a hermit and an eccentric. The years went by and little was heard from him—from time to time, he would turn up in various towns to buy his supplies, but he claimed to be working in the mountains, looking for the lost silver mine.

Then, in 1930, when he was more than 90 years old, "Uncle Al" sud-denly showed up at the house of a friend, Al Greer, in a very dishevelled and excited state. He told Greer and his family a strange tale. He had been work-ing in an abandoned Spanish silver mine in the Pico Blanco region when his pick had gone through a wall into a mysterious underground cavern. He had entered a huge cathedral-like place, the limits of which he couldn't de-termine in the pervading darkness. Thinking that this was indeed a silver-working, he had explored further, moving slowly and carefully because he had little light. From rocky overhangs above his head hung great "icicles," which looked "like glass." Eerie flowers that seemed to be made out of stone sprouted from the nearby rocks and walls around him, and some of them even seemed to crumble at his touch. Scattered just beyond the brilliance of the light were a number of small shiny stones that looked as if they might be nuggets of silver. Further along in the darkness of the great cavern, he came across a bubbling stream in which a number of small fish were swim-ming. They were so pale that they were almost transparent, and it appeared as if they had no eyes. Away in the dark around him, Uncle Al was sure that there was someone or *something* else—that he was not alone in this lightless underground world with its glass stalactites and blind fish. From time to time, he was sure that something moved—a low, whispery kind of sound, like the movement of dry paper. He thought too that something long and thin, like a white rope, moved along the ground in his direction and was then withdrawn. What struck him about the place was that the dry stone floor beneath his feet and the walls of the cavern were pitted with Indian mortars and had been marked in some kind of unknown pigment with some curious designs of which he could make no sense. It was, he said, almost as if ancient Indians had been working the place into some sort of underground temple. But was this a temple where a god of some sort still lived? The further he went into the darkness, the sense of being watched grew more. Of course, he may have been led astray by the echoes in the vast place, but he couldn't be sure. A feeling of menace increased the deeper he ventured into this subterranean world, and Uncle Al suddenly thought the better of his adventure. He made his way back towards the entrance and, as he did so, he became aware of a slithering noise, as if heavy cords were being pulled back across the uneven ground. He made it out of that lightless world and out into the more wholesome sunlight, but the experience had shaken him greatly.

This is the chilling tale that the delirious old man told his astonished listeners, and it bolstered the idea of a strange lost world, which was something that Clark hadn't really seen. But there may well be another explanation behind the strange tale. The area around Pico Blanco is said to boast the highest concentrations of dolomite limestone anywhere on the coast. This is a highly porous limestone that lends itself to the carvings of underground rivers. The cavern might have been created by a prehistoric flood in the area leading to a subterranean confluence of several small streams and the South Fork of the Little Sur River, which disappears underground at several locations and re-emerges a few miles each time. The albino fish that Clark described could be troglobites, blind fish that lose their pigmentation due to the amount of time that they spend in the darkness. The "stone blooms" that he also touched might have been what geologists refer to as gypsum flowers, petal-like discharges of a substance known as selenite. The "icicles" might well be stalactites and stalagmites, formations of mineralized water, which are a common feature of underground environments. And although the shiny rocks that Clark's light picked out might not have been nuggets of silver, they might have been rocks containing flecks of silver ore—or they might have been some other mineral. The suspected movements in the dark of the place are not too easy to explain away.

After his startling discovery, he spent his days keeping inquisitive strangers from finding the entrance to the strange underground place, but he died before he could reveal its exact location to Al Greer. The latter searched the Pico Blanco region for many years afterward to see if he could find the entrance that Uncle Al had spoken of, but without any success.

The 19th century and the early- to mid-20th century showed a slightly renewed interest in the ancient vampiric plant-gods of the Native Californians. Perhaps this was due to the explorations in South America and the alleged finds of both exotic and dangerous plant species there. Some of these may have been tall tales from the southern continent, but they served to fire the public imagination in no uncertain terms. Thrilling stories of adventurers fighting through the Amazonian rain forests and fighting off huge carnivorous plants, whether simply fiction or supposedly true, appealed to readers everywhere, and it soon became an accepted fact that such things lurked deep in the jungle gloom, devouring or drinking the blood of those who came within their reach. There were stories of gigantic, prehistoric mushroom-like growths found in isolated clearings that enveloped adventurers who ventured too close to them.

Public imagination on this topic was also fired by stories of a giant man-eating "tree," which was allegedly found in Madagascar. This was supposedly a plant that not only ate its victims, but also drew both the blood and vital fluids from them. The actual origins of this story may lie in the *nepenthes rajah* plant, which is actually found in Borneo and Malaysia, and is a distant relative of the plants that are found in the Mount Roriama area. This plant, while it does not eat humans, can certainly eat larger birds.

In the jungles of Madagascar, a German explored named Carl Liche supposedly witnessed a frightful ceremony carried out by the Mkodo people of the area. He claimed he witnessed a human sacrifice to a great tree-like thing, which lived in the jungle and partly resembled a giant pineapple hung about with great tendrils. A woman of the Mkodo tribe was offered to the plant which sucked and pulled at her, crushing her and then digesting her. Liche's account, which was published in the *South Australian Register* (one of the first Colonial newspapers in South Australia), is so full of exaggerated and purple prose that it might have come from the pages of H.P. Lovecraft. However, it's probable that the whole thing was just a fantasy or a joke, because this is the only piece of writing, either fictional or geographical, that Liche penned. In fact, there are questions as to whether he ever existed, and if the whole account was written by a prankster. No further reference to the Mkodo people has been found, and no other tribe in Madagascar has ever heard of them, which is astonishing. Liche claimed to have "discovered" these people and they allowed him to witness their most secret rites; one would have to think that, given such unprecedented access to a relatively unknown people, he could have flooded anthropological journals with valuable material. But no—after news of the "discovery" of the tribe, Liche becomes immediately silent and writes nothing more.

The idea of a man-eating vampiric tree gained widespread currency in the popular imagination and, in 1924, Chase Osborn, governor of Michigan, wrote a book entitled *Madagascar, Land of the Man-Eating Tree*. The work was a mish-mash of fantastic and dubious tales. Osborn claimed that all the tribes on the island knew about the tree, as did the missionaries who came there, but they kept it a secret. The governor's account was accepted as true, and a number of readers drew parallels between this horror and that which was mentioned by the Spanish priests in early California. Could this be the same sort of hideous growth?

In 1955, however, the respected American-German science writer Willy Ley suggested in a book entitled *Salamanders and Other Wonders,* that the whole thing had been an elaborate hoax and that the Mkodo people, Carl Liche, and the vampire man-eating tree itself were all fictitious. Nevertheless, a number of people refused to accept this, and the terrible growth remained part of popular legend. And moreover, it was believed that perhaps such plants also lay within the American hinterland, perhaps in places such as California. Believers pointed to yet another work written in 1887 by the hugely prolific American author James William Buel. Buel had written on a number of subjects, but is best known for his works on ape men (of the Tarzan variety) and savage lands. In his book, which dealt with alleged natural curiosities before and since the Deluge (the great Flood), Buel mentioned the *Ya-te-veo* ("Now I see you") plant, which was supposed to bear some resemblance to the vampiric, man-eating Madagascar tree. He argued that the plant was to be found in areas of both Central and South America, with perhaps variants of it to be found on the North American continent. These plants usually captured birds and small animals, drank their blood, and ate them, but they might attack humans as well. These things had, according to Buel, existed since long before the Deluge and were incredibly deadly. A number of writers have subsequently pointed out that these prehistoric plant-things may not have existed anywhere outside Buel's own imagination. Nonetheless, this didn't stop some people asserting that they truly dwelt somewhere on the Western American coast—probably in California.

The stories still exist today, and there are still some people who believe that somewhere in the dark depths of some underground world—maybe even somewhere near Monterey—such a vampiric growth may exist. Nowadays, however, they are not classed as supernatural gods, but as cryptids, some strange form of life that exists somewhere outside regular natural orders that remains more or less hidden from general human observation. And, despite this slightly more scientific classification, such plants are often still seen as being inimical toward humankind.

And the idea mentioned earlier of a huge vampiric fungus also hadn't gone away. In the natural world, some of the predatory fungi actually captured, exsanguinated, and then devoured their victims.

Tales of monstrous growths have been with us for almost as long as we can remember. Some of them are deadly, some of them are allegedly blood-drinking. Although gigantic vampiric growths are yet to be found, who knows what lies out there in some subterranean cavern in Western America, or waits rustling in the darkened forests there?

WYOMING

Although we tend of think of Wyoming as part of "the Wild West," the state is perhaps one of the most mysterious, and yet, the least explored, areas in America. Despite its size, it is the second least-densely populated state of all the 50 states. The name of the state allegedly came from a Delaware Indian word meaning "land of alternating mountains and valleys," and this does indeed describe the geographical landscape. Two thirds of the state is covered by mountains and is bordered by South Dakota, Montana, and Colorado. In spite of this wild terrain, there is evidence that there have been people living in the region for thousands of years. In the Big Horn Mountains, there is a large medicine wheel that dates back for almost 1,000 years. Various Indian tribes have controlled these lands, such as the Arapaho, the Bannock, Shoshone, Ute, Blackfeet, Crow, Kiowa, Gros Ventre, Nez Perce, Sioux, and Cheyenne.

The region was also known to Spanish explorers, though only in legend. Leading an expedition into what is now Alabama in the mid 1540s, the conquistador Hernando de Soto heard old Indian tales of a land made up of canyons and mountains where strange beings lived in caves, deep gullies, and just below ground level. The creatures were cannibalistic in nature, supposedly eating flesh and drinking blood. They were the descendants of an ancient race that had once lived on earth before Man. Some descriptions said they were some sort of giant, others that they were "little people," and others that they were of the same height as ordinary people. They were counted as extremely savage and were fond of the dark, hunting only at night. De Soto listened to these stories but largely dismissed them as old Indian fancies. He didn't bother to investigate, but his expedition passed into what is now northern Alabama and onto Arkansas and Georgia. However, the stories continued, and other Spanish explorers through the region, such as Francisco Vasquez de Coronado, also heard of these strange cave-dwelling people in a land of canyons and peaks.

In April 1803, the United States purchased a massive tract of land (828,000 square miles) that was known as "Louisiana Territory" from France—the famous Louisiana Purchase. Great areas of the Purchase were largely unknown, and had never been properly explored by either the French or the Spanish before them. President Jefferson therefore requested $2,500 from Congress in order to finance an expedition into this mysterious region and to provide a detailed account of what was there. To lead such an expedition, he picked two army officers, Captain Meriwether Lewis and Lieutenant William Clark.

The "Corps of Discovery Expedition" (better known as the Lewis and Clark Expedition) was the first transcontinental expedition of the United States and comprised more than 33 military men. The purpose of the expedition was two-fold, both scientific and commercial. They were to study the Indian tribes, flora, and fauna of the area and to find a direct water route to the west coast, which could be used for trading purposes. The Expedition formally began on May 21st, 1804, when the men marched out of their camp in St. Louis, Missouri, and began to follow the route of the Missouri River. Their trek would take them through Montana and Idaho, and eventually into Oregon. The Expedition lasted from 1804 to 1806, and although it was a reasonable success, Meriwether Lewis did not survive long afterward and died in 1809.

One of the members of the Expedition was John Colter. Like both Lewis and Clark, Colter hailed from Virginia. Although famous as a member of the Lewis and Clark Expedition, Colter is also famous for conducting his own expeditions between 1807 and 1808 into the area that is now Wyoming. He is said to have been the first white man to see the Yellowstone thermal springs and the famous geysers, although his accounts were dismissed as mere fiction by most people. However, his accounts of the strange, broken landscape, which he claimed to have encountered, inspired other explorers such as Robert Stuart to investigate the region. Stuart was a partner of John Jacob Astor, who headed the American Fur Company and had been instrumental in the founding of the Fort Astoria trading station in Oregon Territory. In 1812, he led a party of five men into South Pass in the Rocky Mountains and into southwest Wyoming. This would form the basis of what became known as the Oregon Trail and also the California and Mormon Trails. Although Stuart had kept a meticulous diary, which he presented to Astor and also to President James Madison, the trail into Wyoming was not used for many years and trappers and traders followed a more northerly and more difficult route, which led through the Bitterroot Mountains in Montana.

It was not until the legendary mountain man Jedediah Smith—"Old 'diah"—along with Thomas Fitzpatrick began the famous coast-to-coast trek in 1824 that the South Pass was "rediscovered" and became used as a route. In 1832, a French military officer named Captain Benjamin de Bonneville took a caravan of 20 wagons and 110 men over the pass. This was the first of the wagon trains to cross the mountains down to the Sweetwater River in Wyoming Territory. In 1850, another mountain man, Jim Bridger began to explore the region, traveling as far as Yellowstone and discovering what became known as the Bridger Pass through the mountains. This would later become a route for the Union Pacific Railroad in 1868.

One of things that had been discovered in the mountains prior to the 1860s were veins of precious metals, including small quantities of gold. The big resource found in the area, however, was coal. The Homestead Act of 1862 brought a number of farmers and ranchers to the region, and began to establish a pattern of settlement on what had been once open land. Settlers from everywhere flooded into Wyoming and established themselves in communities that were isolated but developing. Unlike some other States and regions, Wyoming did not have an underlying core of settlement by the European powers, but usually relied on immigrants from elsewhere in America. The folklore of the region, while certainly containing European elements, was also tinged with the old Indian beliefs from earlier times.

Once again, there were stories resurfacing among the new settlers that de Soto and the other conquistadors had heard as they passed by the area. The geographical features of the landscape gave a sinister color to such tales. This was a region of deep caves and gullies, of remote and hidden valleys and of twisting canyons where anything could shelter. There were hills that appeared to be honeycombed with caverns and tunnels, which seemed to lead down to unknown realms and sinister lairs where all manner of things were said to lurk.

Chief among these traditions was the idea of malignant dwarves who lived in the bowels of the earth. It is thought that they had lived among the caverns and gullies of Wyoming for at least 9,000 years. The Nez Perce called them *Its'te-ya-ha*, while the Arapaho and the Umatilla of Oregon referred to them as "Stick Indians." There was also a legend that they were another form of man, or that they had once been men but had died and become something else. They were said to be incredibly belligerent, and, according to ancient Spanish tales, both devoured flesh and drank blood when the mood was upon them. The common expression among many of the Native American peoples was, "Beware of the little folk!"

Apart from legends that reached the ears of the Spanish expeditions further south, stories of these deadly dwarves were related in 1804 to the Lewis and Clark expedition. Meriweather Lewis had led a party of 10 men along the Vermillion River in what is now South Dakota to negotiate with a tribe of Wichiyena Sioux. During the course of these negotiations, he was told of a curious mountain nearby, which was infested with the dangerous little people who lived in caves and tunnels and killed anyone who came near them and drank their blood. They offered to take Lewis with them to show them the mountain where these dwarves lived and the explorer went with them. Lewis would later write that these little people were "deavils" (devils) with large round heads and very alert to intrusions into their territory. They were also said to live in caves and in the dark, hence, their eyes were very big. They carried very long spears or arrows, which they could aim over long distances, and kill anyone who approached their hill or mound. It's unclear as to whether Lewis saw a mountain, a hill, or perhaps an artificial mound.

Although the little people were extremely fierce and vampiric, they were also extremely old and could impart great wisdom if they so chose. The Crow, who referred to them as the Nirumbee or the Awwakkule, claimed that they were an old race who had lived in the world for thousands of years and had accumulated great knowledge in the process, which they passed on to certain individuals, usually communicating with them in dreams. They were, said Crow folklore, great magicians and had ways of healing and poisoning that were unknown to humans. They were also vampiric, using blood in their potions and magical rituals. They had, to some extent, shaped the Crow Nation through communicating with a legendary Crow chieftain known as Plenty Coups, originally known as "Buffalo Facing the Wind." Plenty Coups was not only a chieftain, but a great medicine man, subject to spells and visions. It was he who, as chief of the Mountain Crow, allied the Crow tribes with the white man in order to take vengeance on their traditional enemies: the Lakota, the Sioux, and the Cheyenne. He was the youngest of all the chieftains of the Mountain Crow, elected at the age of 28. Not only was he a fearsome warrior, having between 50 and 100 feathers on his coup stick (a stick with which a warrior touches his enemies as a sign of courage), but he was also a skilled negotiator, representing the Crow nation at talks in Washington D.C. when U.S. senators tried to take away their lands. He was also the only representative of the Native American peoples to officiate at the dedication of the Tomb of the Unknown Soldier and the only Native American allowed to speak at the ceremony. However, much of his valor and wisdom was said to come from the little people who, rather than attacking him, had taken to him and shared their wisdom with the chief.

Plenty Coups had first encountered the little people when he was nine years old at his initiation ceremony as a warrior. After the traditional sweat baths, he went into some hills in order to experience a vision. In this vision, the chieftain of the little people came to him and took him to their lodge where he showed Plenty Coups the future and many of the great exploits that he would achieve. The chieftain told him that he was especially favored among the little people, and that they were an ancient race that had once lived on the Great Plains long before the coming of the Red Man. He also told Plenty Coups that they were blood drinkers and to summon them, he must spill blood. When the vision passed, Plenty Coups returned to his own people.

At 11 years old, he experienced a second vision concerning the little people. At this time, his tribe was living in the Beartooth Mountains in northwestern Wyoming. Young men were driven out into the wild to experience visions that would make them great warriors. Plenty Coups and his friends journeyed as far as the Crazy Mountains in Montana where his companions left him to experience his vision. But no vision came, even though Plenty Coups waited for three days. Then, remembering the words of the chieftain of the little people, Plenty Coups cut his index finger and allowed the blood to fall onto the ground. That night, he experienced a vision of the little people again. This time, the chieftain metamorphosed into the semblance of an old man with a buffalo face, who led him into a system of underground tunnels that stretched toward the Pryor Mountains and contained a number of great caverns that were filled with buffalo, which emerged from a great hole in the ground and then disappeared. Plenty Coups then had a vision of himself as an old man living near the Medicine Rocks in the middle of a great and empty plain. Only one bird—a chickadee—moved in this emptiness. The buffalo-man told Plenty Coups that the time of the Native Americans was coming to an end, and, that, in the future, the white man would cover the plains as thickly as buffalo. All would be eventually swept away by the white man, but the chickadee survived because it was a good listener and was able to adapt. The Crow people would also adapt if they listened with their ears and their minds to the words of the white man and were able to adapt to them. Using this vision, the Crow people were able to retain much of their lands in Wyoming and around the Pryor Mountains in Montana. In fact, the Crow are said to have survived the critical events that beset many Native American tribes toward the end of the 19th century because of the intervention and wisdom of the little people. The place where Chief Plenty Coups emerged from the underground world of the little folk is now found within Chief Plenty Coups State Park in Montana

According to the Crow, the little people live in caves and gullies in the Pryor Mountain Range in southern Montana, but branches of them are also found in the Big Horn Mountains in northern Wyoming and the Wolf Mountains in southeast Montana. However, their home area is not to be approached lightly. Some of the natural rocky spires in the area are thought to be arrows that the little people can magically fire at intruders in order to protect their lands.

The Crow consider the little people to be great healers. One Crow folktale involves an individual called Burnt Face. A young boy fell into a campfire and completely burnt his face, thus leaving him disfigured. When his family moved north to hunt buffalo, Burnt Face moved south to a remote valley in the Big Horn Mountains where he built himself a Sun Dance lodge. There, he spilled fresh blood on the ground and the little people came down to him from the caves and gullies of the mountains higher up. They healed his scars and gave him great knowledge, as well as supernatural healing powers so that he could help his own people. He returned to his tribe where he became a great chieftain and, although he retained the name Burnt Face, his skin was free of any blemish.

For the Arapaho, however, the experience of the little people was somewhat different. They referred to the little people as *hecesiiteihii* or *nimerigar*, which were cannibal dwarves. They were extremely dangerous man-eaters, and at one time in their history, the Arapaho had fought a war against them, which they had won by trapping many of them in a gorge and killing them.

It took them a long while to die, for the use of arrows seemed to have little effect on them. Even so, they were eventually wiped out. However, it was also believed that although small, the dwarves were very strong, and one of them could carry a full-grown warrior on his back to the caves in the mountains where the family could devour him.

It was believed, however, that these vicious dwarves could not cross running water or any deep place, and the only thing one had to do to escape them was to jump a deep, running river. However, one had to be careful, for the little people were also skilled magicians and could bring misfortune by use of their dark arts. Some legends said that they also trapped the souls of dead warriors who had somehow crossed them and held them prisoner in earthen jars for all eternity.

Among the Cheyenne and the Shoshone, the little people were also viewed as vicious cannibals who lived underground in types of cave "cities" cut into the rocks of dark gullies. According to some of the medicine men, these beings could not stand the light, as they had a close connection with the spirits of the dead. They shut themselves away in underground places, hunting only when the moon was out. They were also known to kill their own kind when individuals became too old to be of any use to their communities. This was done with a straightforward, single blow to the head. After that, the community drank the blood of the slain. In this way all the wisdom that had been accumulated by the individual was passed among the community. In some cases, the little people also did the same to old and feeble members of human society, usually under the cover of darkness.

But did such beings exist? Somewhere among the mountains of Wyoming and Montana is there (or was there) a community of vicious dwarves who were hostile toward humans? For many years, the stories of the little people were simply considered to be old Indian legends. In 1932, however, two prospectors—Cecil Mayne and Frank Carr—were digging for gold in the San Pedro Mountains. About 60 miles southwest of Casper, Wyoming, they located what they thought might be a small vein in the mountainside, and used dynamite to blast the rock. When the dust of the explosion cleared, they found that they had blasted through the wall of a small cave,

which stretched back into the darkness for more than 15 feet. Entering, they found that the walls of the place contained several petroglyphs, but, more importantly, seated on a ledge directly above them, was the mummified body of what seemed to be a very small man of about 14 inches in height. His skin was brown and wrinkled, and his face displayed a fat nose, heavy-lidded eyes, thick lips, and a thin slash-like mouth. It appeared to be the body of an old man. It was so well preserved in the airless cave that both toenails and fingernails were clearly visible, and the head of the body was covered in a strange, black, jelly-like substance, which neither of the prospectors could identify.

What became known as "the San Pedro Mummy" was taken back to Casper, where it caused a sensation in scientific circles. Initially, the two prospectors were accused of creating a hoax using old human remains that they had found, but gradually their claims were taken more seriously. Old Crow and Shoshone stories of the little people of the mountains began to resurface, and many thought that this was evidence for such a race, dwelling away from mankind. There were further tales of blood-drinking dwarves who were lurking in dark underground caverns all through the region. There were tales of vampire "cave-cities" somewhere far beneath the mountains, as old Indian beliefs suggested. The Mummy was put on display for several years before being formally examined by Dr. Harry Shapiro of the American Museum of Natural History. He concluded that it was indeed human and that it could belong to another species of man. Nothing was said about possible blood-drinking.

In 1979, fresh tests were carried out on the Mummy using x-rays, and it was confirmed that it was some form of human and might have even been a child. Professor George Gill of the University of Wyoming also revealed that the individual had met a violent death, possibly with a single blow to the head; the curious substance surrounding its head was actually congealed brains and blood. Part of the spine and the collarbone had been broken by a single blow. Gill also suggested that the child might have been born with anencephaly (with part of its brain functions missing) and might have been ritually killed. However, his findings were disputed by some other academics from the University of Harvard, who had also examined the mummy, claiming that it was actually the mummified body of a 65 year-old adult male. One curious fact that emerged from both investigations was that the canine teeth of the mummy were curiously pointed. As this seemed to be a natural phenomenon, stories began to circulate of a tiny vampire race living among the mountains of Wyoming and Montana.

Following these scientific investigations, the San Pedro Mummy was eventually purchased by a local Casper businessman, Ivan T. Goodman, who put it on display as part of a sideshow. When Goodman died in 1950, the Mummy passed into the hands of another businessman, Leonard Walder, and seems to have disappeared. Walder died in the early 1980s without leaving any trace of the mummy among his estate. There is allegedly a current reward of $10,000 offered by Wyoming University to anyone who can find or give information towards the finding of the relic.

In 1994, however, another such mummy, this time female, was found in another sealed cave in the San Pedro Range. This was discovered by accident by an unnamed family who held lands in the mountains. Once again, Professor Gill was involved in the examination, as were physicians from Denver Children's Hospital in Colorado. They concluded that this was the body of an infant girl who had been born with some sort of deformity or congenital condition, and had been ritually killed. DNA testing seemed to confirm that the remains were human, and Native American and radiocarbon dating showed that they were at least 300 to 400 years old. Others were not so sure that the findings were conclusive, and hinted at another species of human dwelling in the mountains. After the tests had been carried out, the family who had initially found the female mummy asked for it back, and upon receipt, they disappeared and were never heard of again. Once again, the evidence remains inconclusive, but the Crow, the Arapaho, and the Shoshone claim that races of small people with vampiric tendencies were (and perhaps still are) wandering the San Pedro and other mountain ranges of Wyoming and Montana.

But is there any other evidence for such beings, perhaps even from elsewhere in America? In 1876, a ploughman on the farm of James Brown of Hillsboro, Tennessee, was turning over some earth in a small and remote valley when he stumbled upon what appeared to be human remains—possibly those of children. Upon investigation, it was found that he had dug into an expansive graveyard in which a good number of tiny bodies, some no more than 3 feet in height, had been buried. Although it was said that "thousands" of them were buried there, this is probably an exaggeration. The area became known as "the pygmy cemetery," and, for a while, enjoyed something of a reputation, which has now diminished. When a number of the skulls were unearthed, they had naturally pointed incisors, prompting speculation about vampiric dwarves once again. Indeed, folklore of both the Cherokee and the Chickasaw tell tales of "little vampire men" who are of a much older race than the Red Men, and who fought against them in some distant time in the past.

And there seems to be some evidence of such vampiric entities elsewhere in Tennessee. In nearby White County, for example, another peculiar grave site was found on the farm of Captain Simon Doyle. This was investigated on July 29th, 1820, by a Mr. Turner Lane of Sparta. Mr. Lane, an amateur archaeologist, found evidence of a number of burials of small people on Captain Doyle's property, one of which was remarkably intact, probably due to the soil in which it had been buried. Together with John H. Anderson, a local attorney and investigator, they opened several other graves and found a number of skeletons, the most intact measuring a little more than 3 feet in length. The results of their finds were published in an academic paper in Sparta the following year under the names of Lane and Anderson, but reports concerning the "White County Pigmies" had been printed in local newspapers, with stories circulating that these were some sort of vampire.

Strange finds of curious skeletons were not unusual in White County, which contained several Indian Mounds. Indeed, Mr. Lane had already investigated the opening of one of these mounds on the farm of Andrew Bryan in which they had found the bones of a man who stood almost nine feet tall.

The skeleton wore a necklace made out of stones and curious metals, which were taken away for examination. In some of the other mounds, extremely small skeletons were supposedly also found, although no evidence of these exists.

Of course, it is possible that the folklore of the area contains a germ of truth and that there were more ancient (and physically different) forms of mankind. The famous "horned skulls" of Philadelphia certainly seem to suggest this. In 1880, a burial mound was opened and several skulls were taken out, each of which had two bony protuberances on the forehead just about 2 inches above the eyes. The accompanying skeletons were well over 7 feet tall, but were normal in all other respects. It was thought that they had been buried somewhere between AD 100 and AD 1200. The find was made under the supervision of a Pennsylvania State Historian and a minister of the Presbyterian church, Dr. G.P. Donehoo, and two prominent archaeologists, Dr. A.B. Skinner of the American Investigating Museum and Dr. W.K. Morehead of Phillips Academy in Massachusetts. Their finds were preliminary, and the skulls and some of the bones were sent to the American Investigating Museum for authentication. However, there seems to have been some sort of bureaucratic error and they were misplaced before completely vanishing. However, all paperwork concerning them is still extant.

With horned men walking around in early America, it does not seem beyond the bounds of possibility that a tribe of vampiric dwarves might have been living in Wyoming and southern Montana, and that they passed into the folklore of the Native Americans. Perhaps there was *some* grain of truth in all the old legends. Were the dwarves another blood-drinking species of mankind that had evolved alongside ourselves? And could it be that such a species survived in some parts of America well into the 19th century, largely unknown to us?

These were the stories and questions that the settlers considered as they built their communities in the rugged landscape of Wyoming, and gradually the old folktales of the Native American peoples of the area became incorporated into their own lore. The mountain-man Jim Bridger who had blazed the Bridger Trail into Wyoming in 1864 often regaled his listeners with stories of vampire-like entities that he had allegedly encountered up in the remote and winding mountain canyons and ravines. However, Bridger was known for his tall tales and exaggerations, and had undoubtedly heard some of the Indian folklore and adapted it into his own exploits. Most people took his stories with a grain of salt, and yet others were not entirely sure that these truly were exaggerations.

Bridger had asserted that somewhere among the mountains (he refused to say where) there was a kind of "mound city" that he had seen from a rise somewhere in the southern Rockies. He said it was an artificially created metropolis built by a race of small, gray people, who drank blood. He hadn't approached such a place, as local Native Americans had told him that it was extremely evil and he could feel the dark vibrations coming from it. Of course, Bridger may have been recounting nothing more than an old Native American legend of a great mound, which had been constructed somewhere among the hills by an early people. The great Oglala Lakota medicine man, Black Elk, mentioned a story that he had heard as a child of a great mound somewhere among the mountains that had great healing powers. Supposedly, it had been built by an earlier people who lived among the hills. Bridger may have simply lifted this old tale, or one like it, and incorporated it into his own personal experience. This telling of tall tales was a feature of the lives of many of the "mountain men," the tough, lonely characters who lived out in the wild and traded with the Native Americans, often absorbing much of their ways and lore.

Whether or not Bridger's story was true, similar tales had an effect on some of the settlers who came to Wyoming and Montana. The strange landscape with its mountains and gullies must have had a rather unsettling effect on the pioneers who put down roots in the region, and it was perhaps easy to imagine something monstrous and dangerous lurking out there among the shadowy canyons or in underground caves in some remote mountain valley. In such an "alien" place, the imagination can certainly play strange tricks, and interpretations of events might become a little skewed. And, of course, this feeling of unease could not be helped by the old stories, especially when they were recounted by the likes of Jim Bridger and other mountain men. Hostile and vampiric little people were used as a means of explanation for a number of things that befell the early homesteaders in this unfriendly land. The beings who dwelt there were as hostile toward the whites as they had been toward the Native Americans. If a child disappeared, it had been taken by the little people; if a community fell sick, the little people had poisoned the wells; if an individual wasted away, the little people were visiting him or her during the night and drawing off his or her blood. Even if things went missing from the home, the little people had stolen them for their own purposes or for malicious mischief. They were up in the mountains, hills, shady gullies, and caves watching and waiting for every opportunity to do humans harm.

They were the people who had built some of the inexplicable stone circles that adorned the nearby mountains, or who had carved the petroglyphs in some of the deep caves in the cliffs. They were, according to some, the same people who had constructed the Bighorn Medicine Wheel in Big Horn County in Wyoming. The name refers to a certain alignment of stones believed to be arranged in such a way as to have spiritual or supernatural properties. They are all laid out in a basic pattern, usually centered around a single stone with an outer "ring" from which a number of lines connect like spokes. They are sometimes named "sacred hoops" among certain tribes. Built by a largely unknown prehistoric race, they have been used across the centuries by indigenous North American people for astronomical, healing, teaching, and religious purposes. Some people have argued that they are "doors" to other worlds, which such ancient peoples used (and though which some people could sometimes be dragged and vanish in their own world); others claim they were the center of long-vanished cities and of strange and inhuman peoples (such as the vampire dwarves). The Big Horn Wheel is the most southernly and most ancient of all these structures and therefore has some importance attached to it. One story about such structures was that they "centered" dark powers, which the vampires used to bring evil and misfortune on a tribe through black magic. Many of the settlers accepted such a belief, and when misfortune or illness struck their own communities (especially in Wyoming and Montana), it was claimed that the dwarves were clandestinely using the Medicine Wheel to bring about death, so that they could feed on the corpses. Scattered all through the Pryor Mountains were small stone circles that were often called "fairy rings," which these malevolent dwarves used from time to time in order to do harm. Such places were to be avoided, even by the most hardened and wily of mountain men.

The idea of vampiric little people was not unique to the Pryor Mountains or to Wyoming, even though stories of them appear to cluster in that state. Around the Great Lakes, the idea of cannibalistic diminutive warriors appears in the oral traditions of the Ojibwe. These beings resemble those in Wyoming—they are great magicians and also drink blood from time to time. They live in deep caves and ravines and are creatures of darkness, only coming out at night. They will then approach Ojibwe houses and try to entice those to come out, when they will attack them and drink their blood. Sometimes, they will take on the voice of a friend and call softly or trick the inhabitants of a house by pretending that there is some sort of emergency outside to draw them out. As in Wyoming, they are said to be the remnants of an ancient race and are opposed to humankind whom they think have invaded their lands.

And, like the mountains of Wyoming, there are cave drawings attributed to the little people scattered throughout the Great Lakes region. In the early 1900s, a prospector name Lewis Calhoun was hunting down veins of copper in the Porcupine Mountains, which extended through Ontonagon County in Michigan. Throughout the course of his investigations, he descended into a narrow gully protected by a rocky overhang. There was really nothing down there, but at the very bottom of the gully, where it was almost cave-like, he saw a number of drawings on the rock wall. One of them showed what looked like a number of small, hairy-faced men in a canoe (presumably on one of the Lakes below). Another showed them gathered around one of their own, and they seemed to be drinking its blood. Calhoun was horrified—even more horrified when he found what appeared to be a sharp vampire-like tooth amongst the stones at the very bottom of the canyon (though he later admitted it may have been a piece of rock). He had the feeling that he was being watched from the shadows, even though he couldn't see anybody and heard nothing except the distant cries of birds out on the mountain slopes. He said later that he had never been so anxious to get out of a place in his life. There was a feeling of *ancientness* about the gloomy location, and he scrambled up to the wholesome sunlight once more. Later, he would return to the area in the company of some other miners and more learned men, but he couldn't find the place again. There had been numerous rock falls in the locality and its geographical references changed. Although they explored several gullies and caves, they couldn't find any trace of the drawings at all. However, several of the searchers claimed that, like Calhoun, they too felt as if they were being watched by someone or something unseen.

Another inscribed rock in Michigan was found at a location named Corpse Pond. In the late 1950s, a group of walkers stumbled across a small clearing in the woods near the Pond (a small lake) and came upon a single stone standing almost at its center. This was covered in crude drawings, which seemed not only to show the position of various constellations in the night sky, but also very crude depictions of little men devouring a large individual. The whole time, the group had the impression that they were being watched from the surrounding woodlands—this seems to be a common sensation in these cases. They left the clearing rather hurriedly. Some time after, several of them attempted to return to the site in order to view the drawings once again—particularly those relating to the constellations—but they could not seem to find either the clearing or the stone again. Several paths that looked familiar seemed to lead nowhere and, although they visited several clearings, there was no large stone, marked with drawings or otherwise, in any of them. They wondered if the stone itself had been moved somehow. Even so, the feeling of being watched in the woodlands still persisted and even out toward the Pond. Old tales of malignant dwarves hiding in the thicket must have seemed all too real.

With all these variations of vicious, blood-drinking dwarves from various parts of America, the vampire little people of Wyoming and Montana do not seem that unusual, but it is here that many stories of them seem to proliferate. The notion of a dangerous subterranean race lurking among the deep caverns and valleys is a very powerful one, and seems to have made a strong impression of the folklore (and fears) of the area. And if the finds of fossils and remains in the region are to be believed, there may be something in these tales. Perhaps some remnant of an exceptionally ancient elder race waits out there in cowboy country, watching human life with a jaundiced and malignant eye. And as the western wind blows along the canyons and arroyos, across the bare mountains where the stone circles and great Medicine Wheels lie, perhaps it is stirring, ready to reach out to nourish itself on the blood of the intruders within its primal domain.

CONCLUSION

What have we learned about vampires? Maybe the first thing is that they are not always what we expect. As we said from the outset of this book, of all the horrors of both fiction and cinema, we believe that we know all there is to know about the vampire-kind. But little could be further from the truth. In many respects, our study of the American Undead has served both to illustrate and confirm many of the things that we suggested in our Introduction; perhaps now is a good time to expand upon them slightly. Vampires come in all shapes and sizes, and are not always recognizable. Nor are they the charismatic, handsome nobleman or the voluptuous, beautiful woman that the classic films have led us to expect. Nor are they even the angst-ridden teenager who seems to be so in-vogue at the moment. They can be anyone or anything, from a Melon-Headed orphan to a well in the ground. And it must be remembered that, although some do, not all vampires drink blood. Others may drink human fluids or simply take energy. This widens the options as to exactly *what* form they can take, and allows them to be chairs, shadows, or reflections in a mirror and growing vines—all non-human entities. We simply don't know what to expect, so there is no room for complacency.

Nor are vampires mainly wealthy and cultured dilettantes as they often appear in *Dracula* or in, say, the works of Anne Rice. In many cases, they are of a low or peasant status—the poor or working classes of society. This is not to say that the genteel or aristocratic vampires—the sort that come from old families—do not exist, just that they are usually the minority. Mainly a community's response to the threat of vampires centered on those around them, people whom they knew. They were the neighbors who rose from their graves to wander about and who sometimes did harm to their own families or to those around them. They were part of the wandering dead, sometimes known as revenants. So forget the cloak, cape, the grand clothing, and aristocratic ways, and think instead of the homespuns and ragged, mismatched clothing. This was very much the case among the inhabitants of a shunned and eerie place such as Dogtown on the New England coast.

Western vampires—the types of the Undead with which we are most familiar through films, stories, and comics—were a part of the idea of the returning dead, but did not always drink blood. In some instances, they simply ate what was available, raiding the pantries of the poor in order to feed themselves. They might drink blood, but only as a last resort, and even then only from livestock, or from their own families or relatives. Certainly they were noisy and terrifying, but were often not the malign monsters that are so readily portrayed in books and films. This is not to say, however, that they were not to be feared or that they were not to be discouraged from returning. Even the Blessed Dead had the capacity to do harm to or make demands on the living. After a period in the cold earth, they were bound to be both hungry and thirsty, and their visitations had the capacity to eat their families out of house and home, causing hardship for the living. If interrupted or denied, they might physically attack or cause supernatural harm to the household involved, so it was better to placate them. But there was worse, for they often brought disease in their wake, which could sometimes decimate a household or a community. This notion was common in medieval England and in parts of Europe, but, as we have seen, it was accepted in some parts of 18th and early 19th century New England as well. Vampires were strongly linked in the popular mind with diseases, such as tuberculosis and its attendant symptoms (difficulty breathing during the night, feeling weight on the chest), and it was also thought that they carried plagues such as smallpox and cholera as well. When communities struggled in the face of illness, many often thought that the Undead—the recently buried—were to blame. Such fears were sometimes compounded by dreams and night-time visions of the dead, which usually added strength to the assertions and belief.

In many parts of the world, vampirism has been also strongly linked to witchcraft and sorcery. In many African cultures, this is still the case, but it was also the notion in many early English, Irish, and European societies. For example, in Holland, the idea of the nachtmerrie were not uncommon. These people were usually considered to be witches and their appearances were counted as part of their witchcraft. But it was not simply a case of drinking the blood of a vulnerable sleeper, for such appearances were meant to terrify or to do physical harm to the person involved. Of course, like the succubus of Greek mythology, the appearance might have a sexual element to it, and the sleeper might awaken exhausted and out of sorts after uninvited and unwanted sexual attention and exertions during the night. The purposes of such nocturnal visitations, then, were often much more complex than first appearance, and the notions of witchcraft and evil-doing were usually pretty much to the fore.

When a vampire was discovered, it was not simply enough to drive a wooden stake through its body as it lay in its coffin. Such a spectacular device, though certainly employed in some parts of the world, has more to do with film and television scenarios than with actual folk belief. The process was nevertheless a risky one—certain rituals had to be performed; the stake might have to be of a certain type of wood (which varied depending on the location), and if these were not observed, or the wood happened to be of the wrong type, then the activity was incredibly dangerous. The vampire might rise and destroy the would-be slayer. However, in many communities, the only sure way to destroy a vampire was to burn it (or at least burn its heart). First, though, it had to be established that the corpse in question actually *was* a vampire. Such investigations were usually carried out shortly after the body had been interred (which is usually when there had been outbreaks of alleged vampirism).

Normally, if the coffin was opened, the corpse had an unnatural *freshness* about it, or it might be bloated with blood. There might also be dried blood around the mouth, signaling that it had been drinking from victims. These signs were often taken as incontrovertible proof that the cadaver in question was indeed a vampire. But, there were other explanations for these signs. Chemical elements both in the body and perhaps in the earth in which the coffin had been buried might have acted as a kind of preservative, keeping the body fresh in appearance. Furthermore, gasses that build up in the body following death may give the body a flaccid or bloated appearance, while the leakage of internal fluids (including blood) may dry around the nostrils and mouth. This might serve to give the impression that the corpse had been drinking blood, and in a number of medieval (and slightly later) societies, it was interpreted as such. Indeed, none of these qualifications were known, and the vampire hunters were called on to destroy the creature as one of the Undead.

In some cases, the vampire could be staked, but sometimes, this was not enough to destroy it completely. The creature might only be suspended, and if the stake were to be removed, it might rise again (this has actually formed the basic plot of some vampire films). Some of the dead were also pinned down in their coffins using iron nails; some have had a large stone weighted on their chest in order to hold them in the ground.

Between 2005 and 2009, archaeologists investigating the site of a Bishop's Palace at Kilteasheen, Knockvicar, near Lough Key in County Roscommon, Ireland, were digging into an extensive, but previously unknown, medieval graveyard containing at least 137 skeletons from the early medieval period. Two of these skeletons were of particular interest, because they were "deviant burials" (burials laid out in a different way to normal interments). One was of a young man, and one was a more elderly individual, both dated from around the 8th century. Interestingly, the skulls of both bodies had large rocks rammed into their mouths, and it had been done with some force, possibly after they were dead. These stones might have been placed there to prevent evil spirits from entering and reanimating the bodies, perhaps as vampires. Strangely enough, this was not an uncommon practice for the period, as similar skeletons have also been found in parts of England. Rocks, stoppers, and bits of cloth have been found in the mouths of some corpses, possibly for the same purpose. It is thought that the Kilteasheen "vampire corpses" might have been suicides or some form of anti-social figures within the community. Such people were especially susceptible to the visitation of evil spirits, and might rise as vampires in order to torment the countryside. This explanation would tie in with some of the medieval manuscripts from the same period that have been found, which hint at an underlying fear of the returning dead. Plague victims were also susceptible to the attentions of dark and evil spirits. Their weakened condition often made them prey to malevolent forces, which were always wandering about. However, there were other reasons for the supposed evil of vampirism in a small community. According to folklore, the activity of incest was a sure way of drawing evil spirits after death. In isolated communities, incest may have been more common than we assume, however, many of those who practiced it appear to be werewolves rather than vampires. Anyone who had been suspected of such practices might be nailed down in the coffin after death, or have their mouths stuffed in order to prevent dark spirits from entering their bodies and causing them to rise.

In order to dispose of a vampire, certain procedures had to be followed. According to Romanian lore, the head had to be struck from the body using a sexton's or gravedigger's shovel. The mouth then had to be stuffed with garlic—considered to be a deterrent to the vampire kind—and placed away from the decapitated corpse. As a final act, the heart then had to be cut out and burned. In some cases, the entire body was burned, and those involved had to be sure that it was completely reduced to ashes. The removal of the heart, as we have seen, was, in fact, a common feature in New England vampire cases, and was considered the only proper way to completely destroy the Undead. If this was not carried out, then the revenant would return at some point and perhaps menace its loved ones or the wider community.

Vampirism might also be linked with some physical deformity. Those who were strange either in appearance or in their ways might be candidates to become vampires when they died. Although there is no evidence of this among the Kilteasheen "vampire corpses," it was well known in folkloric circles that this belief existed. A physical deformity could very well be the outward sign of inner evil. People who were so deformed had to be viewed with some suspicion—they could be witches, vampires, werewolves, or some other evil thing. When they were interred, therefore, precautions had to be taken against their return from the dead. Such deformities might be natural, but latterly others might be scientifically induced through clandestine experimentation as the legend (or urban myth) of Ohio's Melon Heads illustrates. Even if such creatures were "created" by scientific means, this in no way diminished their evil, nor the terror of their presence. The Melon Heads, for example, had been bred to drink blood in some secret laboratory, and their physical grotesqueness only added to their menace. In fact, the scientific element adds a certain amount of viciousness to these individuals. Deformity (whether natural or scientifically induced), witchcraft, and possible violence (whether actual or supernatural), were all interlinked. It is worth noting that in many South American societies, witchcraft and vampirism are inextricably connected.

One other element that characterized possible vampirism was poverty. As we have seen in some American settlements, such as Dogtown on Cape Ann, those who lived on the fringes of "normal" society, those who didn't work, and those who were anti-social, were often believed to become vampires. Those who were destitute or idle were almost certainly agents of the Devil, because God would look after and provide for his own. And, in any case, man had been put on the earth to work and provide for himself; to ignore that was to defy the Divine Will, so those who were poor and who did not work were counted as sinners.

There is also the common belief that, after being bitten by a vampire, one automatically becomes a vampire. This idea is, of course, one of the staples of vampire films, and it is even used to some extent in Bram Stoker's *Dracula*. But although it *may* be the case in some folklore tales, it cannot always be readily accepted—not even as a rule of thumb. Visitations from the Undead, or from beings such as the nachtmerrie, are certainly dangerous (and may ultimately be potentially fatal), but they do not usually actively increase their numbers by turning their victims into creatures such as themselves in the style of books and films. They may, however, have the power to do physical and lasting harm. Having said that, of course, there are some folkloric tales, told within certain cultures, concerning the victims of such attentions, who have become part of the retinue of the walking dead. And in some cultures, it is believed that those who are sometimes visited at night by supernatural creatures are doomed to eventually become such creatures themselves. These people might take on some of the attributes that are readily associated with the night-walking dead: marbled skin, sunken eyes, and a gaunt and haggard expression. Such appearances might be attributed to the advance of some disease such as tuberculosis, but within certain beliefs this is viewed as the transformation of the victim into something resembling his or her attacker—one of the supernatural Undead. Indeed, in some cases—such as those in 17th and 18th century New England—it was extremely easy to make such a direct connection. And there was, in fact, a further connection in the dreams and imaginings of the alleged victims. Those who experienced fevers and illnesses sometimes dreamt of dead relatives during the hours of darkness, and thus the dead were blamed for intervening in the illnesses of the living (and perhaps even causing them). When they died, it was down to the dead relatives, and there was a suggestion that they might become very similar creatures. The idea that the trait of vampirism might be passed on some strain of virulent disease became accepted in some communities, although not all. Apart from a few exceptions, there is little to suggest that the walking dead multiply through biting or infecting their victims.

Although in books and on screen, vampires seem to be our most familiar horror and the ones that are most easily dealt with, they are a much more complex entity than this would suggest. Vampirism is also a much more complicated and diverse subject than we might at first think. It is concerned not only with drinking blood, but with drawing or leeching energy, vitality, and "goodness" from various sources. And in this, vampires can often take many forms. So not only must we guard against the night-walking dead, but we must also be careful of the chairs we sit on, the vines we cultivate, the wells from which we drink, and the mirrors we look into—vampires may be everywhere, and certainly not in forms with which we are familiar. And yet, all are based in the cultures and in the beliefs of the peoples where they are to be found.

Vampires, it seems, have been with us since earliest times. Belief in them has been based around a fear of the returning dead or of the influence that they can sometimes exert over the living. And vampires *should* certainly be feared in their own right. However, they are also products of the cultures that have fostered such beliefs. So there is no certain way of dealing with them as they are portrayed in films and stories. If our trip around America has taught us anything, it is that all vampires can be different and cannot be generally categorized or lumped together. The response to each one of them might be different, depending on the culture and belief system from which they come. Would a vampire from the Jewish sector of New York, for example, respond to the sight of a Christian crucifix? America, with its melting-pot of races, societies, and cultures, is a place where the vampires of such cultures can meld, change, and adapt. In a land where a number of different types of people have lived cheek by jowl with each other throughout the years, many have found their way into other forms of folklore and have been partly changed by them. Perhaps, then, no American vampire tale is *completely* straightforward, but contains a number of diverse elements from Native American to the various colonist. American vampire tales certainly deserve a closer examination—maybe an even closer look than it has been possible to do within the confines of this book. This has only scratched the surface of a deep and fascinating subject, and maybe much more waits to be uncovered.

Because, not only have they been with us since early times, but vampires have continued to both terrify and fascinate us in equal measure throughout the years. Maybe it is our fascination with death and what might lie beyond; maybe it is our fascination with living forever; maybe it is simply our fear of dying, but vampires have exercised a pull on our imagination throughout the generations. And this fearful interest shows no real sign of waning—vampires are as much at home in the 21st century (with the likes of *Buffy, True Blood,* and *Twilight*—and film and television producers are always looking for new angles to take the concepts further into the future). And they seem to be everywhere, not just in crumbling old castles in far-away Transylvania or forgotten graveyards in Serbia. They are lurking in many places in the United States of America, maybe even in your town!

So when you go out tonight, whether you live on a rural road or near the heart of a bustling town, take a look around you, beyond the furthest streetlight. Look carefully at the point where the friendly light turns to the darkest shadow. See that movement? You never know what might be lurking there! Maybe something with fangs! Maybe something equally as dangerous and not what you quite expect!

Bibliography

Allison, A. Lynn. "Navajo Witch Purge of 1878." *West Literary Magazine.*
    May 2001.

Evans-Wentz, W.Y. *Fairy Faith in Celtic Countries.* New York: Oxford
    University Press, 1911.

Gilbertson, R.B. *A Frontier Land.* New York, 1923.

Jones, Reverend Edmund. *A Relation of Apparitions of Spirits in the
    Principality of Wales.* Cowbridge, UK: D. Brown & Sons Ltd., 1780.

Kelleher, Dr. Colm A. *Hunt for the Skinwalker.* New York: Paraview Pocket
    Books, 2005.

Letherbarrow, Mary. *Folklore of Herefordshire.* Battsford, 1955.

Ley, William. *Salamanders and Other Wonders.* New York: The Viking
    Press, 1955.

Mayer, Johannes. *Tuefelbushen.* 1690.

Osborn, Chase. *Madagascar, Land of the Man-Eating Tree.* London:
    Republic Publishing Company, 1924

Skinner, Charles M. *Myths and Legends of Our Own Land.* Whitefish,
    Mont.: Kennsinger Publishing, LLC, 1896.
Stetson, George R. "The Animistic Vampire in New England." *The American
    Anthropologist.* A9 (1896): 1–13.
Trewhitt, Frank G. "Ghost Tales from Bradley County." *TN Folklore Soc.
    Bull.* 29 (1963): 10–12.

INDEX

About the Author

D r. Bob Curran was born in a remote area of County Down, Northern Ireland. The area in which he grew up was rich in folklore—especially the folklore of the supernatural—and this gave him an ear for and an interest in the tales and beliefs of many people. He worked a number of jobs before going to University, where he received a doctorate in child psychology. Even so, his interest in folklore and folk culture was still very much to the fore, and this prompted him to write a number of books on the subject, including *Celtic Lord and Legend*; *Vampires*; *Werewolves*; *Zombies*, and *Lost Lands, Forgotten Realms*. Having taken a degree in history, he now lectures and broadcasts on matters of historical interest, and acts as advisor to a number of influential cultural bodies in Northern Ireland. Most recently he has been working on advisory bodies regarding cultural links between Northern Ireland and the West of Scotland. He currently lives in Northern Ireland with his wife and young family.